Ruth Dupré

Vlado Kreslin, Slovenia and Me

Ruth Dupré

Vlado Kreslin, Slovenia and Me

How a Slovenian Legend and a Texas Housewife Found Themselves in a Wild and Crazy Friendship

JustFiction Edition

Imprint
Any brand names and product names mentioned in this book are subject to trademark, brand or patent protection and are trademarks or registered trademarks of their respective holders. The use of brand names, product names, common names, trade names, product descriptions etc. even without a particular marking in this work is in no way to be construed to mean that such names may be regarded as unrestricted in respect of trademark and brand protection legislation and could thus be used by anyone.

Cover image: www.ingimage.com

Publisher:
JustFiction! Edition
is a trademark of
International Book Market Service Ltd., member of OmniScriptum Publishing Group
17 Meldrum Street, Beau Bassin 71504, Mauritius

Printed at: see last page
ISBN: 978-613-7-38532-6

Tista črna kitara

Bil sem še Vladek,
ko so – kot vedno za praznik
prišli
brkati cigani v hišo igrat
oče je stopil v sobo po tisto črno kitaro,
ki jo je kupil
za prvo plačo.

Gospod tisto kitaro še imate,
gospod, tisto črno kitaro še imate?
Gospod, tista bila je res dobra.

So ga spraševali
še dolgo po tem,
zmeraj, ko hoteli so prositi drobiž.
Zmeraj, ko igrali so vaški gostilni
in hodili v pavzah do šanka.
Pa njihove žene,
ko prišle so pred vrata
po stare obleke,
so rade vprašale:

Gospod, tisto kitaro še imate,
gospod, tisto črno kitaro še imate?
Gospod, tista bila je res dobra.

Včasih, ko pridem domov,
sedim pod kostanji in pijem,
piljem s prijat'li,
ki tam še živijo.
Takrat, skoraj vedno pri mizi
za nas zaigrajo in vprašajo,
otroški obrazis
hripavim glasom:

Gospoud, tisto gitaro šče mate,
gospoud, tisto čarno gitaro šče mate?
Gospoud, tista je bijla dobra,
Tista je bijla dobra.

Chapter One

Ljubljana, January 2010

Pinch me. I'm dreaming.

Snow flies up, kissing windows, delighting children and fools while burying us deep inside the *gostílna*. Somewhere out there in all that blinding softness, beyond black, spiky trees and an endless ravine, lays the road to Ljubljana.

Vlado Kreslin, the most beloved singer and songwriter in Slovenia, taps my wrist to make sure I pay attention to his latest story. He's quite the storyteller. This time he's telling us about how he got stymied in meeting Bob Dylan again. He's opened for him twice but opening for Dylan is no guarantee of meeting Dylan. I'm not sure if even Dylan meets Dylan these days.

Vlado meets everyone, works with everyone, plays for everyone, even hapless fans. Rick and I had traveled halfway around the world for a concert that had gotten canceled. A river had flooded the club. And the blizzard? With this storm, even if we'd found the club we might have been snowed in for a week. We're from Texas. Driving in snow is not our best skill.

But Vlado had swooped in and saved the day. He'd swept us into his arms and carried us — the hapless fan and her long-suffering husband—to his house. He'd sat us at his table with his family, fed us real Slovene food, poured out his own river of wine until we could barely see straight and then put on a concert right there in his dining room. Just for us. He was making *damn* sure we knew what Slovene hospitality was all about.

That was last night. Now he's doing it all over again.

So here I sit, full of mushroom soup and wine, listening as he makes us smile He likes to make people smile.

The snow, disguised as ice now, chatters against the building. Inside it's as hot as a Texas barbeque in July and just as crowded. Evidently in Slovene, "blizzard" is the secret password for "Let's go find a tavern on the top of an icy mountain and drink as much wine as possible". Lunches last for hours here, maybe even days, but that's okay. Who wants to get back to Ljubljana anyway?

Thirsty people are packed together like sweaty hams in a market. Most of them have peeled down to their short-sleeved shirts, leaving coats and sweaters and scarves hanging on various hangers placed around the room. The owners of the *gostílna* dash between tables, setting pitchers of wine and baskets of bread down in front of customers. Those sitting closest to the huge green masonry stove have a distinctive dewy look. Only one person is naive enough to be wearing a too heavy sweater and now is suffering the consequences. I'm stuffed into a turtleneck like a red-faced sausage.

Vlado fills my wine glass. Twenty-four hours ago I hadn't met the man. Twenty-four weeks before I hadn't even heard of him. Twenty-four days… well, of course I'd heard of him by then. You don't just wake up and say, "Hey, I think I'll go to Ljubljana today," not if you live in Texas. You have to want to go to Ljubljana to get there, and you have to be willing to work at it. You're never sure where you'll end up when you start out for Ljubljana. We got lucky this time. Our only unplanned stop was Zagreb at midnight in a blizzard. This blizzard. Yet here I sit, next to Vlado.

Like I said—pinch me.

So how does someone with no connections to this part of the world end up sitting next to a Slovenian rock star on a blizzardy day, eating and laughing and getting more than a little buzzed? Kindness on his part. Curiosity on mine. A thank-you note.

I never expected this when I wrote to him. Hearing from any musical icon, even one from another country, was not on my to-be-expected list, especially when I lived across the ocean from him. Different languages. Different culture. That little fantasy of striking up a friendship, getting to know the family, dropping by for coffee and having barbeque and all that kind of stuff? Dream on.

When it comes to Vlado, normal rules do not apply.

I came across his music this way: Someone posted a video on a friend's Facebook page. The song was *Rulet,* with a Croatian singer named Šajeta and the Slovene singer Vlado Kreslin. And then that same someone sent me a message, urging me to go listen.

Please. I'd rather watch paint dry.

Besides, I had eye cramps from my laptop. I was working on a novel, and my train of thought was sacrosanct. Never mind that the train had broken down in a mucky sinkhole.

On the other hand, nothing else had sparked my imagnination. If I watched the video maybe the train would fire up again.

At least the video wasn't bright and chipper. Noirish in black and white, it opened with a watch and toy sword, a pen in an inkwell and the figurine of a young girl. Evidently, an artist and a businessman were vying for a maiden's heart. Then a young man, terribly earnest and good-looking in that intense continental way, started singing as he typed on a manual typewriter. Obviously, he was the pen, and he sang—strong, clear and totally incomprehensible to me, since it wasn't in English.

The camera switched to an older bald guy playing a piano. An aging rocker, probably retired, brought out and dusted off to play the successful businessman versus the artistic young man. Poor guy—he didn't have a chance. Still, he sang in this husky baritone, so tender it made me want to sit next to him to make sure I didn't miss a word, even if I couldn't understand him. Maybe he couldn't project, or he'd blown his vocal cords. Maybe he was holding back. Then he glanced at the camera. Soft voice, angry eyes.

No need to watch any more. I knew who was going to win the girl. Besides, it felt as if the older guy was chiding me for listening to the video instead of writing. I didn't need that, especially since I was rooting for him to get the girl.

The bald singer-man stood up. He started into the chorus, his voice now deep and rich, no holding back, "*Še zmeraj me skrbi…* "

God only knows what hit me.

Never have I been struck by such a voice. In that instant I became St. Teresa, shot through so deep that my soul cracked apart, but instead of being pierced by the arrow of God, the voice of this man pierced me. With every note he sang I trembled like a bell rung for the very first time, begging to be rung again.

Twenty, thirty times that day I listened to that video. My writing was forgotten, meals forgotten, everything forgotten except listening to that song, that voice, one more time. Just one more time.

Šajeta means lightning in Croatian, but it was the voice of the older man that shot through me and snatched my breath away.

So who was he? Anyone whose voice compelled me to listen twenty times a day was someone I needed to know about. I feared being swept away like a raft on the sea and I needed a lifeline back to all that was sane.

I scoured my friend's Facebook page, looking for the video. It was gone. No problem—I'd find it myself. The song was *Rulet* and one of the guys was named Vlado. How many songs could be named *Rulet*? Especially with a singer named Vlado something or another. Even if it meant wading through fifty or so videos on YouTube, I'd find it.

There it was. First one up. My bald-headed singer was Vlado Kreslin.

His friend Noah Charney calls Vlado the greatest rock star you've never heard of, and that'll do for a start. He was born in Beltinci, Prekmurje in what was then SSR Slovenia, Yugoslavia. His father Milan, first a bookkeeper and then a banker, played guitar in a band for a while back when he was single, then picked it up again when he'd retired. His mother Katarina sang when she was younger. Vlado had a younger sister, Gita, and a best friend, Štefan. As a child, he'd lie in his bed at night and listen to bands playing on the other side of the wall in his grandfather's *gostílna*. He now lives in Ljubljana with his wife, Eva, and their three kids—Čarna, Naj, and Ajdina. He has an older daughter, Nina—and he drives like a bat out of hell when he heads to back to Beltinci.

The usual list of facts, in other words, which anyone could piece together with a little research. Except for the last one. That one I learned firsthand when he took us to Beltinci one rainy day.

Good Lord, how many videos had this Vlado guy made? I stopped counting at forty, and I wasn't close to exhausting them. Most of his titles were in Slovene, but there were a few English ones in there, too. Those I scratched off my list. English is fine but the magic came when I didn't know what he said. It was his voice I wanted to hear, and his words in his Slavic mother tongue. If I was going to swim in his music, I might as well plunge into the deep end.

I found other things, too. Countless interviews he'd given in at least five languages, some translated into English. Movies he'd been in, including one based on a poem of his. Plays he'd performed. Books of poetry he'd written. Concerts, averaging at least two a week for the year. And songs. Always writing songs.

Vlado Kreslin was a one-man entertainment dynasty.

After a few months of gorging on his music, I could warble the songs fairly well in really bad Slovene while working on my book. *Nota bene*: Slovene and Texan accents do not mix. The song I warbled most was from a video eight minutes and seven seconds long, which was how long it took me to write a paragraph. I rode that song all the way down to the finish line, and when I typed—*fini*—on the last page, I thought about letting him know how much help his music had been to me. A thank-you note—short, polite, genteel—something harmless. He might get a kick out of it. Anyway, when I had this flash of brilliance late one night it sounded good.

Of course, there would be problems contacting him. Linguistic problems, cultural problems, accessibility problems. But all these were minor. Difficult, yes, but nothing that couldn't be handled with enough time and self-delusion.

In the murky light of morning, sunlight, that lazy thing, wasn't the first to greet me. That honor belonged to the knotted ball of nerves in my stomach. I couldn't write to the man. Obviously, when the idea had first come to me, I was drowning in a sea of delirium, drunk on finishing the book. But with sunlight staring me in the face? *Get a grip, kiddo, and thank God you didn't write. What kind of fool would he think you were anyway?*

I trudged through my days with a nasty case of the grumps. With enough time I figured the urge would go away.

The urge didn't go away. It made me itch.

For one long itchy-scratchy week I did this, worrying about writing this "Dear Vlado" note, which had now grown into a humongous albatross. I tried reasoning with myself. Weren't we both were both carbon-based life forms? Of course we were. And with the internet the way it was, he probably wouldn't even see it. The note would disappear into the ether and never get to him.

I'm no good at listening to pep talks, especially my own.

I finally gave in. I wrote the note late one night with my stomach still in knots and my hands sweating, just to get it over with. Besides, I needed sleep.

I wrote the note precisely. No insincerity. No gushing. No sucking up. This would be my one and only contact with him. *I wanted to make a good impression.* I thanked him for his music, saying how much it had touched me, that one day perhaps I could see him in concert in Ljubljana. I sent it off, expecting nothing. At best his secretary would write, thanking me for contacting Mr. Kreslin and reminding me to buy his latest CD. In other words, the usual commercial sales pitch. That would have been okay.

Just a note. Nothing special.

I slept well that night.

The next morning I had an email.

Dear Ruth!

I was very pleased to receive your letter. It is always great to hear that your music touches somebody's heart.

If you come to Ljubljana I will try to take you to some of the concerts.

Until then I can send a CD, if you want, just send me your address!

Thanks again and all the best!

Vlado"

Just like that, everything changed.

Vlado was nice. He was a real live person who read his emails himself, a really nice person, who was really nice to me, who invited me to write to him again.

And now I sit next to Vlado in the *gostílna*, drinking Tito's favorite wine while Vlado tells another story. Just as if I've known him all my life.

Vlado has this skill, this gift for making friends. Maybe it's a Slovene thing. He's a whirlwind, excited to see you and eager to please. None of this faux reserved, standoffish "Let's see if we relate" mentality. You enter his life and that's it, no questions, you're in. Right away, he tells you what's going on with him. The easy intimacy of an old friend. He smiles a lot. If he wines and dines you, you're lucky if you're only five pounds heavier when you go to bed that night. For sure you'll be feeling no pain.

I still couldn't figure out why his music moved me so. I didn't want to be a pest, asking a lot of "what does this mean?" questions. But this was a brave new world for me and his music was the door. So, I asked, apologized, and asked some more. He answered every question and sent me his *Koncert* CD set. For the next few months I was worthless. I walked around in a daze, my ears attached to the iPod, trying to memorize the songs.

Then my husband made the biggest mistake of his life. He asked me what I wanted for Christmas.

"I want to go to Ljubljana to hear Vlado," I replied.

He gulped once, blinked twice. "Okay."

Bless him.

Going to Ljubljana isn't as far-fetched as it sounds. Years before, Rick had promised to take me one day. He'd gone to Ljubljana on work, packing as if he were flying to Siberia.

Once there, he called. "This is the most beautiful country I've ever seen. I've got to bring you here. I've never seen a country so beautiful, and the food… oh, the food is outstanding. This is The Little Country That Could."

That was all well and good, but at the time I was The Little Mother That Couldn't. Not with two kids in school.

But now? I smiled back at him.

I found a concert for the 30th of January in Kranj and wrote to Vlado.

Vlado wrote back. "Kranj is such a small town, you sure will not have problems find the place. Are you really coming? Great! I will take you for some good dinner!"

"Yes, I am really coming!" I replied. "And we would be honored to have dinner with you!! I am so excited..."

Excited? I was scared out of my wits.

Vlado wrote again. "Hi, Ruth! Just arrived from Africa. Now I can write again. Do not care about tickets and such things. You will be our guest; we will take care! Bye till then!!!!"

Relieved, I replied, "What? Me worry? Ha!"

I worried. Sometimes it's good to worry.

"Oh gosh, a terrible thing has happened! The gig in Kranj is canceled! There has been quite a flood and the water poured the place, so they don't work for some time. Uh, you already have airline tickets, right? What can you do? Can you change them for some other time?

Pozdrav

Vlado"

Yes, we already had tickets, and no, we hadn't bought trip insurance. Of course we hadn't bought trip insurance. What possibly could go wrong? The screw-up gods were laughing. If we couldn't change the dates, we'd have to go to Ljubljana. We still could walk around, enjoy the snow. Do the tourist thing. But really, how bad could that be? It wasn't a concert but we'd cope. Snow is good. Mucking about a strange city is good. Trying not to think about what we'd miss is… well, if not good at least necessary. I sighed.

The thought never crossed my mind that he might want to meet us even if there wasn't a concert.

I had two hours before I could call my travel agent. Maybe I could find a different concert in case the tickets could be changed. Maybe.

Then I saw Vlado's postscript:

"My wife says, you should come for a dinner and I will play for you in our flat!!!!!!"

I sat down and read it again, five or ten times to make sure it said what I thought it said. The words never changed. This man who knew nothing about us was inviting us to his house to eat with his family and hear him sing and talk and laugh and drink and do all the things one does with guests. With friends. Not fans. Not strangers.

Of course. He was just being kind, taking pity on us. At times pity can be a good thing, but this wasn't one of those times. I didn't want him to feel beholden. Certainly we didn't blame him. It wasn't as if he slipped away to Kranj and flooded the club himself.

I wrote back:

"If your wife really wants to cook dinner for us and you play for us in your flat, we would be very honored. :) Although isn't that risky? You may meet us and not really like us, so don't feel you have to do that if it is in any way inconvenient for you to do so..."

I waited. Held my breath.

"Ruth, don't worry, it will be OK!!!!!!!

Pozdrav,

Vlado"

Going to Ljubljana is like going to Tibet. Nothing goes straight to Ljubljana. No train, no plane, no road. An invisible wall separates Slovenia from all points west. Fly from Dallas to Paris? No problem. Fly from Paris to Ljubljana? Piece of cake, if you don't mind canceled flights for lack of passengers, never-ending layovers, and landing in a different country at midnight and getting bussed in through a blizzard.

I had no idea what we were getting into, heading off on this wild adventure to a snowbound land to meet Vlado and his family—and then what? The morning we left I dashed off an email to give him our schedule, packed up the dog, secured the house, grabbed the luggage, and checked email one last time. Just in case he'd written.

True to form, Vlado had sent one last post:

"I promised to my youngest to go fall asleep with her (two of us are away Friday night), so maybe I will be asleep at 11 pm. But if needed, just call me (or my wife). It is cold (-10) C, but on Saturday it will be -3.C.

Don't bother about flowers-She likes all of them.

Get a good sleep Saturday morning. Maybe better that I do not wake you up-you call me! OK?

Good trip!"

vl

Chapter Two

Cesta
Dolga dolga je cesta iz vasi do mesta.
Dolga dolga je reka iz plenic do človeka..
Polna lukenj in hrepenenja,
tolmunov, želja in ihtenja,
dolga, kot je lahko le noč,
dolga je ta pot
od nekje do nekoč.

"The road is the way between the past, present and the future. For Prekmurje, this very specific, distant, small part of what we call 'homeland' seems that it lives outside of time in some kind of hidden, sleepy, concealed, somnolent, somewhere taking-up-into-the-clouds paradigm. In fact, Prekmurje with its magnificent offspring Vlado Kreslin is something absolutely special, something what we profane Slovenes cannot reach, neither with our minds nor with our hearts. In the music they play down there, no doubt there is something more, something that puts a spell on us profane subjects of society, and we are aware—we know—that we will never really, totally understand it." -- Boris Jež, Slovenian journalist.

Everyone comes from somewhere. For Vlado that somewhere is the heart of the Prekmurje region, the most northeastern part of Slovenia, deep in the Pannonian plain. Flat land, in other words. Flat as a pancake, flat as a plate, flat as only river bottomland can be. The town he's from, Beltinci, is a neat and tidy place, just like every small Louisiana hamlet I've ever driven through, but the road that runs through this little town is wide and so well kept that it looks hardly used at all.

Beltinci has no train station, odd for the center of the local governing district. It's not that there are no trains— late at night, when the air is still, they can be heard chugging along a few kilometers north of town. But the Zichy counts who lived in the castle wanted no trains to foul the thousands of acres of arable land they controlled, and so the railroad had to go around their holdings, bypassing Beltinci.

The Zichy estate employed as many of the townspeople as possible but they couldn't employ everyone. The remaining fields were nowhere near enough to sustain the peasants. So many fathers and sons had to leave Beltinci to make enough money to feed their families.

It was the Slovene Diaspora, and the exodus continued until Yugoslavia embraced the red star of communism.

The building at Panonska 27 was home to the Gostílna Central and, being a *gostílna*, it had lots of food, lots of wine, and live music on the weekends. Loud music, sometimes all night long.

Vlado says, "When my father married, he and my mother moved to a small flat in the house. Now it's Gostílna Tonček. My wall where I slept was next to the notorious 'last room' where Kociper Brothers played. Eh, I listened to that *boom-boom* on Saturday, Sunday nights. Not every weekend, because they also played weddings and such elsewhere but many weekends, yes. I heard those guys from when I was one-years-old, never dreaming that I would play with them thirty years later."

Vlado wrote a book called *Venci*, which covers the time he spent making music with the old men from Beltinška Banda. One of the stories is about how the Kociper brothers played at Gostílna Central for many years, even between the two wars, when his grandfather Jožef Kreslin was still alive. Every now and then, when the *gostílna* closed and the last patron headed home, Jožef Kreslin shut the curtains. Locked the door.

"Now, Irma," he called out to his beautiful wife—beautiful, and the best cook in all of Beltinci, "make us something to eat!"

So, for the band and the waiters and Jožef her spouse, Irma did her magic and laid out a feast. Jožef grabbed a bottle of his best wine, passed it around. The band started jamming again. When they played happy music, everyone laughed, and they lifted their glasses and Jožef poured some more.

But when they played the notorious *Gloomy Sunday*, a song that was banned on radio in Hungary because of its connection with suicide, Vlado's grandfather took the bass away from Jožek Kociper and played it himself. They drained their glasses and hurled them through the cellar door to shatter on the floor. They ate and drank and jammed through the night, until they lost track of time, and the band members and staff had to stumble home with the sun in their eyes.

By the time Vlado came along, the *gostílna* wasn't the only place to have fun. Down the street, a cinema showed films from everywhere, not just Yugoslavia. Even during the communist years they had films from all over Europe and even Hollywood.

"It was only a hundred meters down the street," says Vlado. "When the film would tear, my father ran home and listened in front of the window to hear if I was crying. So on Saturday evenings, my parents went to the movies. When I was a little older I did not sleep, waiting for them to tell me the story of the film they watched in the cinema. Movies like *Never on Sunday* – did I tell you that years later I met Melina Mercouri in Athens? Movies like *The Duel at Silver Creek, Red Garters…*"

The *gostílna* housed other things. Depending on which door you opened, you could find a theatre stage or a billiard hall.

Vlado laughs. "One day I was hiding under the billiard table. I was young—you know how it is. I stole the mushroom—the figure that stands in the middle of the pool of the billiards—and ran away while they played. It was impossible to play without it.

"And then again I took out all the ventiles—valves, you know—from the hundreds of bicycles parked in the back of the *gostílna*. Angry guests—they were chasing me."

Yes, Tom Sawyer was alive and well in Beltinci.

But every Tom Sawyer needs a Huck Finn, an old soul in a young body and the ability to keep his mouth shut. It's a rare combination, which is why Huck Finns are thin on the ground. But sometimes God smiles on little boys, even those who steal mushrooms and bicycle valves. Štefan Smej, who had the River Mura in his veins the way Vlado had music, was Vlado's Huck Finn, right down to his pipe. Like Tom Sawyer, Vlado led and Štefan followed, but when Štefan said do this or that, Vlado listened—eventually. Most of the time. Štefan was older, more cautious and definitely inclined to play Vlado's conscience. And Vlado? Vlado was Vlado, the sensual one, the one out front. The wild one.

So by day, Vlado and Štefan played along the waters of the Mura, fishing from a sandy spit, hunting for Attila's grave. They poked in every corner of the countryside, slipping out at night to wander the outskirts of the village, then crawling back in through a window or sometimes just crashing in a barn. They hunted for mushrooms in the forest and for a while tried to emulate a local character they idolized, a man named Dimek.

"Let me tell you about Dimek. Such a fascinating man with long hair and a beard. He looked like Jesus. Very much into ecological things. He'd go on these long walks across the land. He even introduced mountaineering to Prekmurje—the concepts, you know—even though Prekmurje is a plain. And cycling? It was nothing for him to take his family and cycle to Mount Triglav from Prekmurje, and then they would climb the mountain. He'd put the baby in a basket on his back and off they'd go. He loved the Mura, too." Vlado pauses. "He drowned there, trying to save the kids when his boat overturned. Štefan was quite taken with him. I was, too."

Then there were the bullets. One day, after digging around, they found a cache of old bullets. Of course they had to see if the bullets were live. Without a gun, the easiest way to do that is throw them in a fire. So they built a nice big bonfire and tossed all the bullets right into the heart of it…

"No, no, no. We just sat around the fire and tossed one in every now and then, and then ran and hid behind the tree. Sitting under the stars, being philosophical. Haha… like boys!"

So they didn't throw the whole box on at once. It still wasn't the most brilliant thing to do. Neither was their game of playing chicken with cars.

"It was merely a traffic accident. But our teacher, Professor Ostercova, did not believe us. Eh, maybe we had a reputation, because we were never interested in the expected thing, what was on the surface. Never. But she did not believe it was merely a traffic accident that we were right there, next to the road. She thought we were jumping in front of a car like a game. I narrowly escaped but Štefan? He was tossed into the air and landed in the garden next door with a broken leg. Our professor was so angry! 'I do not believe you guys; you guys have got one dangerous game where the last one jumps in front of my car!' "

When Vlado and Štefan weren't out having adventures, they filled their imaginations with them. They devoured books, especially the ones by Karl May. With his adventures of Apache Chief Winnetou and his blood brother Old Shatterhand, the stories set them dreaming of the American West—hot, dry canyons full of villains, both red and white, frontiersmen and cavalry soldiers on the wide open plains, trusty guns and faithful friends.

But after night fell and Vlado had pulled the blankets up to his chin and closed his eyes, the memories of that old Prekmurska music booming through the wall at his grandfather's *gostílna* thrummed in his veins. Even though he no longer lived at the *gostílna*—the Kreslins had moved, but not far; they'd built a house right next door—and Vlado couldn't hear it through the wall any more, the music still had him. He just didn't know it.

As a child, I'd always heard that kids who grew up in communist countries were horridly oppressed and terribly unhappy. Never had fun. Never smiled. Never did anything but study and stay home and walk around cowering like whipped puppies. If they did anything wrong, the authorities would take them away. They'd never see their families again. This was how things happened in communist countries. Yugoslavia was communist.

But this childhood of Vlado's? This was about as close to idyllic as any boy could get. How did a boy in Tito's Yugoslavia end up living the American dream?

Outside of showing Vlado as a normal kid, I know nothing more about him. Not the essence. Not the 'why'.

"Jože Hradil," says Vlado. "He was my professor, taught me English in gymnasium. Last week I met him at a Budapest Book fair. He gave me his new book. Great book about Beltinci and his family, called *Pictures without Faces*. My father has a great role in it. He was Hradil's idol when they were kids. And Hradil was mine when he walked into the classroom, haha! He is a great guy; try to contact him! Write him! "

So Vlado sends me his professor's email. He's nudgy like that. And because I'm easily nudged, I write to Jože Hradil and ask him to tell me about Vlado Kreslin, the student. And Jože Hradil writes back to me with a story:

"Whenever I entered any classroom of the grammar school where I had been teaching for the first time that year, I did my best to make my pupils trust me. In the beginning I always asked if there was anyone from Beltinci, a village which I described as 'one of the most beautiful parts of the world'—the village where I lived between 1940 and 1945, the place where I attended elementary school. If there was at least one person in my class coming from the village, I named him my 'First Assistant' and emphasized that the schoolboys should take this fact into consideration.

"So I remember well how Vlado—sitting to the back of the classroom in the middle row—slowly got up on his feet, probably trying his best to show he was almost as tall as me (186 cm). He was an excellent student. He never had problems with any subject. Upon seeing his features, poise and smile, I was so surprised I blurted: 'I am certain that you must be one of Kreslins!' What striking resemblance to his father!"

Vlado shows me a photo of Milan Kreslin as a young man. He's outside with Katarina before they were married, and in the photo I see what Jože Hradil saw. In the planes and shadows of the father's face, I see the son.

"...to his father, whom I had always considered to be a small god. He had been my idol for a long time, ever since he—Pubi, as we called him—was a student at a respectful grammar school while I was still in elementary. He was wearing a school cap, a very beautiful one made of red cotton velvet. It was so lovely I could only dream about it. Sometimes Pubi was kind enough to allow me to put this crown on my head."

A red cap?

Vlado shows me more photos, snapshots from 1941-1946 of his dad, standing with other young people, and he's always wearing what looks like a flight cap.

"Students had to wear their cap when being out and in school. The colors were different for different schools, and it had lines on it, every line for a class—first, second, and so on." Vlado pauses, and then adds: "It actually was a tool of control in town during WWII when Hungary was ruling Prekmurje."

Jože Hradil continues:

"In the middle of a lesson with a very strict teacher, Vlado, all of a sudden and quite coolly, left the classroom without saying anything. Not a word. When he came back several minutes later, he went straight to a girl with tears in her eyes to return the book one of their classmates had thrown out the window. The teaching staff had to decide on a suitable punishment for the two boys. The problem seemed to be quite a difficult pedagogic dilemma, until the headmaster, whose name was also Vlado—cut the Gordian knot by asking: 'The question is, how to reward the gentleman and how to punish the naughty boy?'"

They must have come up with a special punishment for Vlado, something clever, something he would never forget. But when I ask him, all he says is, "Oh, I don't remember that at all."

Ljubljana, January 2010

Paris, with a nine-hour layover. Plenty of time to find a café and sip espressos in the sun while pretending to be sophisticated Texans. The French find Rick and me amusing.

But Paris is depressed today, raining all over those plans—a dreary droning rain, and cold enough to snow if it ever gets over being depressed.

Five long, boring hours later, Ljubljana comes up on the board, and just as quickly, it disappears.

"The flight has been canceled. We'll have more information for you in a little while." The perky ticket person flashes her best patronizing smile. "We will call you."

Hours later, the agent calls us up to the desk. With as much grace as she can muster while dealing with such dolts as we, she informs us that the plane had experienced mechanical problems and will not be arriving that night. "We can send you to Zagreb and from there you can go to Ljubljana. If you like… " She dangles the offer in front of us.

We pounce. Of course we'll go to Zagreb. We'd love to go to Zagreb. Going to Zagreb is nothing for seasoned travelers like us. A mere trifle, really. She smiles, we smile. The ticket machine spits out our new boarding passes. She staples our luggage tags to them with the enthusiasm of squishing a bug, and off we dash to catch our new flight, and just to show that yes, every once in a while life really can be magical, the rain turns to snow.

A flight is a flight is a flight. Still, only a Macedonian girl, two women, and Rick and I make up the passenger list, a merry band of five. We're fighting our way to Ljubljana against all odds, or at least iffy airport service, stuck together in an ersatz camaraderie. As soon as the two women, English teachers in a school in Ljubljana, discover our reason for heading there, they chortle, "Oh,

Vlado! Everyone knows Vlado. You should call him *Vladek*. It means 'little Vlado'."

Evidently Vlado is everyone's friend.

Vladek. I cringe. As if I could call him that. I don't even know the man and already I should call him *Vladek*? That sounds like a fast way to offend him. For all I know he might insist I call him Mr. Kreslin. No, it's *Gospod Kreslin*. Something like that. I munch my airline salmon paté sandwich and wonder how to reconcile all the formality I've been told is imperative in Slovenia with this laid back casualness I've seen so far.

I figure the airline will put us on another flight when we get to Zagreb. Wrong. They hustle us out to a van with barely enough time for me to hit the WC. "Ljubljana isn't far," they assure us, "no more than an hour or two. Really, a bus is much faster. Besides, only five of you are traveling to Slovenia, and with the snow…"

The airline men shrug. We shrug.

That done, they load up the bus with everyone's luggage, except for the poor Macedonian girl, whose luggage is nowhere to be found. Never fear, the airline men tell her, your luggage is almost positively on its way to Skopje. Or so say the teachers, who speak all sorts of languages and spend most of their time interpreting for everyone.

Thus sorted, the five of us crawl into the van and settle in for what, please God, will be an uneventful ride. If all goes well, we'll pick up the car at the airport and find our way to the Hotel Slon. In the snow. After midnight. In a foreign country with an incomprehensible language. All this because a stranger in a strange land said, "Come, I will play for you in my flat, and my wife will make for you a good Slovene meal."

We ease out of the airport and trundle off through the snow towards Ljubljana.

I've been awake for twenty-four hours now. God only knows what I say to the teachers. One of them asks me to sing a Vlado song, but I'm so tired I can't find the tune, let alone carry it. They talk with the driver. They talk with the Macedonian girl. Back and forth, back and forth. It's like being on a bus headed to camp.

Had we entered Slovenia the usual way—flying to the airport, putzing about getting the car and then creeping through the snow down a road just like every other airport road—maybe it wouldn't be so magical. But traveling from Zagreb at midnight? I feel like a spy in a trench coat and hat, sneaking into the country under the cover of a blizzard. I have the hat, but it doesn't make me mysterious, and the only thing I can sneak is a yawn. Only one, though. The second one dies in my mouth.

Lights on the hilltops catch my eyes. Alabaster churches wink into view, first one, then another, and another one still, each glowing with transcendent golden light and surrounded by deep blue snow. Mouth still open, I press my nose against the window. I forget about the yawn, forget about how tired I am, forget about everything in that cold and crystal moment except the fairy tale magic of those exquisite lights.

The teachers jump off at a gas station to catch a bus going straight into Ljubljana. The Macedonian girl and the two of us head on to the airport—she to catch her flight to Skopje and we because our rental car waits there. Right? Of course it does. Avis won't let us down.

Avis lets us down. Getting in after midnight probably has something to do with it.

The airport is deserted but for a few empty cars. We haul our luggage off the bus while the Macedonian girl dashes over to some security guards. The guards shake their heads at her and she turns away like a lost puppy.

The wind whips my hair about my face. How odd, since the last time I checked I had a hat on. I reach up to push the hat down. No hat. It's back on the bus, which at that very moment pootles away. Rick chases the bus down and reappears, clutching the hat. As he jumps off, the Macedonian girl jumps on and disappears into the night.

So instead of being stuck at Charles de Gaulle for who knows how long, we're stuck at Brnik Airport. Everything is closed. I look at Rick. Rick looks at me. It's going to be another long night.

"I can take you."

English? Can it be there is still one last taxi driver at Brnik Airport, and she speaks English? Hallelujah, yes. The taxi driver gestures to her van.

Vlado said they would charge us twenty-five euros to go into Ljubljana. She charges us nine and drops us at the Slon.

We squeeze into an elevator the size of a birdcage, and it groans, protesting at the violation of its inner sanctum. You'd think it had never carried anyone before. We each straddle a bag, my head braced against the back wall to keep from falling over. In a snit, the elevator chugs upwards and, trembling, deposits us at the correct hallway.

Despite the last twenty-four hours—canceled flights, canceled reservations, mysterious ferryings through even more mysterious countrysides—we've made it. Somehow, we get our clothes off without falling on the floor and tumble into bed. I desperately need sleep. It's nearly two a.m. Today we meet Vlado.

But first, an email to Eva. She's the one cooking dinner.

I collapse onto the pillow. I can handle this. I'll pretend I'm dreaming. That way I won't make a fool of myself. I turn off the light. Watch the ceiling in the dark. Wonder if we'll make a good impression—being quasi-semi-sort of ambassadors for Texas, America even, and all that. I worry about slippers and fall asleep.

Chapter Three

Morning tiptoes into the room and pricks us in the eyes. We haul our jet-lagged bodies out of bed—Rick to shower, and me to fret. I have a nine o'clock appointment to call Vlado. It's only seven. Two hours of worrying. I've barely enough time to build up a nasty case of nerves over breakfast.

Never have I seen such food at breakfast as the buffet at the Slon—eggs, bacon, sausages, hams, steaks, mushrooms, fried potatoes, tomatoes, cheeses, cereals, grapes, pickles, pineapples, oranges, bananas, kiwis, toast, bagels, sticky buns, doughnuts, muffins, breads, jams, jellies, honeys, yogurts, fish, oatmeal, coffee, tea, juices, hot cocoa, and milk.

If I were smart, I'd settle for toast and a cup of water for breakfast. But instead of being smart, I'm hungry. Slovenes feed their guests copious amounts of food—the breakfast banquet tells me this—but I don't get the implications. I missed dinner the night before. One quarter of a salmon paste sandwich doesn't constitute a real dinner in anyone's stomach. So, after justifying my gluttony with only a twinge of guilt, I pile sausages and potatoes and mushrooms, and more mushrooms, and even more mushrooms onto my plate. Content with my haul, I thread my way through the people to a tiny table by a window.

Ljubljana in winter morning's early light: It snows, then it doesn't snow, and then contrary-wise, it snows again. Fat flakes fall onto spiky strips sticking up from the windowsills. They must be some kind of anti-pigeon device, although what self-respecting pigeon would be caught dead flying around in this cold? Quite a few, it turns out. They dip and soar and spin in the snow, and then, once their show is finished, huddle under the eaves across the street and stare beady-eyed at us.

Rick and I talk about the usual over-breakfast things—how we slept (fine), what ached (everything), how good the food was (very) and the pillows (less so). Every five minutes I ask what time is it. He tells me. We talk some more, and then again what time is it? After the fifth or sixth time I merely point at my wrist and he shows me his watch. It's less intrusive that way, especially when chewing.

There comes a point, though, when I've had all the breakfast I can stand. It's finally quarter to nine. I have a call to make. My stomach cramps up into a bubble-gum sized wad of fear.

Phones make me stammer. It isn't calling Vlado Kreslin that bothers me. I get frazzled calling anyone I don't know. I forget words, jumble others up, and get totally lost when trying to push a sentence out. Fear of calling strangers on the phone, whatever the long Latin name is for that, I have it. In spades.

However I've come halfway around the world to make this phone call. If I get so scared that I throw up, then so be it. Praying my breakfast stays down, I punch in what I hope is his cell number. If I haven't gotten it right, this will be a most unproductive conversation.

A gravelly voice answers, saying something like "hello" and "eh" rolled into one. "Hello? Vlado Kreslin? This is Ruth—"

"Ruth! Where are you? *Mamma mia*! Are you okay?"

I collapse on the bed in a puddle of relief. "Oh, yes! It was the best adventure! It was great!!" It *was* great. The whole mess had been a delight, akin to hacking away at a jungle to arrive at Shambhala. Totally worth it. Isn't this the man I've been corresponding with for months? Why would I be afraid of him? To top it off I haven't made an idiot of myself yet. That makes it an absolute miracle of an adventure.

"An adventure? Good, good, haha! We had adventures, too, in Africa. We just got back from holiday. We had this happen, and we had that happen—you know how it goes, but we had a great time! An adventure! Now, for lunch you need to go to the As, around the corner from the Slon. It really is the best, and then go up to the castle this afternoon, and then the market by the river. You will like it. I will pick you up at six. Goodbye."

I put the phone down. It rings again. "At five. I will pick you up at five."

Ljubljana looks frumpy in snow, frumpy and exotic and eerily familiar, like a dowager aunt from the old country whispering in my ear. Dark windows like marcasite jewels are set in the dull skin of her buildings. It isn't her fault that she looks frumpy. Dirty snow does that to even the most beautiful city. I expected Ljubljana to be exotic. After the journey of the day before, I wouldn't be surprised to find the city on a different planet. But the familiarity shocks me.

Red-cheeked and wary, we crunch our way through the ice down the sidewalk.

Sure enough, around the corner and halfway down the block is the courtyard to the As. What if I end up ordering something like chewy tongue in squid tartare? On this snowy day that cries out for stick-to-the-ribs food, I better go with something safe. Maybe a salad…

Or maybe not. I've already forgotten my gargantuan breakfast and my dinner to come. The menu has English subtitles, and the description of the dishes looks so seductive. The wait staff gloriously, wondrously speaks English. We might survive this after all.

Tonight, Vlado will pick us up for dinner at his house. I'm not thinking about this, no, not at all. Thinking about it will make me worry. If I worry too much, I'll get sick. But if I don't worry, I'll forget something. So I worry anyway about all sorts of things: Slippers. Manners. Gifts. It's customary to bring gifts. Everyone gets gifts. This is great if you know what your host likes, but if not? Traditionally, the gifts are wine for the host, flowers for the hostess and candy for the children.

How hard can that be?

I have no idea how traditional the Kreslins are, but why tinker with a blueprint that works? Since we're coming from Texas, I wanted all the gifts to be Texas-themed. The children are easy—Lammes pecan pralines. A Texas wine for Vlado.

The saleswoman swore the wine was good. No, it was better than good. Excellent, actually, the best she'd ever had. She drank it all the time. It was her favorite. Really. She smiled. Blink. Blink.

"You think the wine is okay?" I glare at the pasta as if I'd caught it in bed with the aforementioned saleswoman.

"You worry too much." Rick sips the blood-red Slovene vintage we ordered. It's a fabulous wine. Of course it is—he chose it. A chipper saleswoman would never have taken him in.

"What about the pralines? The kids may not like them." The pralines were my idea. That makes them suspect.

"Stop worrying."

"But what about Eva?"

Yes, what about Eva? I could get her a cactus. Maybe not. With all those prickles it would send the wrong message. Bluebonnets? There's no way I'd find bluebonnets here. They're far too temperamental to grow in Slovenia. I can't even get them to grow in Texas. I have to find a local florist and explain with my non-existent Slovene what I want. If I can even figure out what I want.

So after a lunch of boar and pasta and more wine than we should have tried to drink, we slosh through the snow and find a florist a few blocks from the Hotel Slon. Maybe with enough finger pointing we can communicate. That is, if they have something we like. If nothing else, we can go with roses.

We shuffle into the shop, shaking snow off our coats, and find ourselves in the tropics. The shop is sweltering, and the sweet, thick smells of a hundred roses and plumerias wrap their sticky tendrils around us. It's like walking into Hawaii.

"*Dober dan*," I say to the girl behind the counter. This tells her right off that we're not Slovene, not even European and probably have trouble conjugating simple verbs no matter where we come from. It's the curse of the southern accent. "Do you speak English?" we ask her.

"Ye-es."

Okay, so it's a tentative yes. It's still a yes. She even smiles at us. That's more than most French would give us. And I've given the proper polite greeting so we don't seem like total hicks. It's a success so far.

But what to get Eva from this hothouse jungle? Even more important, what will survive the trip from the florist to the hotel in the blizzard? The last thing I want to do is show up with a bunch of dead and dying frozen flowers. Jade plants, anthuriums, bromeliads, succulents—would any of these even survive the trek to the hotel? Roses?

Roses might be dangerous. The language of flowers can change at a country's borders. Even though Slovenia feels as familiar as my grandmother's kitchen, underneath her skin thrums something wild and thick, a liqueur brewed by a dark and lusty stranger. No roses.

The anthuriums have been cut, useful in an arrangement, which is okay but still, the subfreezing wind might turn their edges black, and they'd be pretty only for a short while. Maybe only that night. Besides, they're too sexual. Am I the only one who thinks anthuriums look sexual? I wouldn't be able to hand them to Eva with a straight face. Jade plant? No, too informal. At least this time.

But there's an orchid, a little cymbidium orchid sticking its head up from behind a bunch of undefined greenery. My daughter has grown a cymbidium for years and it survives all sorts of trauma—lack of heat, lack of water, cats. This one is beautiful, perky with its white petals trimmed in purple, and small enough to stick inside my coat to ferry back to the hotel.

I don't need to stuff it in my coat after all. The girl wraps the orchid up in plastic sheeting for us and, smiling and waving, we make our way back to the Slon. I cradle the cymbidium in my arms against the wind and the snow.

Back in the room, I start wrapping presents, laying them out all over the bed with the paper and tape and ribbons I've brought from home. I cut and fold and tape very carefully since my deficient wrapping skills are legendary. I've been known to use half a roll of tape on one package. It's bad enough that my family snickers at my tenderly wrapped gifts. "Obviously that's from Mom." Heaven forbid the Kreslins find out about this little shortcoming of mine.

We have three hours until Vlado picks us up. Three hours in which to worry about meeting them, or three hours to take a nap. We set the alarm, crawl into bed and crash.

"It's time," says Rick.

My stomach ties itself into knots all over again.

We grab the presents and catch the elevator. This is crazy. No matter what country they're from, musical icons don't do this, just up and meet with fans they've never seen before. Not with folks like us. He doesn't have to do this. Why is he doing this? He won't like us. He won't like me.

In the time it takes for the elevator to creep to the lobby and spit us out, I work myself into a swivet. We set up camp by some chairs at the front window. Rick sits; I stand. I pace. I practice what little Slovene I know—*Dober dan, Gospod Kreslin*. Good day, Mr. Kreslin. No, no, that's not right. It's evening. Well, then *Zdravo, Gospod Kreslin*. Hello, Mr. Kreslin. That's safe and reserved. And formal—just in case he's formal. He might be. Everything I've read says Slovenes are reserved and formal, and I don't want him to know I'm not. *Dober dan...*

"That's him."

A stork-legged man wearing a knit cap lopes by outside, followed by a boy with a camera. Sure enough, the man blows into the lobby and turns towards us.

I stand there, trying desperately to remember what to say, "*Zdravo, Gospod Kreslin*". Hello, Mr. Kreslin. But I can't get the words out. My tongue glues itself to the top of my mouth.

I don't have a chance to say anything.

The man opens his arms and grins. "Ruth! I can't believe you're here!"

He sweeps me into a bear hug, crushing my face against his chest. Then, still holding me close, he turns and grabs my husband's hand. "Rick! Hello, hello! This is my son, Naj—take pictures, take pictures." Naj does so. At least I think he does. It's hard to tell with my face smushed into Vlado's shirt. He squeezes me once again and says, "Eh, come on. Let's go!"

So much for being formal.

We snatch up our gifts and, like leaves drawn in the wake of the wind, hurry after Vlado to the car. Rick ends up riding shotgun. Naj and I pile into the backseat. In the back I can hide behind Vlado. Much better to watch him.

I should have known anyone over fifty who dives off a concert stage into the audience might not be the most formal and reserved person in Slovenia.

Vlado talks as we creep down the street through the ice: "My youngest daughter and I were in Prekmurje visiting my parents, and a journalist friend who lives there came to see me. He asks if we're staying over. I say, no, no, we have to get back, some Americans are coming in from Texas. They were planning to go to the concert in Kranj but it was canceled. Then they got to Paris and their flight was canceled, and instead they were sent to Zagreb, and this and that... ehhhh. And my friend said 'What a great story.' He wants to interview you tomorrow."

Interview us just because we came to see Vlado? Who is this man?

I lean back against the seat and watch somber buildings slide past. It's barely light enough to see through the gray, falling snow. Night is almost here. Dinner lies ahead. Fish, Vlado had said. No telling what else. Breakfast had been wonderful, but of course, it would be with mushrooms. Mushrooms cover a multitude of sins. Lunch was even better with the wine and pasta with wild boar. Now fish for dinner in Vlado's home, with his wife and children.

We slip through the city as snow falls and dark closes in.

The fun has just begun.

The fragrance of burning rubber fills the car.

"Ewwww!" Naj waves his hand in front of his face, laughing. And me, being the mature person that I am, I bite my lip to stop the giggles.

The car merrily spins its wheels at the bottom of a hill while the men go over what might be causing the smell. Vlado opts for the belts. Rick blames the tires. Satisfied with the attention, the car lurches forward. We crawl up, up, up the road and into Vlado's driveway. Naj heads into the house. Rick and Vlado do the male bonding thing by sticking their heads under the car's hood to check to make sure everything's okay.

I stumble through the doorway and glance up the stairs. Steep stairs, and not only am I carrying gifts—including the fragile orchid which is probably squished by now—but my too long coat sweeps the step in front of me. I lean forward in my best bag lady imitation, figuring it's better to fall up the steps than down, and waddle my way up.

My, my, Vlado's got a ton of hats here. At least twenty or thirty of them hang above the entrance stairway, most of them fedoras but a few with larger brims, like homburgs. Maybe this wall is Vlado's hat cemetery, where his hats go when he retires them.

In a proper Slovene house, people either wear slippers or walk about in socks. Since guests don't usually bring slippers when visiting—although it's possible they'll keep a pair at a good friend's house—a good host provides a selection of slippers in various sizes.

I have a hang-up about feet. I hate showing them, seeing them, touching them. I'd rather suck a slug. Had I thought about it, I'd have asked if I could bring my own slippers but maybe that's going too far. I sit on the bench and tug my boots off.

That's as far as I get when the men bustle up the stairs, telling everyone that the belts are fine, nothing's wrong with the car at all, it's just the tires and they're fine, too. Vlado bends down by my legs. I scoot my feet sideways out of his way, demure on the outside but on the inside screaming, 'Please, please don't touch them.' " He reaches under the bench and fetches some slippers out for us. Puts a pair down by me. I tuck my feet as far under the bench as I can get them. He smiles. I smile. Safely shod, the men head into the kitchen. I wiggle my toes into my own borrowed shoes and hurry after the men.

Just like back home, the kitchen is the place to be. Naj, we've already met. Čarna's at the stove, cooking, and Ajdina, who's the youngest, regards us with a solemn look and doubtful eyes.

And Eva, who's a perfect complement to Vlado. Dark hair, with eyes still like a child's and a face so familiar that I swear I know her. She's in the group photo taken at the Beltinška Banda's anniversary party, standing in the back, smiling down away from the camera while Vlado is stretched out on the ground in the front. And so it is—Vlado out front and Eva in back. Vlado takes care of the music. Eva takes care of everything else.

The Kreslins' house buzzes with energy, full of vibrant colors—reds and oranges and yellows, a ton of open space, and windows everywhere overlooking Ljubljana—so they tell me. I can't see the city or the river, or even the street below. All I see is snow, lots and lots of snow, blowing and falling, smothering dark lumps and dips, with deeper darks behind the house. Some of them move.

"Wolves followed my mother home from school one day, when she lived in Bela Krajina," Eva says, looking out the window with us.

It's time to eat. We flutter about the table like birds to a feeder, finding chairs, sitting down, jumping up and changing places, with the kids popping in and scattering off again. We finally settle so Eva can place the first course on the table, a huge platter of smoked fish.

Vlado pours the wine and passes around the platter. "These are from some friends of ours. They have a farm. Dried sea bass—it's very, very good."

I've never had smoked sea bass in my life, but sea bass is fish, and fish is good. I take a bite. Dried smoked sea bass is even better. I take another bite. Oh, yes, indeed it is good. We devour the sea bass, and I thank the good Lord that it's not going to be a large meal.

Eva brings out more food—a salad of mache dressed with pumpkinseed oil and slivered almonds, and steamed asparagus, potatoes, pineapple slices dusted with sugar and crushed mint leaves, bowls of pumpkin soup and baskets of bread.

The kids scurry back to the table. Ajdina's at one end, Naj's between Vlado and me, and Čarna sits across the table beside Eva, when she's sitting. Rick commandeers the other end, closest to the bread.

Surely, this is it. Surely, there is no more.

Now Eva sets the main dish on the table. It's sea bass again but this time with white sauce and almonds, cooked to perfection. "Čarna's favorite dish."

In Slovenia it's impolite not to eat what you've been served but oh my, all this food. I look at Eva's smiling face and the table groaning with this wonderful home-cooked delectable meal. Goodbye, diet. Hello, feast.

With enough time and enough wine—and Slovenes believe you must have both for a good meal—it's amazing how much you can eat. But at last, we're done. The End. *Fini*. There's no way I can eat another bite.

Then Eva brings out the dessert, an apple tart.

Vlado, guitar in hand, sits down at the table. "I will be in Milwaukee in March. A theatre production. *Three Other Sisters* and I will play this." He starts playing Dylan's *Boots of Spanish Leather.*

"You'll be in the States?"

"Oh, sure. New York, Cleveland… There are a lot of Slovenes there, and in Milwaukee, too."

Later, I wonder how Vlado fared in the US.

"You should talk with Isabelle Kralj," says Vlado. "She's the director of Theatre Gigante in Milwaukee."

"Our audiences loved Vlado," writes Isabelle. "We had both an American audience when he performed in our theater piece, *Three Other Sisters,* and a Slovenian audience, when he played a solo concert. My favorite anecdote about Vlado, however, is this one:

"My husband, Mark Anderson, and I have a friend in assisted living. He is over ninety, and he is Slovenian. I asked Vlado if he would go visit him with us and bring his guitar along. Immediately, he said 'yes!' He sang *Spominčice* for our friend. Needless to say, our friend was very moved and happy."

"Ah, the priest—Fr. Jože Gole!" A huge gin spreads across Vlado's face. "For many years he was a professor at Marquette University. He's ninety-six years old and speaks twelve languages! What a guy!"

Vlado begins *Odhaja Dan*. I've gone through several glasses of wine by now, and, feeling brave, start singing with him.

He stops. "You're singing."

"I'm sorry. I didn't think you'd mind."

"But you're singing in Slovene."

"Well, yes. That's how you sing it."

"But in Slovene!"

"I don't know it any other way!" I'm almost in tears by now.

We lock eyes, neither of us saying anything. I have no idea what's going through his mind. I'm terrified he's about to chastise me for my rudeness. I hold my breath and wait, watching his face for some sign of everything still being okay.

Suddenly he grins, a grin that starts with his mouth and spreads to his nose and his eyes and his ears and probably even his fingers and toes and everything in between. He looks like a little boy on Christmas morning who realizes he's just gotten everything he's ever wished for.

I smile, too, and let my breath out.

He starts *Odhaja Dan* again. I sing, too, but a little quieter this time. At the end of each line he stops and listens to me, shakes his head and grins.

In this instant, I know that of all the things I could give him, this is the purest and sweetest of them all. He finally knows I really, really love his music, that somehow his music had gone all the way from Slovenia to Texas and touched someone who has no connection to anything Slovene except his music, that his music was enough to make me come almost ten thousand miles to hear it from him in person.

This is a dream; it's only a dream. I'd better not wake up until I'm on the plane back to Paris. Otherwise, I won't be able to get through this evening with Vlado. My timidity will win out over anything else. But if it's only a dream I can get through anything without making a fool of myself. Much.

The toilet almost does me in.

Everything about the Kreslins' house is comfortable. Homey. Friendly. I feel very homey and friendly right now, like an engorged tick, just the way you'd expect to feel after a five course meal and three glasses of wine. However, parts of me are becoming more engorged by the second.

So, after discreetly asking directions to the restroom, off I toddle.

The toilets of my childhood are of the American Standard/Kohler/Crane variety. All the flushing mechanisms are little handles on the left side of the tank. Nothing sleek about them—no, sir. They mean business. One glance and you know exactly what you need to do to flush away the evidence of a sumptuous dinner, complete with numerous bottles of wine.

European toilets are different. Each toilet is a crapshoot. Handle on the left, handle on the right, handle on top, on the side, the front, below, above. It's as if designers have a mandate to make every toilet unique. A work of art. European. And very confusing.

The restroom is lovely in a comfy upscale way—spacious with a huge jetted tub and subdued lighting. Right there to welcome me is my bête noir—a sophisticated European toilet with no apparent handle or flush mechanism of any kind. I only notice this afterwards.

I stare at the toilet, looking for a handle. Or a light. Or something. Anything. Nothing on the left side. Nothing on the right. I bend down—nothing underneath. I wave my hands around it in case it's motion-activated. Nothing happens. It can't be sound activated, can it? Surely not. I lean over, and say, "Flush." Nothing.

Here I am in the house of the Slovene national icon Vlado Kreslin, and I can't flush his toilet.

Mortified, I close my eyes and count to ten. I will not, cannot, ask for help. Not from Eva, his charming wife who's a saint for putting up with these crazy strangers from halfway around the world, not from my husband who'll tease me about it for years to come, and absolutely not from

Vlado, who's given up his weekend to be the perfect host. Especially not from Vlado.

Maybe I can pray it down. I run my hands up the sides of the tank and onto the top—and feel a crack. A barely visible but long purposeful crack, like a crack that surrounds a place that you push to flush a toilet. I push. It flushes.

Hallelujah! I throw my hands up into the air and spin around, laughing. I can face the Kreslins again.

Wine gets me musing. As I sit here with the Kreslins at their dinner table, I'm musing about this curious friendship. We're both married. We love our spouses. Eva certainly loves Vlado, flirting with him in front of us. With one glance, their world is complete with just the two of them. She takes the scarf I'd wrapped around the wine bottle and pulls it across her neck, smiling. He smiles back.

I look down, thinking perhaps I should go muse somewhere else for a while. But Vlado jumps up and says, "Come, come."

Rick and I scurry behind him, passing Eva's desk. She has an orchid next to her computer like the orchid we've given her. This pleases me to no end. Eva's not a woman to be flummoxed by a mere orchid. Where one orchid thrives, so can another.

He leads us into his office.

Four members of the Beltinška Banda face the door—four photographic portraits not yet hung. Each has a ribbon crossing the bottom left corner but in colors instead of black. I recognize the Kociper brothers from some of the older videos I've seen but the other men? I figure they're deceased but I don't know them, and the colored ribbons confuse me.

Vlado picks up a portrait. "We had these done. They were used in a concert—Anniversary of Prekmurje Independence."

"But colors—what do they mean?"

He stares at the portraits and slowly shakes his head. "Nothing. I just did not want them black."

The story of the Beltinška Banda reaches back almost a hundred years. In *Venci,* Vlado writes that the band started when the guns stopped after the First World War ended. That's when Jože Kociper joined his father's band in his hometown of Beltinci. Both he and his brother, Janez-Janči, ended up playing with the band the whole of their very long lives.

Prekmurje borders Hungary, Croatia and Austria, which means a lot of cross-cultural pollination goes on there. This makes for a lively cultural soup, especially when it comes to music. The band played everywhere they could—at balls, Catholic holidays, at funerals and marriages. Fiddle, clarinet, accordion, double bass were the instruments, later joined by tzimbals. As time went by, the Kociper Banda morphed first into the Kociper/Baranja Banda and then into the Beltinška

Banda. As is usual with bands they added some members and lost others, but the Kociper brothers always stayed with it, playing everywhere and with everyone they could.

But they'd never played with Vlado.

"They knew me—of course, they did. The Kociper brothers often played at my grandfather's *gostílna* years before. But we'd never jammed together."

With Vlado being a rock singer and the Kociper/Baranja Banda playing folk songs, it would take something extraordinary to bring them together. Or someone.

Enter Štefan. It was 1990, and his daughter was being confirmed. Vlado, being Štefan's best friend, had driven up to Gornja Bistrica for it. After all, if your best friend's family is celebrating, you go and celebrate with them.

Confirmation over, everyone headed out for the picnic celebration. Janez-Janči and Anton Rajnar, being musicians, brought their clarinet and accordion. Vlado grabbed a guitar and started strumming and singing with them. Nothing planned, just the inevitable jam session musicians do when they get together. Well, these guys jammed for almost ten hours straight, playing the traditional music of the region and much else, until their fingers were about to fall off and their voices raw.

"When dawn was crawling in, Štefan and I lit up our pipes as we stood in front of Štefan's house. It was one of those traditional Prekmurje houses made of mud and wood. Like Johnny B. Goode's house. " Vlado laughs. "So we stood there, puffing on our pipes, and Štefan leaned over to me and said, 'If you do not do something with this music, I will throw you in the Mura myself!'"

Up until then, Slovene popular folk music had been defined by the waltzes and polkas from the Gorenjska region. Nice music, but there was so much more to Slovene musical heritage than happy songs and romantic dance tunes. Music from Prekmurje? Completely different—wilder and haunting, sadder and more bittersweet. More melancholy. Even when happy, Prekmurci remember the grave, and that bleeds through in their songs.

So Vlado did something about it, and soon afterwards he and the Beltinška Banda were making music together. Wearing signature white shirts and black hats, they played their first gig in Filovci for the crowd at an eco-pottery workshop Štefan helped to organize. After all, another thing you do is you help your friends out, especially when they've helped you.

"Actually, I helped him get the audience to that workshop," says Vlado. "I was pretty well known then. Just the connection with Beltinška Banda was new.

"See, Štefan was a fighter for the Green movement, and I strongly supported him. In the eighties they wanted to make electric plants on the River Mura. We fought it back. We succeeded. Štefan was fighting against regulating the river, against drying out the moor and such problems. They did not listen, of course, and now we have problems with floods. They are making the moors back.

"Štefan saw the future of Prekmurje in soft tourism, production of industrial cannabis, etc. Of course, it had no response. A friend who tried to grow industrial cannabis -- it is a medical wonder and not just medical; they are using it in cars—had twenty years of trouble with the police, yet now he has a very successful farm.

"The first democratic elections were coming close. Štefan was one of the founders for the Green Movement, and they were forming a Green Party. He even persuaded me to be a candidate. I insisted on being the last on the election list so I would not be elected, but I gave my name to them. We needed the band to play on the Green Party election meetings, and Beltinška Banda would be the right thing for it. So in a way it was a political project of mine. The first gigs were quite funny, but then it became more and more serious. I took my father and mother, started playing songs which were missed and almost forbidden—like *Lili Marlene* and *Gloomy Sunday*.

"When we came to Ljubljana, it was quite a shock."

So the new, improved Beltinška Banda was on its way, this group of octogenarians fronted by the not quite forty year-old Vlado. They sang old songs, folk songs from Prekmurje that people had grown up singing, popular songs from Mitteleuropa, and even rock—Dylan, Stones, and Iggy Pop. With his younger band, Mali Bogovi, Vlado sang his own songs. But whatever songs he sang, and with whichever band he played, the people went absolutely wild for it.

What had seemed to be a funny experiment between tradition and modern touch ended up some years later to be the greatest live attraction in Slovenia.

Vlado's study is a regular room, not too big or too small—the kind of study you'd expect a musician to have. A piano over here. A computer over there. Leaning against the wall is a long necked lute-like instrument, looking like a wooden giraffe, albeit one that's lost its legs and sprouted a trio of strings.

"What's this?" I ask, pointing to the giraffe-thing.

He nods. "It's a saz, an instrument from Bosnia. Our ambassador gave it to me in Sarajevo after a concert."

Vlado opens his computer and clicks on the *Prošetao Mujo Mladi* video. "Vali," he says, pointing to the group singing with him. "They were refugees, you know. Teenagers."

Young women dance by the river and sing as they weave in and out among themselves, their harmonies tight, young men playing guitars, slapping bongos. One woman sits on the riverbank, strumming the saz, her red gold hair spilling about her shoulders as she glances up at Vlado. Bright open faces, smiling, relying on the kindness of strangers.

The sound of cymbals and drum brings me out of my reverie. Vlado has another video playing.

"'Joužek,'" he says. "Jožek Kociper." He points over at the portraits. "He played contrabass for the Beltinška Banda and his brother Janez-Janči played violin. I used to lay in bed and hear them through the wall of my grandfather's *gostílna*. You remember."

A weathered face with laughing eyes peers out of the screen.

"He was ninety-five when he died, and he played until the end. He was the best.

"We were at the monastery Pleterje, and Jožek, who only spoke Prekmurski, was talking to a French monk who spoke no Prekmurski and no Slovene. 'And what did you speak about?' I asked Jožek later. 'Oh, nothing important.' 'Then how did you know what he was saying?' 'Oh!' Jožek laughed and said, 'Like everybody else, he asked me what I ate and drank because he wanted to live as long as I did.' Haha!"

Jožek appears merry, eager even, ready to meet whatever's coming. Maybe that's the secret of a life well lived.

"This says," Vlado murmurs, pointing to a comment below the video. "'This is how people should be.' Yes."

He laughs, but when he studies Jožek's face on the screen, there's no laughter in Vlado's eyes. And on the video, Vlado sings: "Jožek, wait for me at the end of the road."

"Have you seen this one?" Eager to change the mood, he lets his fingers fly across the keyboard again. *Preko Mure, Preko Drave* starts playing.

On the screen, a capped and coated Vlado steers a motorbike down a Parisian street, passing mounds of snow and lovers kissing. Of course. He goes up to a wall covered in graffiti.

"Serge Gainsbourg's house," he says. "This is the wall around it."

This Serge Gainsbourg must be really somebody. He must be dead, too, or he'd keep his wall clean, but until Vlado I'd never heard of him.

"People write all over the wall?" I ask. "Just like that?"

"Oh, yes. Me, too. Haha!"

Then the video moves on to the Cimitière du Père-Lachaise and Jim Morrison's grave, where Vlado lets a pencil portrait of Morrison drift from his fingers.

"Did you draw that?"

"Oh, no. It was already there. I picked it up to look at it and then put it back down again."

All this, with *Preko Mure, Preko Drave* playing in the background of the video. A river of life, flowing out to the sea of forever…

"You have a video that opens with you and a baby, where the baby's saying *'ne'*." I stop, take a breath and pick my way around the syllables. "*Ljubav se ne trži*?"

Vlado peers at me.

I close my eyes. Slowly, slowly I say the words. "*Ljubav se ne trži.* With Lidia Baiuk. You're showing a baby a candy bar, and the baby is grinning and says '*ne*!' You know—'no.' A baby's favorite word? I mean, the world over, no matter what the language, it's their favorite word."

I stop. Bite my tongue to keep from babbling. Wait for him to say something.

"Oh, yes. That's Naj!" He grins and points to the ceiling. Click, click, click—up comes the video. Sure enough, there's Naj grinning, saying "*Ne!*" Vlado smiles down at him with that face parents get when their offspring does something cute.

I wait for the music but he starts to close the video.

"Please. Can I hear it?"

"Oh, sure, if you like." He starts the video up again.

Lidia's alto first fills the room, followed by Vlado's husky baritone as he slowly walks up to her and unbraids her hair.

"We filmed this on the Isle of Love, off the Mura River. It's very popular. The title means 'love cannot be bought or sold'."

"I like that. Slovene?"

"Croatian."

Vlado runs through all the comments that have come in. He pauses on a few, and then skims a few more, his eyes serious.

"What do they say? If you don't mind me asking…"

He shrugs. "These comments…" He scrolls down through a few more. "These people... they really liked this. This man… he said he had tears in his eyes." He stops, and then says, softly, "I hadn't read these. I didn't know."

"Roberta Flack. You know her, yes?" We're all huddled together on the sofa in the living room, delicately holding our half- empty wine glasses. Except for Vlado, who's holding his guitar. "I introduced her at a concert in Ljubljana. I didn't know anything about introducing people so I just said her name, and then I kissed her. On the mouth! Haha!!" Vlado starts playing *First Time Ever I Saw Your Face.*

He sings, and we join in. Somehow we end up on different verses. We sing the one about the bird several times. It's possible we stick the bird in a few verses where it's never been before, but it's still great fun.

Vlado likes fun. The next day, while at the *gostílna*, he pulls out his camera. "This is what we did this morning." The photos show Vlado wearing his knit cap, and Eva and the kids, sliding down the snowy hill next to their home, all of them laughing and grinning.

But that's a different wine, a different day.

Back in his living room, Vlado says, "This is our concert at the Cankarjev dom last month."

He starts a DVD on their television. Sure enough, there's Vlado up on stage, singing and playing his heart out. Miro Tomassini is off to the right, his once long hair looking as if someone had chopped it off shoulder length.

"It looks like Mr. Tomassini has cut his hair."

Vlado breaks out laughing and calls someone on his cell. Still laughing, he talks for a few seconds and then passes the phone to me.

"Here! You tell him!"

Oh, good grief. I handle his cell like it's planning to shock me, which means holding it with as little contact as possible. What do I say? Does Miro Tomassini speak English? Surely Vlado wouldn't hand me the cell if…

"H-hallo?" I say.

"Hello," Miro Tomassini replies.

Well, we got past that hurdle okay, didn't we. I launch into my nervous explanation of what I said about him cutting his hair. Miro Tomassini explains that oh, no, he never would cut his hair, that his wife would be most upset. Then we laugh that funny laugh two people do when they're both they're thinking, what do we talk about now?

Vlado rescues his cell, which also rescues me. He laughs at something Miro Tomassini says and hangs up.

Much later Vlado tells me, "Miro Tomassini—Tomas—was already a rock star when I came to Ljubljana to study in 1972. He played bass guitar in great rock trios—Bumerang, Oko, Jutro—and some more bands. I used to stand in the throng at the first row under the stage in Študentsko naselje—Student campus—and gaze at those heroes, dreaming of being onstage. Years later, we got together and wrote *Tista črna kitara*. Then he joined the second Martin Krpan lineup. After the band split I persuaded him to change to guitar, and since then he's recorded some of the greatest solos I ever heard. Most of the time we write together; he does music and I write lyrics.

"When I first was with Beltinška Banda I was the youngest; now I am almost the oldest in Mali Bogovi. Tomas is a little older. It is great to play with young people in a band. But it is precious to have someone who is your connection to the past, who remembers things—musical and others. Half of our talks in a car, when we drive to the gig, look like history lessons. Today's generations have the memory only as long as a few tweets. I remember Jožek when he was ninety-four, and Janez passed away. Every one was so much younger, even my father. You have no one to talk to about your youth."

Vlado sits down and clasps his hands together. He sighs.

"My father? He likes to tell his stories. He talks and he talks, and you know, the stories can go on for a while. The people like them. But the time… eh. And I think, 'Come on, Pubi, the concert schedule. We have to go on.' "

Vlado shakes his head. I shake my head. Time can be such a pain, especially when it comes to schedules. Concert schedules, airline schedules…

Suddenly Vlado stares at me, and jumping to his feet, he slaps his hands to his chest. "But you know? Fuckin' shit, he's my father, he's eighty-three years old and he's got the right to say anything he wants!"

"Absolutely!" I blink up at him. I almost say "damn straight", but even with all the wine I've had—and I've had a stupendous amount, at least a bottle and a half on my own, maybe more, certainly more than I've ever drunk at one time in my life—I've kept my wits about me. Women might not swear in Slovenia, and I'll be damned if I'm going to be the first to do it.

Vlado smiles at me then, nodding. "Right."

Right. I smile back, and then I grin. He grins. It's okay.

Standing alone at the corner window in the dining room, I can almost see the city. The blizzard makes sure the view is iffy, but here and there lights flash through the snowfall. It's enough so I think I'm at least facing the right direction.

I try to gather my thoughts, a neat trick if I can do it. Maudlin metaphysical thoughts. It must be really good wine to get me thinking about things like this. Things like kindness and saints and how did I ever get to be here. Right now all these thoughts are floating and bumping through my mind like drunken balloons. I could use a pin. Or coffee.

Vlado turns the lights out in the dining room and opens the door to the balcony. "Come, come. I have something for you. "

We creep out on the snowy ledge in our slippers.

Everyone has on slippers, even Vlado. Eva, who passes on this adventure, told us how Vlado likes walking barefoot in the snow. The snow and the night have turned me into a voyeur. I want to see him do such an outrageous thing, but Vlado's slippers stay on.

Snowflakes swirl around us. Vlado, with his glasses perching on his nose, has transformed himself into a schoolmaster. In one hand he holds a flashlight, in the other a small book. Maybe he's about to read from his book *Pojezije*. Even if we don't understand him, it will be the perfect cap to a perfect night.

The quiet settles in. The snow slows its fall. He opens the book, smiles and reads to us Robert Frost's *Stopping by Woods on a Snowy Evening.*

Back inside, we scramble to pull off slippers and find our shoes.

"I'll be in Milwaukee in March, and then New York and Washington. At the Slovene Embassy…" Vlado's voice trails off on a hopeful note.

"Milwaukee's pretty far from Texas." Eva finds me a piece of paper and I draw a very not to scale map of the United States. "Milwaukee's up here," I say, pointing on the paper. "Texas is 'way down here." On the paper Milwaukee looks impossibly far from Texas.

"Oh. I see." Vlado's smile disappears.

"Still, Washington may work. Rick goes there sometimes."

Vlado's face brightens. "Good, good. Maybe Washington then."

Hugs all around, with Eva promising we'll see her tomorrow. We clatter down the stairs and out the door.

I tip my head back, laughing as I spread my arms and turn around and around, doing my best to catch snowflakes in my mouth. It's the perfect ending to a perfect night; at least, it is for me.

Vlado takes us back to the hotel, driving deliberately, both hands on the wheel. No one else is out. It's only his car and the snow, piling up here and there with more coming down. Soft, quiet…

"The street. Someone should be taking care of this. All this ice. " He shakes his head.

The street looks fine to me, but I have nothing to compare it to. My sole experience of driving on ice consists of my old car, creeping up a very long ice-coated hill at a forty-five-degree angle. Vlado's car has no problem with the ice—no fishtails, no spinouts, just a quiet midnight *whoosh* through the snow.

"Now tomorrow. I will pick you up about noon."

Rick and I immediately protest. "Oh, please, you needn't. You've done so much, and we don't want to put you out. Really, we'll be fine."

"Of course we'll do something tomorrow." And that's that.

Vlado pulls up across the street from the Slon, and Rick hops out. I get tangled up trying to gather my things, which have disappeared under my legs, my seat, maybe even the car itself, god only knows. I dig around by my feet, feeling for my cap as I thank Vlado for his hospitality and food and wine.

He motions me forward. We try for the traditional "kiss kiss". I forget to kiss the other cheek, still worried about my cap. He waits until I finish dithering and then motions me forward again. With an "oh!" I lean over the gearshift and we kiss cheeks again, although I aim for the wrong cheek and catch the side of his mouth. No matter. He smiles. I smile. I scramble out of the car and over an ice berm, completely graceless. With a wave, he makes a U-turn and heads home.

Chapter Four

Ljubljana, January 2010

The dreaded morning after. I keep my eyes shut and brace myself against the headache that must be lurking somewhere in my skull. How much wine did I drink? Way too much to get off pain free. Over a bottle by myself, maybe two. I lost count. Now I'll suffer for it. My first hangover.

Or maybe not.

I open one eye. No pain. Morning light fills the room with its weak winter glow but nothing hits me over the head. I open the other eye. Nothing. No pain. No queasiness. Nothing.

Vlado's wine is magic. That must be it.

Nothing beats mushrooms for breakfast, except maybe lots and lots of potatoes, fried in butter and salt and a little pepper, but—no really, mushrooms before potatoes. It's a close race, though. And hot chocolate. But mostly mushrooms. Dear God, please, can I have this every day for breakfast? At least this winter? I'll be good, I promise.

Stuffed, we head upstairs to swaddle ourselves into too many clothes. It's cold out there. If our sweaters and scarves and more sweaters and coats can't keep us warm, at least they can cushion our bodies when we fall on the ice. Once we're wrapped thick as marshmallows, Vlado calls. He says he'll pick us up at one-thirty. That gives us plenty of time to get into trouble.

We go kicking around Ljubljana, our faces bared to the freezing wind. The snow has stopped, and the sun is doing its best to warm the cobblestone street running down to the square. Its best is pretty good. Puddles are everywhere, and people hop and skip around them, trying to keep their shoes dry.

Still, it's January. By the time we make it to the end of the street the sun has given up and gone into hiding. Like magic, the people disappear too. We're left to cross the stones on our own. Fat flakes twirl around us, giving me hope, but the clouds stay sulky. Maybe someone shut them up with their prayers, but not for long. Even now the clouds swell and bulge, and then here comes the snow! Swirling and dancing in the lightest breeze, kissing our cheeks and lashes, flying merry, merry everywhere.

A few blocks away, we come across an intriguing statue of a man wearing a heavy coat. This was Ivan Hribar, the former mayor who rebuilt Ljubljana after a devastating earthquake in 1895, and he did so with great success until he fell out of favor with the emperor. It wasn't until the dark days of 1941 that he was selected to be mayor again. Ljubljana was to be annexed to Italy, though, and this filled him with despair. In protest, Hribar wrapped himself in the Yugoslav flag and leapt into the Ljubljanica River.

We head back to the Hotel Slon. Around the corner and down a few blocks is the heart of Ljubljana—Prešeren Square. On one side is Plečnik's Three Bridges, the Tromostovje (*tro-* meaning three, *-most-* meaning bridge, and *-ovje* which makes it plural and adds a *-ness* on the end, Vlado says. The state of being three bridges. Threebridges-ness). The bridges cross the Ljubljanica River there, enticing folks to the market and on into Old Town. The Franciscan Church of the Annunciation sits on the other side, its rosy bricks looming over everything, the way big, impressive churches generally do. The building that looks like a prow of a ship sailing into the square is the Hauptmann House.

In the middle of all this stands the national poet of Slovenia, France Prešeren, forever staring past Hauptmann House towards a figure on the building's wall, the figure of the woman who spurned him.

If not for the unrequited love he had for Julija Primic, who married a respectable merchant instead of the far from respectable Prešeren, he might have remained a minor poet. But in first wooing Julija and then losing her, he made her an icon of Slovenia, and immortalized them both.

Julija may not have loved him, but the Slovenes do. They love him so much that, rather than a king or president, they chose him to be their most beloved national hero. He's their Dante, their Goethe, their Shakespeare, and if his genius was recognized too late for Prešeren to enjoy it, at least it was recognized.

But I wonder if Julija had any regrets when Prešeren was honored, if people watched her and whispered as she passed them in the street, if she kept the little book of poems he'd given her when he'd hoped to win her love.

Go to the market, Vlado told us, so we leave the unhappy Prešeren in his square and cross the Tromostovje to find the market. However, he told us to go on Saturday. This is Sunday. No one's here but us. We kick slush all the way down the street to the colonnade, and then we walk, skirting ice patches. On the way back we study the shop windows and little cafes.

Everywhere there's English. All the shops and stores have signs outside chalked in Slovene and English. English? Italian or German or Hungarian I understand, since Slovenia touches nations that speak those languages. But English? Yet, there it is. How can one ever get lost in a city so full of English?

Ljubljana Castle sprawls out high above us, watching over the city. Below it, a railcar beetles its way up the funicular. Rick and I debate whether we should go up to the castle, but heaven only knows how long it would take. Normally, we'd have plenty of time until one-thirty, but so far things have been anything but normal. Exciting, unbelievable, magical—yes, but normal had been left back home. Since Vlado seems to be an early person, a cushion of an hour or even more might be wise. So, doing the smart thing for a change, we head back to the hotel.

But first, a detour. There's enough time for this.

We turn down the street where we'd found the florist.

A haberdashery sits a few doors down. The day before I spied a hat that I want to see again, just in case it convinces me that it needs a home. But the store is dark, locked. I see the hat through the window, looking forlorn on a shelf.

It isn't to be. We leave before dawn the next morning, long before the store opens again.

So up to the room we go. Sure enough, someone has slipped a note under our door: "Twelve-thirty. We will pick you up across the street. Vlado."

It's already twelve-twenty. We clatter down the stairs and across the street. A car pulls up, headlights flashing. We dive into the back seat. Good thing it's Eva and Vlado, or who knows where we might have ended up.

Vlado drives carefully, his cap sitting on the dashboard again. "We're meeting some friends. You'll like them. Chris is from Seattle. This place we go to—very nice. I go about once, twice a year. They're only open on the weekends, very good food. "

I settle back in the seat, feeling like Lara in *Doctor Zhivago*, and watch the scenery zip by in a thousand silvered shades.

Vlado pulls behind a gas station and jumps out. Standing on packed ice in an open space, he plays hacky-sack with a frozen snowball as he scans the passing cars for a familiar one. Sure enough, a car slips in besides ours. Vlado dashes over, talks to the driver. He smiles and waves at us, and then speeds away. Vlado hurries back to our car, and we're off again.

The Gostílna na Zaplani, near Vrhnika, lies halfway up a mountain on a twisty road. Even with Vlado's deliberate driving we shimmy and shake around the corners, tires and snow doing a jitterbug. The road falls off on my side into a forest of giant needles. Most of them stretch out of sight above us, but the trees closest to the road are broken off as if cars crash into them on a weekly basis.

Vlado turns up a driveway, and we scramble out of the car to meet Chris and Anda. Kisses all around, even Rick and Chris, who are both American men but, hey, when in Slovenia do as the Slovenes do. The six of us crunch our way through the snow to the *gostílna*.

Gostílna—tavern, or pub, or even inn—comes from *gòst*, which means guest. All sorts of words dealing with taverny things come from *gòst*—*gostíja* (feast), *gostílničar* (innkeeper), *gostíšče* (guesthouse), and *gósti* (playing the violin—trust me, it fits). If Vlado is any indication, Slovenes love showing *gostoljúbnost* (hospitality) and they really love *gostíti* (feeding guests), which makes it easy to go from *gòst* (guest) to *góst* (thick), especially around the middle.

Blueberry liqueur. Wine. Bread, which Vlado snags by slipping his arm behind my back. More wine. More bread. More snagging.

"I'm sorry," I say, reaching for the basket. "Would you like some bread?"

He replies, "Oh no, that's okay," and smiles.

Cold cuts sliced as thin as cellophane. I hold one up to the light and make out Chris's face through it.

"I had something that looked like that once," he says. "It ended up being stomach."

Erm. I'm not so wild about it being stomach. "How'd it taste?"

"Really good."

Stomach? Tiny flecks of fat pock the meat, which is more amber than the cold cuts I'm familiar with. It looks like beer brushed salami. Surely one piece won't hurt me. Besides, backing down now would be impolite. The cold cut doesn't smell gamey, a good sign since for me that renders everything inedible, leading to disastrous consequences. But this aroma? I barely keep myself from licking my fingers.

I pop the slice into my mouth and close my eyes, holding off on swallowing so I can savor the salty, smoky taste. It tastes almost like prosciutto but more subtle. It's better than good. It's to-die-for delicious.

We talk about music, the challenges of putting on concerts and the folly of eating a large dinner before going on stage, which is why Vlado tries to only eat the backstage chicken soup before a gig.

"Who is this?" Vlado later asks me. "We really eat chicken soup in the Cankarjev dom, but that is because of Beltinška Banda's teeth. I rarely have time and nerves to eat it. On the contrary, I always joke about Sting, who says that he eats the day before the concert only light meals so that it doesn't come up from his stomach. And, of course, does not drink! We eat and have a big meal before the concert if we only can. Haha!"

Somehow we end up talking about *Vsak si želi*, one of Vlado's songs.

"It's the perfect go-to-heaven song," I say, not even knowing if they believe there's a heaven, but what does it matter? We're all old friends now; we can handle these little assumptions with grace. "When I hear it, I see a sunny green hill where people are laughing and dancing, hugging one another like they haven't seen each other in years. It's forever springtime, and as the couples dance together, they spin faster and faster until they rise up in the air and *whoosh!* spin all way up to heaven."

Vlado looks at me.

Maybe I shouldn't assume quite so much. But I'm brave. I meet his eyes and wait.

We stare at each other for a very long time. Vlado wears the most placid, unreadable expression. He studies my face. Maybe the song has nothing to do with laughing and dancing and flying away to glory. Maybe I'm tramping around in his memories.

But when I hear *Vsak si želi*, that's what I see—a reunion. Vlado's reunion, with Vlado and Eva and their children, his mom and dad, a small crowd of friends—everyone he loves, all laughing and hugging and dancing. Cool breeze, hot sun, and lots of laughter. Some tears. All these people, so very happy, spinning up, up, up into the sky until they disappear in the light. Slowly, slowly Vlado turns. He sees me, and he grins. His arms open wide. He gathers me up and spins me around, laughing. Around and around and around, laughing and laughing...

Vlado whispers, "I played that song at President Drnovšek's funeral."

More wine, this time Cviček. "Tito's wine," says Vlado, pouring me a glass. After the first go around, we're the only ones drinking it. "Not everyone likes it."

I call down the table to Eva who refuses a glass. "Don't you like it?"

She laughs, her face lighting up, and she shakes her head. "It's great as a cleaning fluid."

Okay, so maybe Cviček tastes a little thin and ever so slightly sour. It doesn't taste vinegary, which is good, and it doesn't pack much of a punch, which is even better.

"It has less alcohol," says Vlado. "Tito would drink it when everyone else drank other wines. That way he wouldn't get drunk."

"And they would," I reply.

Vlado smiles.

Cviček—I like it. Vlado likes it. It appears we're the only ones who like it. We finish the bottle off.

"Now, when I was in Cleveland..." Vlado sees the surprise on my face. "Oh sure, I've been there a few times, and once when I was there, this young lady comes up and says I'm not playing correctly this Slovene song—*Nocoj je edna luštna noč*. I'm not playing it like this Slovenian pop singer plays it. And here's the thing—it's an old folk song, but Beltinška Banda were the ones who brought it out to a wider audience, and then this pop singer probably took it and performed it. I never heard his version. But she was convinced he had the real authentic version of the song and that I was doing it wrong." He shakes his head. "It reminds me when I performed with the Dubliners, and Sean Cannon made an announcement 'Now we play a song by Metallica—*Whisky in the Jar*.'"

Vlado tips another bottle around for everyone. This time the wine is something rich and dark, and we have boar, sitting right in front of us. Succulent, savory, sexy boar.

I close my eyes and take a bite. "We don't have food like this back home," I murmur, blissfully trashing the entire US food industry. "Nothing even comes close." Maybe it's the wine, maybe it's the company, but if I'm struck dead this moment my mouth will die happy.

Somewhere between the cold cuts and the boar, Vlado orders mushroom soup for me. Just me. The broth is pale buttery gold and stuffed with mushrooms. I sip it ever so delicately, taking my time so no one watches me. It's very much worth savoring. I'd pick up the bowl and drink it, but I'm determined to be on my best behavior.

We gather up our coats and head for the door. Music and laughter drift down the hallway from somewhere deep in the building—happy, homespun music. Like a hound on a scent, Vlado dashes off to investigate, Chris close behind.

The rest of us huddle together in the bar.

Chris comes back, saying it's a wedding reception. Vlado follows. "Oh, yes, a wedding reception," he says, "and someone played a gut bucket." He has a muffled excitement about him, as if he's discovered something he wanted ends up not being what it's supposed to be.

We head outside and stand in the cold, surrounded by drifts. There's a chapel next to the *gostílna*. Chris says he attended a wedding there not too long ago. Out in the snow, a black cat as big as a lynx leaps from drift to drift, disappearing into a hole and reappearing again somewhere else.

It's time to kiss-kiss and say goodbye, so kisses all around for everyone. I wonder if Chris and Rick, being American, will shake hands this time but no, they kiss again, too. Gotta love these European customs.

We pile into the car, Eva driving this time. The drop off looks just as harrowing. Ice has turned the road into a deadly, crackly crunch. The car fishtails, a good one, and the ravine creeps much too close. What would it be like to be found dead at the bottom of a ravine, impaled on those black trunked needles with Vlado and Eva, to slip over the edge into that sweet sheer snow?

But the car fishtails only once. Soon we're zipping down a flat road past ochre buildings settled in snow-skinned fields.

Eva and I say our goodbyes. The whole time I wonder when I should do the kiss-kiss with her. Now? But she's saying something important. Now? But I need to respond. Maybe afterwards. No, she's talking. Is it rude to kiss when someone's talking? Maybe if I just zoom in, but is it left cheek, then right cheek? My left or her left? Maybe she initiates the kiss. Maybe she already has, and I missed it. How am I supposed to know when to respond? Then she smiles, hops in the car and drives away.

I'll never get this kiss-kiss thing right.

"*Dušobržnik.*"

Vlado eyes grow sharp as a hawk's eyes. "Where did you hear that?"

I blink. "The Internet. I found it on the Internet. For my book. Someone suggested it to me. I wanted to a word to describe what the woman called this man in her life, who was becoming her lover."

"Hmmm." He sits next to me. "Maybe not that word."

We sit there on the settee. Our heads are together, like family whispering at a funeral, knees almost touching. He cocks his head, considering, his eyes moving back and forth. Thinking. Waiting.

Finally I ask, "Is there another word I could use instead?"

He nods. "*Moja ljubézen*. It means 'my love'. But if you want to be more intimate? *Ljubézen moja*." He speaks slowly, distinctly. I repeat the words, working them around my tongue.

"*Ljubézen moja*. Okay." I nod. "I like that."

"Here." He writes it down on a napkin and hands it to me. "If you need translation, you ask me. I will do your translation for you, okay?"

Oh yes, very much okay.

Something across the room catches his attention. "Look."

A young woman unwraps a present—a book. Vlado's *Pojezije*. Her companion leans forward, smiling, and points in our direction. The young woman whips her head around. Her mouth falls open.

"Here she comes," Vlado whispers.

Sure enough, she grins, grabs the book and heads our way.

Vlado sits up straight as she apologizes for interrupting. She stammers out her request. He murmurs something as he reaches for the book, signs it and hands it back. She thanks him, then thanks him again, and scurries back to her table.

Vlado slumps back into the settee.

I nudge him. "You see? People are buying your book."

He sighs.

"They're giving it as gifts," I add.

"Mmm…"

I lean over and whisper, "They like it. They wouldn't give it if they didn't like it."

We sit side by side, both looking ahead—Mr. Dejected and his chirpy sidekick. He squirms a little, nods a little. I sit very still. When I finally glance over at him, he's smiling.

"I need to get my own copy of *Pojezije*."

"I gave you one last night, but you didn't take it."

"Oh, no." Ouch. Now I've done it. "I thought you were only showing it to me. Like you did your friend's book. I didn't realize you were giving it to me. I'm sorry."

He nods. "I will give it to you when you speak Slovene."

And because it's a dream—it has to be; I'm here, aren't I?—I say, "I'll do it."

Of course I can learn Slovene, right? Piece of cake. Sure it is.

I don't know what I'm getting into.

Vlado smiles. He knows.

Slovene is excruciating. The alphabet is Latin with a few letters taken out (Q, W, X and Y) and a few added in (Č, Š, and Ž), and yes, the basic sentence structure is subject/verb/object, the same as English. Everything after that induces brain cramp.

On my dining room table I've got a dog-earred Slovene/English dictionary. Fewer than twenty-five percent of the Slovene words Vlado uses with me are found in it. If I'm lucky I can find the root word and figure out what he's writing. Online translation programs are not much help either. Adding to the confusion, not only does Slovene have the usual singular and plural nouns and pronouns, it has dual as well. Plus there's standard Slovene, and then fifty other dialects to contend with. Prekmurjian, for example.

Vlado's friend and fellow writer Feri Lainšček says:

"Vlado Kreslin rose to prominence in Slovenia when a leading Slovene linguist, Toporišič, was destroying the Slovene language and creating people who were afraid of speaking dialects. They were afraid of their vocalizations and of using the wrong accent, which comes from the local environment. Kreslin in Ljubljana consciously spoke the Prekmurjian. Besides all the rest of what he has done, this is the most significant. He dared publicly and manifestly to speak Prekmurjian. He raised people's self-esteem. Besides the fact that he made the Pannonian sentiment and folk music the urban phenomenon, this is perhaps the most important."

The only Slovene I know is what I've learned from Vlado's songs. Eva sent me a course with CDs, but the instructions are in Slovene as well. I'm lost right from the beginning. I've gotten to Lesson Seven about ten times now, and I'm still floundering. Plus, there's that pesky little accent issue. A hearty "*Dober dan*, y'all!" would probably come off as incomprehensible. I doubt that would endear me to a native Slovene.

But I try. I really do try. One day I want to carry on a conversation beyond what's found in tourist books and Vlado's lyrics. I'm not looking to participate in a philosophical discussion on the socio-psychological effect of the Slovene diaspora on her culture in the early twentieth century. But something beyond, "Hello. How are you? Where's the restroom?" would be nice to know.

Bojan rushes in, young and handsome with dark hair and dark eyes, showing very white teeth when he smiles. He smiles a lot. Energy zips around him like a crackling Tesla coil. This interview is going to be fun.

He pulls out his DVR and sets it on the table, asks if we mind if he uses it.

Mind? I'm just glad he speaks English. I'll never get used to everyone speaking English here. It makes me feel woefully uneducated because I'm trapped inside one language while everyone else is out there playing around with everyone else's words. But that will change.

He also has a camera, which is less fun. Cameras hate me. With luck, all the photos will be of Vlado, and I can hide. Still, if he points that lens at me, I must be confident enough to keep my eyes open and my smile wide when the time comes.

Unless I shouldn't smile. Maybe smiling isn't what's done in photos here. Vlado rarely smiles. But I'm not Slovene, I'm American. We always paste a smile on our faces. I try not to smile.

Smiling or not, the interview must go on. Vlado sits next to me, his arm draped over my shoulder. I give Bojan's camera a wary eye. Then I smile, and Bojan takes the picture. Maybe I'll look good for once. Maybe. Miracles do happen.

Or maybe not. A few months later Vlado sends me a copy of the interview—a two-page spread in *Ona* magazine. He looks great. Me? Not so much.

Out in the lobby, Bojan shoots a few more photos of us. It takes a while. Vlado fidgets, standing by me. It won't be long until it's time to say goodbye.

Then it's over. Bojan shakes my hand, thanks us for the interview, and hurries out into the snow.

At the door, Vlado glances back and smiles. He spins his finger up in the air, just as I had done when we were talking about his song *Vsak vse želi*. I smile back and nod, and he waves and walks away into the night.

Chapter Five

Washington DC, March 2010

The last time I was here in DC, the road to Dulles was an empty little wanna-be-interstate through a tree-filled countryside. Now it's seven lanes each way and packed with so many cars it's almost impossible to navigate. The highway signs are about as clear as anything coming out of Washington—confusing and only marginally useful.

No time to find the hotel. We'd landed during rush hour. The embassy is God knows where, and we have sixty minutes to get there. We'll never make it. Once we get into DC all the streets turn into one-ways. We could spend hours looping around the embassy and never find it.

We manage to navigate our car to within a block of the embassy without hitting anyone, but with all the one-way streets shunting cars here and there away from where we want to go, there's no guarantee we'll make it on time. I call Vlado. It doesn't go through. I call again. Nothing. I try one last time.

"Ehhhhello…" says a gravelly voice. Thanks to the honking traffic now frozen on Connecticut Avenue, that's about all I understand. Vlado and I shout a few things back and forth, mostly about us being about five minutes away and if we can find the right street, we'll be there in time for the concert. Okay, so we're obsessively early. We used to live in DC. We take no chances.

Round and round we go. Somewhere in there lurks California Street and the Slovenian Embassy. Surely we'll find it. Surely…

Ah, there it is. And walking up the driveway followed by a photographer, long legs scissoring as she tries to keep up, is Vlado.

We slow down. Rick yells out the window. Vlado turns, waves, grins, and waves some more.

"Hallo, hallo!" He runs up and kisses my cheeks through the car window. Thankfully, he decides not to crawl over me to get to Rick and waves at him instead: "Kiss, kiss."

This European custom of men kissing men to say hello and goodbye and heaven knows what else is still disconcerting to my macho American male. But when in Slovenia, do as the Slovenes do, and we're on Slovenian soil at the embassy. Rick waves a "kiss, kiss" back.

We park only slightly illegally down the street and let the wind push us up to where he stands, camcorder in hand. "And here are my friends from Texas…"

Rick and Vlado fetch the pralines and rum balls from the trunk of our car. Vlado disappears with them downstairs and returns, surreptitiously licking his fingers.

He introduces us to the staff, all young and efficient, and then he heads off to do sound checks for the concert. Rick and I occupy ourselves by first studying the art exhibit by Z.E.K. Crew, a wonderful exhibit that puts me in mind of what Andy Warhol would have done if he and Peter Maxx had fused brains after dropping some really good acid. After that, we study the food laid out for the guests—all lovely morsels that my fingers itch to pick up. I make sure I stand far away from the table. I'm dreadfully hungry, but snitching food would be rude. My stomach disagrees. I park myself in front of a window and watch snow the size of coconut flakes drift down into the backyard.

Snow is good. So far, I've only seen Vlado in snow.

People float in. I can tell who's there for the performance and who's there to be seen. The latter are embassy hoppers, people whose social life consists of attending as many embassy parties as possible. It's a grand lifestyle if you like living on finger food. Most of these folks are dressed in casual cocktail, otherwise known as business as usual with a splash of glam. It's okay. They came to be seen but Vlado will work his magic. They'll leave as fans.

The former are much more sensible, wearing comfortable business attire and a smile of expectation. They know what it's like to be entertained by Vlado. Most of them have ties, if not to Slovenia, then at least to what was once Yugoslavia. For them, Vlado sings their memories and the old stories of the land their family had to leave behind. Sometimes he brings them news of family back home as well.

Rick and I are the odd ones out, not being Slovene or even Yugoslav—as far as I know—in any way. Nor are we embassy hoppers. We're just there for Vlado. Ergo, we are sensibly dressed, being both fans and friends of Vlado. It's a good thing, too, because I never get the glam thing down.

The concert gives Vlado a chance to catch up with old friends, too.

Vlado spies a distinguished looking gentleman. With a cry, he dashes over to greet him.

Vlado later tells me: "Mr. Žarko—did I introduce you to him? He was Tito's head of catering service at the Protocol of the President of the Republic. He was at the concert in Washington. We first met the year before when he was doing the catering for the Slovene Embassy at my concert. After my performance he came to me with tears in his eyes and said: 'My son, I didn't understand much of what you are singing but you opened my heart!' And then I ask him—what do you want me to play for you? And he answered—'*Zbog jedne divne crne žene,* my son.' So later, between the plates and dishes being served, I sang for him.

"He told me great stories about people he met when working for Tito. When Fidel Castro came to Yugoslavia in eighties, after Tito was gone and there were new 'guys', new politicians waiting outside on the tarmac, Castro stepped from the plane and went straight to Mr. Žarko, who was standing in the back. He shook his hand and said: 'This is the only man I remember.'

"Mr. Žarko is a very charming man. I have hardly ever met such a gentleman and we are big friends. We write all the time."

Vlado gets me a wine, not Cviček that I hoped they'd have. It being the Slovene Embassy, I figured if anyone would have Cviček here, they would, but no. Still the Cabernet is lovely. With a full wine glass in my hand I make my way over to Sonia, Vlado's scissor-legged photographer. Her last name isn't Slovene, so how did she end up here in D.C. with Vlado?

"I grew up in Prekmurje, where Vlado's from." We lean against a bar table in the foyer and sip our drinks. "I always was listening to his music, but I never dreamed when I ended up in Fort Walton Beach, Florida that I'd be doing a photo shoot with him. When I heard he was coming to America, I had a chance to see him live for the first time. I flew from Florida and finally I got to meet him. When I met him here, he asked me to do his photos. And here I am."

Vlado says later. "You know she did the cover picture for *Drevored*? Very nice, very nice."

It all sounds very Vlado-ish, very down to earth and...well, natural. Work with your friends. What a novel idea.

"Celebrity in Slovenia is very different from celebrity here," Sonia says. "People there are very respectful, not nearly so in your face. Someone like Vlado can lead a much more normal life."

Normal, like standing outside in the bitter cold, talking with someone. That's where Vlado is now. He's across the street in front of a house, talking to a woman who's sweeping snow from the steps. She may be the maid, she may be the ambassador with a penchant for wearing a starched white uniform, but whoever she is, Vlado's out there with her. Less than an hour to go before his concert and he's outside in the cold with someone who wasn't invited in. Until now.

I later ask, "The maid, the one you were talking to before your concert—did she come?"

"Oh, sure. She was there. She is the maid for the Brazilian Embassy. I met her two years ago."

Rick and I find our seats in the second row. Vlado takes the stage and sets his playlist down by his side. Checks his tuning. Makes sure he has something to drink close at hand. Says a few words and starts singing.

For an intimate concert it sure is packed. Every chair is filled. People stand lined up two and three deep at the walls, waiting to see if this Slovene folksinger can deliver the goods. By the end of the first song he's won them over. The ones who know the words—mostly the staff but a few others as well—sing along with him. The ones who don't sing sway in time with the music.

I sing, too, but under my breath. I know most of the songs, having listened to them every day for the last six months. However, my accent isn't that great, and Slovene is an incredibly tricky language.

Back at his house the month before, Vlado had asked what song I wanted to hear next.

"*Kakor zvezda na nebu*," I rattled off.

Vlado peers at me.

"*Kakor zvezda na nebu*?" I tried again, much more slowly.

He shook his head.

I gave up. "Your song with Neisha. *Ka-kor…zvez-da…na…nebu*."

"Ah! *Kakor zvezda na nebu*!" He zipped right through the words that sounded for all the world just like what I'd been trying to say all along.

Obviously, Slovene words and Texas accents don't blend well. No big deal. It's not like I'm going to use them anytime soon. Or sing them loud enough so other people can hear. *Sotto voce*, that's me.

Contentment flows through me like rich wine. To think saying yes to watching a video brought me to meeting Vlado, who's about to perform, in person, in front of all these people—and me.

I whisper in Rick's ear my new philosophy of Life: when Life asks something of you, you say yes. No matter what it is.

I sit back, pleased that I'm so radically clever.

Vlado calls the embassy staff up to help him sing *Od višine se zvrti* (Dizzy from the Height). It's a lovely thing for him to do. Vlado gets through the first verse and chorus. Then he stops. Smiles at me.

"Ruth! Come up and sing!"

I can't not do it. It would cause both of us to lose face. Me, I'm not so worried about, but I can't do that to Vlado. I lean over to Rick on the way up to join them. "So much for saying 'yes' to Life."

Someone hands me the microphone. I try to give it back, give it to anyone, but no one will take it. The room really is packed. So many people, more than I ever thought would fit in here. They're all laughing and clapping, eager to see what might happen. Especially if it ends up in the *Washington Post* as *American Woman Makes Fool of Self at Slovene Embassy*.

Vlado is singing again.

I don't get one word right. I get close. I watch the mouths of the other singers very carefully, but what they sing and what I sing isn't quite the same. They put consonants together in ways I've never combined them before. My tongue can't mash them together fast enough.

Then it's over. Vlado stands. We all take a bow, the staff and I'm laughing because we've actually gotten through it. Yes, it's over. Time to say good-bye.

Well, almost.

In the foyer, a few books and CDs are on a table, manned by a lovely young woman, but most have made their way into the audience's hands. People crowd around Vlado, holding their treasures, asking for autographs, shaking his hand. He talks with everyone, thanks them for coming. One woman comes up to me, saying, "Wow, he's not like celebrities here. He's just like a regular person!" as if I'm an expert on all things Vlado. I don't understand why she's telling me this but I smile back at her, agreeing. Eva, where are you?

The crowd thins, and two older ladies, both from Russia, come up to Vlado.

"They said I touched them in their Slavic soul," he says later, pleased.

That I understand. He's touched me, too.

Vlado writes. He writes emails, he sends articles and YouTube links, he sends mp3s of songs he's uploaded, he sends photos—all these things he sends me. "Ruth, look at this!" "Did you see this?" He's so delighted, just like a little kid.

We keep on writing, several times a week and sometimes several times a day. I'm hesitant because, really, he's made up a thousand times over for the canceled concert in Kranj. I don't know if we'll ever see each other again, yet he still writes. I half-expect him to say, "Thank you for corresponding, but I must go now; have a good life." But, instead of brushing me off, Vlado writes back enthusiastically. Every time. He's always enthusiastic. He's probably an enthusiastic sleeper.

A small voice inside me, a tight snobby voice full of swallowed diphthongs, hisses, "You should be ashamed." For friendship? Ha! Silly woman. I know this voice. It belongs to someone who had taught me elocution and all things tea and petit fours while she looked down her nose with arch disapproval at little ol' scruffy me. I ignore the voice, the same way I did then. Anyone who apologizes to snails for stepping on them doesn't need help feeling guilty.

Besides, Vlado is still holding his hand out to me. As long as his hand is there, I will take it.

I still don't know why his music moves me. If something moves my heart I want to know why, and nothing moves me like his songs. But without something giving the friendship a structure, some task that we're both working on, our correspondence will fade away into Christmas card greetings. The question won't be answered. This makes me twitchy. I don't need any more twitchiness than I already have, thank you very much. I doubt Vlado knows the answer himself, at least not consciously. Lord knows I've asked him. But he is the key. Of this I'm absolutely sure.

I'm stuck between the rock of my curiosity and the hard place of my fear.

What to do, what to do?

On one hand, our friendship is humbling. Never in my wildest dreams did I imagine we'd be friends. On the other hand, friendship at our age is supposed to be proper and demur. It'd take a lifetime of pleasantries and once a year meetings before I'd find my answer. I don't have that much time. Besides, I can't glom onto him like a leech and suck the information out. Not that I would, but oh, I'd be tempted. To figure out why I get tears in my eyes when he sings? Oh, yes, indeed.

Then I get an absolutely wild-hair, crazy-brain idea. I could write a book, a memoir about him and me and how we met, our unlikely friendship, a friendship that is totally unexpected.

That would go down like beignets on Bourbon Street. In New Orleans. At Mardi Gras. Oh, yeah.

And in the course of writing this book, surely I'd find out why his music moves me so. Surely.

But instead of letting Vlado in on my absolutely crazy and wild idea, I keep it to myself. I hide it in my heart and pet it and stroke it. Late at night when everything's asleep, I pull it out and study it, weigh it even, because if I ever get brave enough to ask him, and he's crazy enough to say yes, it's going to be a hell of a lot of work. Asking him means my courage needs to be worked up. That takes days, weeks, maybe even months. I don't ask questions well at all.

"Ask me anything," he says. "Anything at all."

I look at him and think—*do you know how dangerous that is?*

It's not the writing that worries me. It's if he says no, because if he says no, that's it. It's dead. *Fini.* So, I think and I wait, and I think some more, all the way up until I get to the point that if he refuses, it will be a relief instead of busting my soul into little bitty bloody shards.

Just like writing the thank-you note two years before.

"What do you think," I start off, "about us doing a book together?" Before he has a chance to say no, I send some ideas: a proposal, how to get an agent, then a publisher, then… I stop.

I resign myself to him saying 'Eh, *draga* Ruth, maybe not' because who am I to write such a thing? I've had… what? A few musical comedies that were locally produced and blessedly forgotten? A couple of books languishing at the bottom of a drawer? Big whoop. That doesn't inspire confidence. I know nothing about his culture, nothing about his land, nothing about his country. I need a crash course on all things Prekmurje, if not Slovene. What if I make him angry? I have a knack for angering folks. And this awe thing—am I supposed to be awed by him? Like a coat, I put it on; I take it off. Neither feels right. I barely know him.

But I know him enough to see if he's just as crazy as I am.

Vlado writes back.

"Sounds very reasonable! But not just about me. We can make it about Slovenia, too. About how a girl from Texas sees Slovenia through music. Through me! Haha! And we can add a few of my poems, your impressions from a concert this December... Uh!!! Big work for you!!!!"

Big work for me? Is he kidding? He said yes. I'm in heaven. First I need to get back to

Slovenia. Research, you know.

"Ruth, please tell Rick this lady is coming to Križanke."

Vlado attaches a video of a woman with flaming red hair singing the blues—Mary Coughlan. Rick and I both listen, and when she opens her mouth and lets go with that sultry voice, now soft and sad, now belting to the rafters, we're in that bar, right there with her. Mmmmm, what she and Vlado could do to a song… If we could only hear them in person. That would be bliss.

I plead, but Križanke is not in the cards for us this year. Vlado and his flame-haired chanteuse will have to wait.

But Vlado's twentieth anniversary concerts at the Cankarjev dom are this December.

Chapter Six

Ljubljana, December 2011

"Let the Music Flow"

I'm crossing the border and I'm heading south
Gonna meet up with my old friend.
We go back some ways, those were crazy days
But I remember when
We were running fast, hoping it would last
We never thought it would end.
So I'm crossing the border and I'm heading south
Going to meet up with my old friend

How does it go for you, are you getting through
Are you still running with the Muse
When you get her close you've got to keep her close
She's too good to lose
But didn't she take you far, with your black guitar
There's no need to sing the blues
Hope it goes good for you, and you're getting through
And still running with the Muse.

It's kind of understood, you did the best you could
There was no other way
When all is said and done it's still a lot of fun
Just living for the day.

Odpiram vrata svoja na stežaj, za prijatelja
dolgo je že to, kar ga ni bilo,tam od severa.
Miza stara je že pogrnjena,
kot da vmes bila sta dan al' dva,
zato odpiram vrata na stežaj,za prijatelja.

Čme kitare glas nam ustavi čas za eno kratko noč.
The morning comes too soon, looking at the fading moon
Thinking it's time to go
The road is calling me, the way it's meant to be
It's the only way we know
We'll take it through the night, and try to get it right
And let the music flow.
---Allan Taylor/Vlado Kreslin

The first time to Ljubljana, we'd slipped across the border at midnight. Slovenia was a snow-spangled fairyland, and magic danced all around us. This time we fly in before noon. It's raining. We're so damp we're moldy. The landscape decides we were wowed enough the last time we came. Being merely quaint with alpine houses and sheds dotting green slopes will have to do. As for magic? Who wants to be magical in rain?

We leave the airport and, with blurry windows on a blurry day and a GPS still trying to find itself, turn towards what we hope is Ljubljana. The GPS has a pleasant British voice—male—once it decides we're worth talking to. This sets Rick off in a grumpy mood. Note to car rental agencies (I'm talking to you, Avis): if a man with a wife rents a car, make the GPS voice female. Trust me—after a long flight, Brit twit male is not what he wants to hear, especially if the voice can't even figure out where we are.

Through the rain I see hundreds if not thousands of photo opportunities. Sticking my head out the window and getting soaked while I take point and shoot photos isn't the best option. None of them will be good enough to bore family and friends with, and I can't sell them to a magazine. I shoot through the glass anyway, and mentally cross my fingers, hoping the camera lens sees better than I do. It doesn't.

At last the GPS decides it will talk nicely to the satellite. It leads us straight to the Hotel Lev with only a few minor hiccups.

The Lev is nice, very nice. Eva reserved us an actual suite. Not only do we overlook the road to the airport, but across the highway up on a hill is the most desolate house. It seems abandoned, shuttered against the wet and cold with all its ghosts locked inside. I love it. It's the Cekin Mansion, which houses the National Museum of Contemporary History. No wonder it looks sad.

Once inside our warm and dry room, Rick's phone rings.

"We're on our own to get to the Cankarjev dom. Vlado's had a wreck. Eva isn't sure when she'll get there."

Vlado's had a wreck… I can see it now—Vlado carted off in an ambulance, Vlado's car mangled on a wet street, the announcement that Vlado wouldn't be at the concert that night…

"Don't worry. He's okay. Only the car and the fence got hurt."

So much for catastrophic thoughts. Eva's stress levels must be spiking through the roof. The last thing we need to do is add to her stress, and ours. Walking to the Cankarjev dom sounds more and more peaceful by the second.

If we can find the Cankarjev dom.

Rick points his chin in a random direction. "It's that way."

So, with mist sticking to our hair, we hurry to the Cankarjev dom by way of Rick's chin. Between the hotel and the convention center sits a park and the Opera House, which means we have to walk a mighty crooked path to get there. People loom out of side streets, out of the park, out of every which way and pass by us as though we're ghosts.

"We could go through there." I point down a narrow path that disappears between huge shrubs and on into the park. I figure a straight line between two points is just as short here as it is back home.

"We don't know if the path goes through. Or what's in there." Thus spake the American male, long wary of muggers.

Maybe throwing caution to the wind on the night of the first concert isn't the best idea. Taking the path still looks like fun. Instead, we meander this way and that to get around the park, becoming wetter and wetter. I try not to twist my ankle on the intermittently cobblestoned sidewalk.

Finally, we fetch up, more dripping than bedewed, on some steps of what we hope is the Cankarjev dom. I say "some steps" because we get to choose among a lot of steps that lead to various doors. This prompts a lively discussion about which is the correct entrance. I have it wrong, as usual, but at least it's the right building.

Down at the other end of the entrance hall we see Vlado's photographic display. This concert series is a double anniversary for Vlado—the 20th anniversary of the December concerts. And tonight's concert is the 50th anniversary of all the concerts he's had here. Thus Vlado's gallery here in the hall, showing pictures from every December concert since their inception.

Photographers and fans and various other people swarm around the photos. Bobbing up from the middle of it all is a fedora. Vlado.

"American woman," he sings *sotto voce*, moving with open arms through the crowd towards me. "American woman."

He kisses me on the cheek, greets Rick, and when I ask how he's doing, replies, "Bad". Then he turns away, smiling, and melts back into the crowd

Like shuttles on a loom, photographers weave among the crowd. They're respectful shuttles, though, so very respectful, not only of Vlado but of the fans watching what's going on. Quiet, too. No one gets jostled or shunted aside, not even by the cameraperson holding a video cam or the pretty young woman interviewing Vlado. High tech and low key—that's Ljubljana.

A video of one of Vlado's songs plays on a screen overhead; another screen is running an announcement of his concert. Eva finds us, standing lost in a sea of unfamiliar words, and we talk mouth to ear while someone new interviews Vlado.

Suddenly he disappears behind huge glass doors.

"Wait here," says Eva, and she disappears as well.

Maybe I have to time to slip away, find a restroom. I dash downstairs and promptly get stuck in a crowd of runway models. That's what most of these women are with their immaculate makeup, perfect hair and scarlet lips. And gorgeous. The women here are gorgeous. The last time I was gorgeous I was twenty-two, and it was an accident. Did I also mention they're tall? Oh my, are they tall. They tower at least a foot over me, even the ones who aren't wearing four-inch candy apple red stiletto heels. Very high heels seem to be de rigueur in this line. Evidently women dress to attend Vlado's concerts. I shrink down into something resembling a short dumpy bag lady.

The line doesn't move. I scratch at an invisible spot on my coat sleeve. No line movement. I shift my weight from one foot to the other. No one comes out of the restroom. Ten women ahead of me—I count them—and none of them are even in sight of the stalls. I can't afford to wait. What if Eva's searching for me right now to go backstage?

I break out of line and scurry up the stairs.

Eva, bless her heart, waits for me at the door. Little ducklings one and two, Rick and I follow her. We leave the throngs behind and take the elevator down.

So this is the backstage. It's like standing in a hospital corridor—narrow halls, low ceilings, and passageways tucked behind these huge metal submarine doors, hiding God knows what as they lead off to God knows where. This place must be an amazing bomb shelter.

And the quiet. It's not Whisper World back here but I'm mindful of making too much noise. Out there is the audience, and in here? Why, we're in here with the performers who are waiting to put on a show. Months and months have gone into getting everything ready for tonight—the music and the performers, getting the playlist just right, practicing over and over until the music drones in their sleep, the little dramas of how all this came together. It's like giving birth. Each one of these folks has done everything they can do to prepare and now they're about to deliver this baby, anxious to deliver this baby. But first they have to wait. And be quiet. Or at least not shout too much.

"Ruth! Come eat!" Vlado makes a beeline for two cauldrons full of chicken soup set out on a table. He snatches up a bowl.

"Err, that's okay," I reply. What if I have to look for a restroom in the middle of a song? I'd be mortified if I had to do that. "I'm fine. I don't need to eat."

"Sure you do. Get a bowl and eat. It's good."

On the other hand, when Vlado says eat, maybe it's good to eat. I mentally cross my fingers for luck and fill a bowl half full with chicken soup. Really, how much harm could a few spoonfuls of soup do? We stand at the counter, me next to the cauldrons, and eat.

"The boys—you know, from the Beltinška Banda—taught me about this soup. We have it before every concert. Eating of the soup is like our transcendental meditation for us. Haha!"

Good for the stomach, too. It's hot and salty which I expected, and really garlicky, which I didn't. That's okay. I can happily live on garlic. The soup is chock full of chicken, potatoes, carrots, and onions. And dumplings—that's unexpected, too. I bite one in half to make sure it's good. It is, even if it's a little bland, but then I belong to the-hotter-the-better club. When you're going to be on stage in the middle of a set, spicy dumplings aren't what you need to eat.

Vlado finishes his soup first. "You okay?"

I nod and wave, my mouth full.

"Good, good. Keep eating. I'll see you later." He hurries off to take care of something else while I finish my soup.

Folks hurry through, jazzed on adrenaline. Some carry guitars, laughing and greeting one another as they head back to their dressing rooms. The soup reels them in. All of a sudden there's a bowl in their hands full of garlicky chicken goodness. The awesome power of magical soup strikes again.

Maybe setting up camp here next to the soup isn't such a good idea. I move along a couple of yards down the counter. Give the soup sippers plenty of room. It's like quarantining myself. Trust me, that's a good thing. I still can see what's going on but if I stay away from the soup, everyone's safe from the Klutz Monster. All we'd need is for me to twist the wrong way and knock me, them, and the two cauldrons of soup to the floor.

Eva and Vlado have vanished to do whatever they need to do. I make an effort to vanish, too, or at least blend into the wall. It's possible with my forgettable face. I've done it before. If I were shorter, I'd back up underneath the counter, but that won't work. Instead I prop my elbow on the ledge and hide in plain sight.

I don't stare, not really. That would be impolite. But being backstage at the concert with all these performers? I watch, observe. I've never been this close before to a group of professional musicians, seeing how they interact right before a major concert. My only saving grace is that my glasses hide my eyes. No one knows I'm almost staring.

I'm discreet. If anyone glances at me, I look away. No eye contact at all.

Ear contact, though, that's fair game. Someone close is speaking English. I edge up to a silver-haired gentleman. He's talking to one of the Mali Bogovi members about teaching piano, and he's got a lovely British accent. Not Brit twit, either, but something close to York, maybe? The inflections sound familiar. Our priest is a Yorkshire man, so maybe so.

Thus we meet Allan Taylor, friend of Vlado and a damn fine folk singer and balladeer in his own right.

The song he sings tonight with Vlado is an ode to their friendship. Vlado says they are very great friends.

Allan is a most interesting guy. He introduced Bob Marley to New York on one of Marley's early US tours, back in the early seventies when Allan lived there for a time. Since Allan was recording for Island Records, Chris Blackwell, director of the label, asked him to show Marley and his band the joys of the Big Apple. So this dapper Brit and reggae Bob Marley and the Wailers spent a week schlepping round New York, all the while carrying these huge joints, big as trumpets.

The three of us—Allan, Rick, and me—strike up a camaraderie, not of the English speaking, because almost everyone here speaks English, but of the I'm-sorry-I-only-know-English group. My Slovene barely covers *prosim*, *hvala* and Vlado's song titles. Oh, and variants of *gósti*. Got to have *gósti*, especially tonight. Otherwise it's our own little island of ignorance in a polylinguistic sea.

However, even though we speak English, it's hard to understand each other. Not because of the English vs. Texas accents, but of the noise. The quiet has vanished. Down here it's now a party. Upwards of a hundred people are stuffed together in an area the size of a bedroom—performers, their significant others and friends, family and friends of Vlado and Eva. The snack bar's tended by a young woman, making sure everyone gets their necessary fix of carbohydrates.

A crowd from Beltinci has driven in to see Vlado on this opening night. One of them, Milan, brought wine from his own vineyard. The container sits on one of the tables, and the level of wine is rapidly falling. Someone—Vlado? —passes me a cup of pale rosé, light and dry. Eva's here too, although she's talking with someone away from the wine table. Other friends from Ljubljana are here. I meet Vlado's parents, get reacquainted with Čarna, who now speaks perfect English, and talk with the loveliest lady, a friend of the Kreslins, who shows me photos of her granddaughter.

Later, I mention the lady to Vlado.

“Ah,” he says, “that is Dr. Gabi, very prominent psychologist. She is Prekmurska, just like us.”

I feel like I’ve crashed a family reunion.

Then someone calls time, and the non-performers follow Eva to the elevator.

We split up at the main floor, the others to find their seats and we to get our tickets. Eva, carefully carrying Vlado’s shirt for the night, leads the two of us on a labyrinthine path down the stairs where the ticket office is tucked away in a dark cubbyhole. She hands the very white shirt to me while she discusses with the lady behind the counter where our seats are. Evidently, she’s reserved the perfect place for us but anywhere is fine. Not too high, not too low, not too far from the door would be perfect but I’m not looking for perfect, just a seat where I can see.

Holding the shirt up high so no stray dirt particles can attack it, I peer at the seating arrangement on the computer screen. Forget high, low or the distance from the door. The auditorium is sold out, even the nosebleed section. I don’t see two seats in the same section, let alone side-by-side, anywhere in the auditorium.

But indeed Eva reserved us two seats and there they are, two seats together. She swaps the tickets with us for Vlado’s shirt, still pristine—you have no idea how remarkable this is—and we dash back up the stairs behind her to our seats.

“I’ll meet you in the lobby after the concert,” she says. “Vlado will be either downstairs or up here signing autographs. I’m not sure which. You’ll have to look for us.” With us safely parked, she heads off to take care of another problem before the show.

We settle back in the chairs. Take a deep breath. Relax. We’ve made it, unlike another couple a few seats down from us who are in the wrong place. They scoot by us, with apologies and a smile, and soon we see them emerge in the balcony next to us. Oh well, it could happen to anyone.

“Excuse us.”

A couple looms over us. We’re in their seats.

We study our ticket stubs. Pinching them daintily between thumb and forefinger, we bring them up to our noses. Nope, can’t read them there. Then we stretch our arms out as far as we can without hitting the people in front of us, who try to be oblivious to our little dilemma. Nope, can’t read them there either. I pull my glasses down to see if that helps. Nope. The light’s too dim in the auditorium. All this while the looming couple stands transfixed, smiling over us.

The corridor, though, is dazzlingly bright. Surely we can read them out there. We haul ourselves up out of our seats, not the easiest thing to do since the balcony floor rises and dips to follow the undulating row. I’ve been known to keel over even when I’m not wearing boots. This time I keep from pitching nose first over the people in front of me, although my feet think it's tempting to do so, and the looming couple and we head back out to the corridor — and immediately get a bad case of the squints.

Don't get me wrong. The couple is most kind, most apologetic, at least I think they are, but with them speaking Slovene I may be wrong. Of course, we apologize as well. More than likely we got confused and ended up on the wrong row. When they hear our English, they apologize all over again in perfect, barely accented English. They're so congenial that for a moment I wonder if they're going to ask us out for drinks afterwards.

Once again we study the stubs. We hold them up side by side. Alas, they have the wrong row. Once more they say how deeply, terribly sorry they are to have caused us such trouble. But it's no trouble at all, we reply, it can happen to anyone. Please don't worry. It's no problem. Enjoy the concert.

We stumble back to our seats. I gingerly sit down as if the seat is now covered in sandpaper, ready to spring out of my chair once again. Waiting. Watching. Listening for those footsteps that warn me another apologetic couple is about to loom over us, oh so nicely murmuring that we're in their seats.

Finally, the lights go down.

Milan Kreslin, both dignified and pleased as punch to be there, strides across the stage. He stands in a pool of light and tells a story, an old story. The audience loves it, clapping wildly. I clap, too, although the only word that's familiar is the one that sounds like *Vladek.*

But what did he say? A niggly feeling whispers that I should know this.

Vlado tells me later, "He quoted the first chorus of *Tista črna kitara*. 'He was a little Vlado then when gypsies came into the house to play.' And then he added: 'Gypsies, rock-n-roll groups, orchestras, bands…' "

Vladek. Little Vlado. Of course. What else would his father quote? Especially with the concert series named *Tista črna kitara*. I've got egg on my face but it's okay. Egg is good for the complexion.

As Milan walks off, Vlado appears, and launches right into *Vsak se želi*. His rock band Mali Bogovi slips onto the stage behind him. No pyrotechnics or funky contraptions for them. The crowd is already enthralled with Vlado, who's strumming like a crazy man. Anyone watching him would swear he hasn't a care in the world, that the only thing he wants is to be on that stage, playing and singing just for them.

In this moment, it is absolutely true.

But later on? He's got to be sore. All the jumping and dancing around like this when you put on a show has to make you hurt, even when you're half his age. Lord knows most folks would be pretzeled in a fetal position, sobbing on the floor. Add the car wreck from this afternoon into the mix, and I don't see how he can keep from being one aching puppy. I hope Eva has a ginormous bottle of aspirin waiting for him back home.

"Did I say that I was sore? I was not. I never need an aspirin. A glass of wine—yes."

There you have it, straight from the expert. He was not sore.

Well, he did dive into the audience when he was fifty. Maybe the usual aches and pains don't bother him. And maybe it's a very good wine.

Vlado sends me a video. "Ruth! Take a look!"

I recognize the song but…wow. Siddharta's *Od višine se zvrti* is loud, clashing, growling, hard driving, adrenalin pumping to the max. Vlado's version is a sweet and tender love song. This is fast sex in a back alley. It shouldn't work for me, but it does.

It especially works when Vlado takes a flying leap into the audience.

The man is fifty years old here, mind you. He's wearing an Armani suit so white it burns the eyes to look at it, and he's got a white hat on, too. God? Satan? Take your pick. There's a whole lot of power wrapped up in those threads. He's singing with Siddharta frontman Tomi Meglič, matching him growl for growl and sweat for sweat. He pounds his notes. He works the song. And, damn, if at the end of the bridge, this Kreslin guy doesn't jump off the stage. God only knows what he landed on.

"Teenaged girls," says Vlado. "We all collapsed to the floor. And I did apologize to them."

However, he wasn't sore. Not at all. No aspirin.

Vlado is singing, hands in his pockets, looking like a grown-up Huck Finn. The auditorium is a cathedral now, the people silent. No fidgeting. No rustling of programs. Even the children—and there's a whole passel of them here. It's a school night but that doesn't matter. This is important, a family event, this coming together to hear Vlado at his December concert. I study the section next to me where several large families sit. Not a petulant face among them. You'd think they were at the symphony.

Never have I seen such honor, such reverence at a rock concert, if you can even call it a "rock concert". That's a little small for what this is, since there's jazz and folk and classical and blues here as well. No country western, although I've heard him sing something awfully close. Vlado isn't one to stay in a box. Atypical rock, then. A musical smorgasbord.

A few rows down from us a sneaky camera starts going flash, flash, flash. Everyone firmly ignores it except a lovely young usher, who scrambles up and squashes the mechanical firefly. Too late. The mood is broken.

So much for dreamtime in Vladoland.

But Vlado sings on, lulling us back into that perfect place. The prickly feelings smooth down. We're back where he wants us.

There was a time, though, when his venue was rough and raw.

*

"Vlad-o! Vlad-o! Vlad-o!"

It's Križanke, 1987.

Vlado grabs the microphone. Tosses his shirt onto the stage. Shouts, and the group Martin Krpan jumps into *To Ni Političen Song* (Not a Political Song). He's slick with sweat. His voice, strong and rough, sings one thing but his lips graze the microphone, promising other things—hard, sweet things. The girls next to the stage go wild. He wipes back his hair, his voice driving, body driving, skin wet, fingers wide, eyes shut, leg pumping in his tight jeans…and the crowd screams, punching the air with their fists.

*

His friend Jure says, "When I first saw Vlado, he had hair and no shirt. And now? Now he has a shirt and no hair."

His lips still graze the mic. Jure wouldn't notice that but women do. No fist pumping, but hey, the night's still young. Who knows what these wild and crazy Slovenes will do?

Crazy comes up a lot when folks talk about Vlado.

Allan comes out on the stage. He's carrying his guitar in one hand and he wears a look of bemused exhilaration, like he's really pleased to be here but slightly shy at the same time. A stagehand fiddles with Allan's guitar, trying to plug it into the sound system while Allan gets situated with the mic.

"Good evening, ladies and gentlemen. It's a great pleasure to be here and to play for you and to be with my crazy, beautiful friend.

"So, one day I phoned Vlado and said, 'Vlado, I'm on my way to Austria, south east part of Styria. I'm staying in a street called Weinstrasse. Sounds like it's gonna be fun."

Vlado cracks up at this.

Allan goes on: "Drive up from Ljubljana and meet me. And he said, 'I can't. I've got the kids in the car. But I've got to go to Vienna to record a song next week with Insingizi. Write a song for you and me.' 'Vlado, I can't write a song in an hour. What about you?' 'Oh no, I take a long time. Twenty years.'

"So I put the phone down, and some times that inspiration comes so fast and so hard. This song came out in an hour. I phone him. 'Vlado! I got a song.' 'Great! Come to Vienna. We'll record it. I'll write a verse in Slovenian.' And this is it—*Let the Music Flow*."

Allan looks at Vlado then. "Is that right?"

Vlado waggles his hand—*comme ci, comme ça*—saying, "Haha, don't let the truth kill a good story."

But it's all good, and the song makes the people smile. Later Vlado and Allan even sing in Slovene—*Daleč je moj rojstni kraj*. They're just old friends, making music, having a blast on stage.

When was the first time I heard *La Brigata Garibaldi*? Long before Vlado's *Cesta* CD, long before I knew it was a Partisan song. The music is too familiar, the words falling into all the right slots in my brain, like leaves reattaching themselves to a tree. But who is this contralto, this Gabriella Gabrielli? To carry that voice she must be a big boned, big breasted, longhaired woman. An older woman, Earth mother diva. Heavy smoker, too.

Then this pixie dances out to sing. Surely this can't be Gabriella Gabrielli, with a grin as big as the sun. Surely it is, and when she opens her mouth, that lovely contralto comes forth, her dark eyes crackling with fire.

"I met Gabriella through her Italian band Zuf de Žur," Vlado tells me later, "With which they used to also play Slovene folk songs and Partisan songs. And she doesn't even understand Slovene! A few times I performed with them. Even in Austria in a church, haha! That was great!"

Vlado joins her on *Bella Ciao*, and once again they sing of the one who says goodbye as he goes off to war.

Then Vlado breaks for intermission. Everyone dashes out. Except me. I've played enough musical chairs this night. 'Tis better to sit with legs crossed and keep my seat, only to leave and lose my place and be cast away into outer darkness—which in this case would be the hallway. So here I sit, leaning back with legs crossed, smiling. I've finally made it to Vlado's December concert series, and I will get to see all three.

The pianist starts the prelude to *Od višine se zvrti*. I half expect to see Severa Gjurin walking out to sing with him. She's the other half of his duet on the eight minute version back when I'd first heard Vlado's music years ago, and she's sung with him many times—"*Abel in Kajn", "Kadar sva sama"* … Her alto is a perfect foil to his voice. Sister to band member Gal, she's also a friend of Ajdina and Čarna.

But Vlado sings alone tonight. He tips his head back away from the microphone, his hands clasped behind his back, and the audience becomes his choir, picking up the words.

Tears burn my eyes. Maybe one day the song will lose its magic for me, but not yet, thank God, not yet.

A hundred or more people press against the door and then burst into applause. Vlado appears, smiling, relaxed, his hat the only beacon to tell folks where he is in the throng. He signs CDs, signs books, poses for photos, whispers asides, kisses cheeks, laughs. Everyone knows him. Everyone is a personal friend.

I stand back from the crowd, watching.

"Ruth! Come here!" He waves me over and drapes his arm over my shoulders while he talks with a woman on the other side of him. I understand "Texasa" but that's about it. The woman beams up at him, nodding, and Vlado whispers down to me. "You understood that? More or less?"

Oh, sure I do. One word, maybe two. "*Prosim*, Vlado."

He looks away, smiling. "More or less."

We regroup backstage. Wine shows up, band members and guests mill about, chat about the concert, compare notes.

A little wine makes me brave.

Gal is sitting at the table, fiddling with an odd horn. I have to know about this funky-shaped thing that may or may not be a trumpet.

"Hi, I'm Ruth." I shake his hand.

He gives me a quick smile. "I'm Gal."

Of course he is. And he plays so many instruments that he probably doesn't even know how many. Right now he's quietly enjoying this beer and I'm about to grill him about this horn.

"I saw a picture of you where you looked like Robert Downey, Jr." Sad to say I can suck up with the best of them, although in his case my observation is true. I saw a photo from the Križanke concert earlier in the year. In the photo he did, indeed, resemble Robert Downey, Jr.

He laughs, shakes his head. He doesn't believe me, obviously. I laugh, too.

"What's this? I've never seen a trumpet like this."

"Oh, it's just a trumpet. A V trumpet. It's nothing special, maybe a little brighter." He studies it, fingers the keys. "Dizzy Gillespie played one."

"Ah, that's where I've seen one. I'd forgotten."

Someone taps him on the shoulder, and he gets up. “I’m going out for five, for a smoke.”

I nod. “We’ll be gone. See you tomorrow. “

He waves and heads out.

“Gal is a great musician, and a great composer with his own career,” Vlado says later. “He could be my son. His father, Velemir, who is famous for acting as Kekec in a legendary movie back in sixties, is just a little older than me. Gal is one of those young people with whom you can talk and not just about music, though he knows it back into my times. Once when I joked and improvised the line ‘this is the end, beautiful friend…’ into the last song, he just slipped in a Doors riff on the organ. Great guy.”

Chapter Seven

Today's our only day for exploring the city. Vlado and Eva are off doing Vlado-and-Eva things. The rest of us are on our own until it's time for sound check and chicken soup backstage.

Which is fine by me. I've got a funicular to try, a market to discover and a castle to explore. I'm going to have fun—or else, even if it rains.

Before we do anything, we have to find an ATM. Not because we don't have any cash. Heaven forbid, we're not that gauche. We brought cash, but who knows what we may find? The city reeks with treasures, and if one begs to come home with us, we'd better have enough euros to redeem it. American credit cards have a knack for not working overseas at the most awkward moments.

Not far from the market is an ATM. Rick puts in our French bank card. *Nada*. He puts it in again. *Nada*. He shrugs, puts in our US bank card. Bingo! Happy again, the machine spits out all the euros we want. Amazing. I'd kiss the machine, but Rick might get jealous.

First stop is the market down by the Ljubljanica River. When there's a full day of exploring, it's always good to shop first so you can lug everything with you all day long. The heavier, the better. Right? Well, maybe not. Still, a tiny astrolabe would be nice. A reliquary from a monastery, or an icon. or a painting…

What I really want is a *zmaj*. A Ljubljanica dragon.

Remember Jason and the Argonauts, and how he sailed down a river and defeated a dragon? He'd stolen the Golden Fleece and now had some half-crazed Colchis after him. Who can blame them? The fleece belonged to their king, and they wanted it back in a big way, along with Jason's head and a few other body parts. Jason and his men had taken a wrong turn and ended up on the Danube, which goes to show even then men loathed asking directions. So, instead of enjoying a nice balmy day sailing home on the Aegean Sea, chucking scraps of fish at the sea gulls and flexing their brawny muscles in the sun, they found themselves having to muck about on a river—the Ljubljanica. Between Vrhnika and where modern day Ljubljana is now they encountered a marsh guarded by a dragon.

Jason, being not only someone who was on speaking terms with a Greek god but also a manly man, fought the dragon, who was more than a little pissed at these puny men messing up his afternoon. Piss and vinegar can take you only so far, though. Jason whacked the dragon's head off, chopped him into pieces (which later became stew because they were awfully tired of eating fish), and kicked the dragon's eyeballs into the marsh. Thus, Jason slew the dragon and became a hero, gained safe passage for his men to return home and upheld his reputation as the manliest of manly men.

However, there's a more mundane story about how dragon came to Ljubljana.

St George, the same St George who is seen the world over cutting off a dragon's head, is the patron saint of the chapel in Ljubljana Castle and all Ljubljana. Where you find St George, you always find the dragon. But where you find the dragon you don't always find St George—at least not in Ljubljana. When Ljubljana decided it was time to decorate her bridges and buildings, she chose the dragon. Just the dragon. St George she left up on the hill in the chapel.

So it's the dragon that's the iconic figure of Ljubljana. Not Jason, who sailed away home on the Adriatic Sea with his mighty men and a hairy sheepskin. Not St George with his sword held high, stomping the dragon's head into the ground. It's the dragon that's atop the castle tower in the city's coat of arms, and it's the dragon that sits on the bridges, guarding the people of Ljubljana. The dragon even has a bridge named for him -- Zmajski Most.

Ljubljana loves her dragon. So do I.

I find no dragon to take home.

There are other ways to get to Ljubljana Castle but the easiest way is going up the funicular. The view from the car is breathtaking. Especially if, like me, you get dizzy from the height.

Like Vlado. Like the song…

"Od vižine se zvrti!
Skrij me v svojo dlan,
svojo mehko dlan,
svojo toplo dlan!
Vzemi me na svojo stran,
skrij me v svojo dlan.
Lahko mi vrneš karto še nocoj,
hočem le,
da me vidijo s teboj."

Deep breath time. I take one. In an act of extreme bravery, I keep my eyes open. I fix them on what I think is Mount Triglav.

Vlado had said, "You need to go up to the castle."

Okay, okay, I'm going.

Here's the thing about Ljubljana Castle. The castle is very old. The renovations are very new. This creates an IKEA meets Dracula's Castle effect. Some folks don't like it, but I think it works. There's a lot of glass and metal where the funicular stops (thank God) but the castle itself feels like a living, breathing building, not a museum. Okay, so it's a little modern in places. At least no one's stuck a rusty air compressor in the courtyard and proclaimed it modern art.

Right now I'm hungry enough to eat an air compressor.

We step out of the funicular and head to the courtyard, looking for a place to eat.

Ljubljana means lovely. In fact, the root word for love—Ljub—is in the name Ljubljana. But when I'm at the point I could suck on stale French fries, Ljubljana also means the city of long lunches.

The castle restaurant, Gostílna na Gradu, is closed. But there's a coffee house, called The Coffee House, and where there's coffee, there's something to eat. Eat—that's what my stomach, by way of ominous rumbles, tells me I need to do right now, right this instant, no questions asked. Now I'm so hungry even stewed coffee grounds sound good.

Except, even though it's getting on to two o'clock, the coffee house is packed. This poses a problem. We can wait for a table, but it may be hours before they seat us. There may be another place to eat up here, although I doubt we'll find it. Or we can get back on the funicular, go down the hill to find something to eat in the city and waste the money we spent coming up.

An elegant woman with dark blonde hair nibbles at the morsel of pastry on her fork. It's obvious that it's her first morsel because only a mouse bite is missing from her cake. *Prekmurska gibanica*—it has to be. I'd be sick with envy if I weren't halfway ill with hunger. The *gibanica* is huge, so huge that it will be an hour before she licks the last few precious crumbs from her scarlet lips.

I sigh. We head to the watchtower.

Rick rushes up the stairs to the top of the tower. It's quite a way up, a very long way, in fact. Notice that he goes by himself. He leaves me behind in the relative safety of a narrow landing surrounded by lovely stone walls. I'm thrilled to be left behind.

Rick scurries back down, windblown and face flushed.

"You really should go up. You'll love it."

I peer up the red stairway. Maybe hell is up. No one's come back from hell to say that, yes, positively, without a shadow of a doubt hell is beneath us. I could use some reassurance about now that, absolutely, hell is down. Because at this moment I'm sure that hell is at the top of those stairs, those steep narrow winding twisting stairs that go up, and up, and up…

"It's wonderful up there," says Rick, who pays money to jump out of planes. "You'll be sorry if you don't go."

Wonderful is relative.

"I'll go with you," he says.

Oh, hell.

Mr. Enthusiastic trots up the stairs like a demented mountain goat. Me? I'm a turtle. I creep up one metal tread at a time. It makes it easier to thank each rivet and screw, each strut and brace, for doing their job and to please, oh please keep doing it just a little longer.

Halfway up, I stop. I've got to flex my hand that's frozen into a claw from holding the bannister in a death grip. In the few seconds between hooking my arm around the railing and stretching my fingers, I glance down.

Into each of the stairs is etched something medieval-looking—a tower, and a figure with over-girding wings.

All this time I've fretted going up the stairs, I was borne aloft on the backs of dragons.

Which doesn't change my worry about hell being up. Dragons fly. I don't. Therein lies the rub. Precipices fascinate me, and not in a good way. What if I lean over the edge, lean way over to see just how far I can go before I topple over? Pancaking myself at the bottom of Ljubljana Castle might cast a pall on Vlado's concert. That would be inconsiderate.

After a time in which several kingdoms rise and fall I make it to the top of the watchtower. Rick is thrilled. That makes one of us.

I creep to where he is. I can do this. I see why people think it's lovely up here. Down below us Ljubljana spreads out all around like a lumpy terra-cotta quilt; the dark seam of the Ljubljanica River peeks out here and there. I lean over a little farther to get a better view of something right below me. Suddenly that's all the looking down I need to do.

Standing next to the outer wall, Rick cheerfully points out the rosy Franciscan Church of the Annunciation down in Prešeren Square for me. I keep my nose pointing away from the edge and glance down. Yes, I see it. And the Hotel Lev and what may be the Hotel Slon? Yes, I see them, too. Over there has to be the Cankarjev dom and the Opera House. Amazing, isn't it, they're all down there, very far down there. No, I don't want to come closer.

Off in the distance, thanks to the clouds, I only see bits of the Julian Alps standing blue and cold against a gray sky. My old friend Mount Triglav, he's there too. It's nice there are things to see without me having to get close to the danger zone.

"What's that?" Rick stares at something in the sky.

Something dark bobs and twirls above us, something longish with legs. Four legs, actually, and a long neck. A dragon.

It's impossible, of course, but there it is, circling out from us, a little higher than the watchtower. It's coming in for a landing—no, wait, there it goes out farther. Now here it comes again.

Oh. It's not a dragon. It's a horse, a helium filled balloon horse. It bows to the castle, then slowly rises in the air, now on its back, now upright, tumbling farther and farther away until it's lost in a cloud.

I look back over the city one more time. Somewhere out there is Vlado's house—north of the city, high on a hill. I try to find its little white square among all the thousands of little white squares. I can't see it. What good is a watchtower if you can't see the house of your friend?

We head back down the stairs, Rick trotting ahead and me inching along behind him. Even Rick is hungry now. Surely we can find a table at the Coffee House.

Surely not. Every table is still full. The elegant woman with dark blonde hair holds her fork, laden with yet another morsel of her nibbled at *gibanica*, halfway between the table and her mouth. She talks and she talks, and as she talks, her carefully speared morsel makes lazy circles in the air.

It's three o'clock. The funicular drops us off at Krekov Square. We meander up one street and down another like half-starved pigeons staggering around the sidewalks. Eventually we wash up at the door to Pizza Osmica. The place is almost full but they're still seating famished tourists such as we. It must be a miracle. I want to kiss the floor.

The menus are translated into English. My admiration for Ljubljana, indeed for all of Slovenia, knows no bounds at this moment. Not only can I read the menu, they even have our favorite European pizza— ham for Rick and mushroom for me, with just enough cheese to make it decadent. We scarf it up like teenagers and wash it down with wine.

Up there under those lights, with thousands of eyes watching him, Vlado is one laid-back dude. Guitar pickups that don't pick up, stools trying to engage him in a waltz—no problem. Nothing fazes him. When he's not jumping around in the middle of a song, or singing a ballad as he strums his guitar, or acting out the lyrics—which he really likes to do, all those expressions rolling across his face—he sits on his stool in front of his mic, crossing his legs on top of his bass drum. He's Mr. Cool, grinning and shaking his head as different guests come out and tell a story about him. They're told with such ease that I forget they must have gone over them a jillion times in rehearsal. Vlado laughs anyway. Each one is a great story. He makes it seem easy, as if he's invited all these people, the audience too, into his house for a little jam session among friends.

But this relaxed stuff? Well, if that means no stage fright, then yes, Vlado's relaxed. He's done this enough to know things happen and you just keep going. But his is a calculated relaxation, something actors learn to put their audience at ease. Vlado is a very good actor. He has to be. Everything on that stage has to happen at just the right time, and for something to appear that smooth, it's got to be rehearsed until the musicians hear it even in their sleep.

"No rehearsal," says Vlado. "We never rehearse."

Lunch is at the Gostílna Figovec, across the street and down the block from the hotel. We dash out of the lobby with Allan Taylor and Gabriella Gabrielli, just in case it's raining. It is, but it's a soft easy rain, not enough to worry with umbrellas.

Vlado meets us halfway down the block, grinning, his arms wide open to gather in his wayward chicks. "Spread out and link arms! Eva's doing a video!"

We link up and march down the sidewalk, laughing and ignoring the camera. Eva walks backwards in front of us, filming, dodging the posts and berms looming behind her, never missing a step. Maybe she has eyes in the back of her head.

Rick and I commandeer the far end of the table next to the window where a huge tabby cat sleeps in a box on the sill. Gabriella sits next to me. Across from her is Eva. Next there's Milan, and then Katarina. Hans's wife, Milica, is next, and then Šajeta at the other end of the table with Hans across from him. Then there's Vlado, then Allan Taylor and back to Gabriella again. Only Aleksej is missing. Different languages all go at the same time while wine is poured, and the breadbasket flies up and down the table as if it's on a zip line. Milica brought a wreath and puts it on Vlado's head. For a while he's the male Euterpe, but I think he does just as well as Caesar Vlado, at least until the pictures are done.

However, we haven't come to praise Caesar but to eat and to look at Vlado's new songbook, *Pesmarica*. He has a copy for everyone, even Rick and me, although we're not performers. Everyone else here has a song in the book they've performed with Vlado and, of course, they're in the photos as well. The book is well done and, bless him, the chords are easy.

That's when the food comes, when the books are spread out over the table. We all fumble around, trying to find some place to stash the songbooks so we don't drop anything on them. "We", meaning me. I've got a huge plate of tagliatelle with truffles, and I don't need to drop my noodles all over it. Trust me, it would happen. I tuck it down between my feet so I'll be sure to trip if I try to get up without moving it.

The tagliatelle is good even though the truffles are shy. The wine is good, too. Then afterwards, finally, nirvana has arrived. I have *gibanica.*

Prekmurska gibanica and Slovenia—forever may they be joined at the hip. But, please, not my hips. With my mouth watering and my head whispering, "You'll be sorry," I stare at this cake that's materialized in front of me.

Gibanica is the traditional dessert from Slovenia. Evidently there are several kinds but I want the original. That's *Prekmurska gibanica,* with tons of walnuts and raisins and ricotta cheese and poppy seeds, and paper-thin layers of pastry on top. A diet buster deluxe. I desperately want to try it before I leave Slovenia. This *gostílna's* version is akin to a New Orleans bread pudding without the pecans and bourbon sauce. It's not gooey. I'd gotten the idea from somewhere that *gibanica* was gooey. Maybe that's the difference between this *gibanica* and one from Prekmurje.

Even without pecans and bourbon sauce it takes me three bites to devour half of the *gibanica.* I burden my fork with another bite. I am such a little pig. Carefully, I place my fork on the dessert plate. Push the plate away. Dab at my mouth with the napkin. Smile.

Like flipping a switch, lunch is over. Eva rushes home to take Ajdina to a doctor's appointment. Vlado has to check on something for the concert tonight, his focus already away from the rest of us here. A snafu with the guitars needs his attention. He looks weary.

The first bone I ever broke was in honor of Vlado.

Rick and I make plans with Gabriella to walk together to the Cankarjev dom later this evening, to make sure we can get backstage. With that anxiety taken care of, off we trot through the drizzle back to the Lev.

At least, that's the plan. But a gray sweater in a shop window lures me in, and I turn into a poor dumb fish chasing a chum line.

It's not that I don't have anything to wear. I have plenty to wear, but it's all back home in my closet. Everything I have with me I've worn over and over, some to the point where they can march out the room on their own fumes. Besides, tonight is the after-concert party. I'd like to wear something no one's seen before, something different. Something clean.

We dash into the shop. Yes, they have the sweater in my size. Yes, I may try it on.

I stand in front of the mirror. Dancing a little happy dance because this sweater will be perfect for tonight, I yank my top off over my head. I bring my left hand down hard and fast—and crack it on the sharp, metal edge of the clothes rack.

The rack rings with the impact but not nearly as much as my hand does.

Oh, god. I don't know if it's even still attached. I can't see anything except bright fizzy lights flashing everywhere. I drag a breath in, as slow and as deep in the murky depths of my lungs as I can get it. I hold it. No air means no sound, and that means I keep my stupidity to myself. I'd rather die of pain than let anyone know what I've done. Sweat pops out on my face.

I bend over to keep from passing out. My nose almost touches my knee. The tiny part of me that's not suppressing pain is amazed that I can even do this. Me, the Human Paperclip. I stay this way until the singing pain changes into something easy to handle, like a cacophony of anger at my boneheaded dance.

Eons pass. I slowly straighten up and touch the side of my hand. It's hot and swelling fast, growing a marble-sized knot. Should I even try the sweater on? My hand hurts no more than it did before I touched it. I push on the bone above the knot. Nothing crunches. I push on the bone below the knot. Nothing crunches there either. Maybe if I'm careful…

I slip into the gray sweater and ease it down over my hand.

I flex my fingers. Not only does the hand still work, it's numb. No need to tell anyone what I've done, not even Rick. I don't need a trip to the ER with the after-concert party tonight. As long as no one grabs my hand, I'll be okay.

Three hours later, fresh in my new gray sweater, and my cracked and possibly broken hand hidden deep in my pocket, we burst out of the elevator, looking for Gabriella. No Gabriella. How on earth will we get backstage now?

But wait. Someone's outside in the rain, waving and smiling at us—Gabriella. It's a soft rain but still a rain. She's waiting for us just beyond the lobby's awning. I understand walking to the Cankarjev dom in this drizzle, but waiting out in it? It's not a problem if we end up sounding like frogs. But we're not singing tonight. She is.

It's only rain. If she's game for walking in this mess, so are we.

All the major players are already backstage, except for Eva. Vlado stands alone, waiting for his best friend to show.

"How's Ajdina?" I ask.

"Eh? She's okay. She's at Eva's folks."

"What'd the doctor say?"

He pauses. "She has pneumonia."

Eva hurries through the door, followed by Naj and Čarna.

"I had to park on the street. I hope I don't get a ticket." She rolls her eyes, shaking out her umbrella. "Čarna had nothing to wear."

People scurry back and forth, checking their hats, checking their coats. It's almost time. Everyone's here, except Vlado.

Down the hallway away from the rest of us, Vlado's talking to Čarna. Very calm. Very intent. Very much a father-daughter discussion.

Mali Bogovi and Beltinška Banda make their grand entrance from the back of the auditorium. Blowing horns and thumping drums, they march down aisles. They march between rows. They snake through the audience every way they can. They're like the Preservation Hall Jazz Band back home when it marches in procession, but without the dancing part, because nobody's died here yet.

Both bands had a venerable tradition that needed an infusion of life. Both had ended up with a younger, brash musician who kept their heritage alive by jumping in to revitalize the band. Definitely revitalized now, with much *oompah-ing* and banging of the cymbals, the Mali Bogovi-Beltinška Banda Marching Band heads up the stage steps and disappears again.

The lights go down. A video comes up on the back screen—"*Tam na koncu drevoreda*". I stare at the screen and dare my eyes to spill their tears.

With his long mane combed back and his deep bass rumble, Hans Theessink pads onto the stage, a lion to Vlado's pacing sleek panther. As soon as he takes his guitar and sits down, he and Vlado swing first into *Bourgeois Blues*, and then right on into *Sitting on Top of the World*. There's not a lot of stage patter with Hans. He smiles a lot but doesn't say much; he doesn't have to. His music speaks for him.

"Hans is originally from Holland," Vlado says later. "Now he lives in Vienna. Very appreciated on the world blues scene. Bo Diddley says he's a hell of a guitar player. And he's an old family friend."

After Hans comes Dražen Turina—Šajeta, almost skipping onto the stage.

I like Šajeta. He's friendly, charming and not much taller than I am. Instant cameraderie. Talking with tall people, on the other hand, can be intimidating, all that looking up their nostrils while carrying on a conversation.

Šajeta's the one who sang with Vlado on *Rulet*, which for me was the seed for everything Vlado. I expect Šajeta to sing a solo and then do his duet with Vlado. Instead Šajeta launches into a monologue. The audience bursts into laughter.

His timing is great. It's easy to laugh even when I don't know what he's saying. But… what if I'm laughing at the wrong thing?

"Okay, so why was Šajeta so funny?" I ask Vlado later.

He thinks for a moment and then chuckles. "You know he is a Croatian singer-songwriter. From Istria. You were there; it is where Savudrija is. He is very witty, very funny, and his concerts are actually stand-up comedy shows with songs. So, before he sings *Rulet* together with me, he is joking about our relationship and the relationship between Slovenia and Croatia. Those two countries with their love-hate relationship are a very rich ground for jokes. Ah, the people love him."

Then it's on to "*Rulet*". Vlado sings "*Še zmeraj me skrbi…*" My heart beats faster, my breath quickens. I step out onto that road, and once again, like the first time when I had no idea how much my life would change because I took a chance and followed that voice, I am swept away.

As they sing, voices all around me, soft as a prayer, join in.

A huge photo of the Beltinška Banda hangs in the foyer of the Kreslin house. It's from the early days, when they'd just joined forces with Vlado. They're all standing on a Mura ferry—Vlado in the middle with a contrabass, then Milan and Katarina Kreslin, Janez Kociper-Janči and his violin, Jožek Kociper-Joužek, Anton Rajnar holding an accordion, and Miško Baranja.

"Miška taught me something very important," Vlado says. "Sometimes a song would last for ten minutes and I'd think, when is this going to end? 'Let the people dance', Miška said. 'The music has a beginning but it has no end.'"

The band starts the intro to *Nocoj je edna luštna noč*, and Milan and Katarina come out to sing. It's so cool the way they're still performing with Vlado after all these years. They're a bridge from today all the way back to fifty years ago or more, and the songs they sing are the folk songs they grew up with.

They're cute when they're up there singing—cute and endearing, and people really get into their music, even young people. I know nothing about this song—

"It means 'Tonight's the Night'," says Vlado.

—but I love watching them sing—the smiles, the nods, the way their eyes flash when they look at each other.

Vlado and company end the concert with *Poj mi pesem,* a rollicking mash-up of polka and Dixieland jazz. Then, as the music still plays, he calls everyone back out for curtain call and they come, waving and even singing. They all bow, Vlado keeping his hat on yet again. One by one they file offstage, laughing, with Šajeta playing Aleksej's balalaika.

What would a Vlado concert be without an encore? Milan comes out with his guitar and, with Aleksej Ermakov on his balalaika and Vlado lending vocal support, he begins the sad sweet song, *Tam Daleč Stran*.

Tam daleč stran,
čez stepo in ravan,
zemlja poljublja nebo,
mu šepeta v uho.

Tja daleč stran,

čez stepo in ravan,
enkrat samo še nazaj,
tam je moj rodni kraj !

"You told me about this song, the first time we were at your house, when you showed us the video of your father and Aleksej playing. Something about being a prisoner of war."

Vlado nods. "We were recording *Goodbye Jim, Goodbye Joe*, the song from the old western movie *Red Garters*. I remember when I was a child and my parents went to the cinema, I waited, awake in my bed—only Joužek's bass was heard through the wall of the Gostílna Central—until they came home. And then my father sang to me *Goodbye Jim, Goodbye Joe* and told me the story of the film.

"So, after so many years we were sitting in Gal's underground studio recording this very song. My father had finished the song, and Gal said. "Ok, this is done. Now you can play something for your soul."

"He was clever enough to leave the record button on.

"My father started a song, very slowly, very gently. Gal and I—we were trying to look like we were uninterested to let him be as much relaxed as possible. But with every line we were more into his singing. When he finished, Gal pushed the button to stop recording, and I asked my father, 'What the hell is that? I never heard that from you before.' And I know that he knows hundreds of songs.

"I thought I saw something shiny in his eye.

"My father said, 'I see them in front of me, as if it were now. They were as young as me—seventeen. Cossacks. We were all prisoners of war in a Russian camp in the place called Tabor in Czechoslovakia in the autumn of 1945. And they were singing those beautiful songs and playing balalaikas. I smuggled myself out of my hut and listened to them. I don't think they survived—as I did. I was forced to be in German Army. Now the song just came to me.'

"I was totally charmed by the melancholy mood of the song but we did not know what it was. My father only remembered the melody. I thought it was a folk song. I wrote the lyrics, and one year later we were back in Gal's studio, and my father recorded the song.

"A few months later I happened to sit in a Sarajevo coffee house with the ex-Jugoslav president Raif Dizdarevič. I was telling him about music, about my father, and so I started the melody of that beautiful sad song. He stared at me, leaned over the table and started to sing: *'Stjep, da stjep krugom...'*

"'What is this? How do you know this song?' I ask.

"'Of course I know it. I was Jugoslav Ambassador's adviser in Moscow back in fifties. It is an old Russian folk song.'

"And that's when I first heard the original lyrics of that Russian song."

We all huddle together like chicks behind the glass doors, waiting for someone to lead us to Vlado's after-concert party. It's in the K Club, somewhere on the top of the Cankarjev Dom but it seems the route there takes one by arcane tunnels through the vasty deeps. There's probably a passkey elevator involved but none of us have the key.

Someone—Eva? It has to be Eva—appears, holding a key up high, and we follow the key into the elevator.

The K Club is a huge, dark cavern, with just enough amber lighting to keep me from stumbling into the person in front of me, but maybe that's because the hallway leading to it is so bright. It's definitely advised to stop for a moment to let the eyes adjust, but being in the middle of a crowd makes that problematic. Once in the club, I step to one side to see where everything is.

Flanking the room are two walls of windows. One wall overlooks a park full of trees, their leaves covered in thousands of sparkling raindrops. The opposite wall is glass and filled with a view of Ljubljana Castle bathed in blue floodlight. I could happily stand here all night, looking up at it.

Cheeses and meats, puff pastries, fruits and cookies and cakes—most of which I've never seen before— are laid out on a giant table behind me. Next to it is a table loaded with lovely wine glasses filled with even lovelier wine. I hunger, and I thirst. The breathtaking view of Ljubljana Castle can wait.

A large crowd, a mix of blue jeans and suits, is already milling around. They must have found the other secret passageway. Everyone's talking in half-hushed voices, waiting for Vlado to appear. Rick and I, laden with cheese and wine, drift around the different clumps of people, trying to listen in on conversations and failing miserably. No one gossips in English.

To one side is a small stage and sure enough, here comes the band carrying in their instruments, including all the pieces of the massive cimbalom. It's like hauling up a grand piano. They must be used to moving it. In less than five minutes they've got it set up and ready to play. All the others have brought their instruments up, too. I bet it won't be long until there's a respectable jam session going.

Gal sits at the piano, his fingers tripping lightly across the keys. Out of nowhere Vlado appears. He moves from group to group, laughing and talking. People relax, eat more, drink more. The party's in full swing now.

"Can you take a picture for me?" Eva says. "It's Šajeta and the former president of Slovenia."

Really? I hurry along behind her. Sure enough, Šajeta is standing with his arm over the shoulders of a man with shocking white hair. All around us flashes go off like crazy, but I manage a shot from the side.

"I want to introduce you to someone." Eva takes us over to a young couple standing by the stage. She introduces us to Noah and Urška Charney, who are good friends of Vlado's, by saying I'm writing a book on Vlado.

Oh, dear.

Her hopes and expectations hang over me like a double-edged sword of Damocles. What makes it worse, Noah's a writer. A published writer. I'm not. What if he thinks I'm a scam artist? Yes, I'm not the one saying these really lovely things, these gracious and truly awesome things, but, silly superstitious me, every cell inside my head is screaming 'Oh god, you're in for it now!' On the outside, I've still got it together, checking all the boxes on my "How to Appear Charming and Delightful at an Important Soirée While Trying Not to Panic" list, and smiling with the Charneys. But inside? I'm a wee bit nervous since I'm not yet published, never have been published, may never ever be published. In fact, God's Big Eraser may even now be expunging my name from every written media all the way back to the dawn of time. I won't even mention my fear of not being able to produce and letting Vlado down.

But we don't talk about specific writing projects. Instead, we talk about books and publishing in general, and how this is such a lovely party, how much work Eva has put into this, and how wonderful Vlado is, both his work and as a person. I'm so delightfully pleasant, up here in the stratosphere with these up and coming artists and writers. Then without warning, because one is never warned about these things, my mouth spits out a wad of cheese.

I feel my face flush red, and the more it flushes, the more I want to melt into the floor. I apologize and silently beg God to kill me. Of course the Charneys laugh it off, and of course, God, in his usual way, does nothing of the sort. Then, to show that the incident is forgotten and all is okay, indeed it never happened, Noah and Urška go on to tell us the story of how Vlado befriended them and of him singing *Od višine se zrvti* at their wedding.

It's really true—everyone has a Vlado story. Vlado's ears must be burning. Just like my face.

Rick and I spy two vacant chairs next to Allan and Gabriella. Friendly faces—the best kind. I nibble on more cheese and mull over what other embarrassments the screw-up gods might have planned for me tonight. It's always good to sit while we eat and sip wine. It's an even better place for watching people. Watching people is safe, if I keep my mouth shut and don't drop my wine glass. Which is now empty. I decide safety is overrated.

I head out to find more wine and run into Šajeta and Aleksej. We talk about balalaikas and *Rulet*, the only things I can really converse with them about. At least this time I don't spit cheese or snort wine up my nose. The band starts up, and Aleksej is coaxed into playing his balalaika. He strums so fast and so long his arm's just a blur. His muscles must be rock hard.

Vlado works the room. He folds one arm across his chest and dips his head down as he talks to this person, laughs with that group. It's a good thing he's taller than most people here or he'd end up bopping them upside the head with his hat brim. My father worked a room the same way. By the time I was ten, I could tell exactly where someone stood in his pantheon of friends by how soon he approached them, how loud he laughed when they talked. Now I watch Vlado do the same. It's déjà vu all over again.

Vlado's mom, Katarina, brings his sister, Gita, over to meet our little group. Gita is delightful and charming, just as much as Vlado, and much prettier than he. This is a good thing because, let's face it, although he's an attractive man, Vlado would not make a pretty woman.

Now Bob Dylan he can do. Oh, yeah. Just add a wig and shades, and he's the Bard.

There's something edgy about Vlado. He doesn't always play by the rules. When we talk and he glances away, in that time between words, I hear the thunder of wild men on horses, and see the fires of Roma camps at midnight, as if he'd led me away to this wild and new exotic land of his. When he turns back to me, his eyes dance when they catch mine, as if he has this secret he wants to share, a secret that's audacious and exciting and just a little wicked. When he's silent, he's completely silent. His face goes still, like a death mask. I can't read him at all. It's not because he thinks in a different language or is from a different culture. Other people—European, American, it doesn't matter where they're from—even when they don't speak, their faces give away a thousand little things. Vlado gives nothing away. Other Slovenes? They also speak when their mouths are shut. Not Vlado. It's a gift, this utter stillness that reveals nothing. This fascinates me.

But it's later when I think of these things, not while Gita is standing here, telling me how lovely it is to meet me and me telling her the same. I wish I could talk to her a little longer but she and Katarina need to move on.

The wine hits. But I am a clever person. I can find the restroom by myself. I head in the logical direction for that kind of facility, and run into Vlado.

"Do you see Eva?" he asks, scanning the crowd, back and forth, back and forth.

I glance around, in case she's reappeared behind him. "No, but when I do, I'll let her know you're looking for her." It isn't much but it's the best I can do at the moment.

He nods once and hurries away.

Well, I'm half right about the restroom. I find the men's room with the international symbol for "man" etched in the frosted glass door. I don't see a symbol for "woman" on the other door, which is half open. Maybe it's a storeroom. If it is, I don't need to barge in. Someone might be in there, or two someones even. Still, the women's room should be right here.

I walk up and down the outstandingly bright hallway two or three times. No women's restroom. Sighing, I head back into the club to ask directions from someone. Anyone. Anyone, but Eva. After what happened when I last visited her house? Please, anyone but Eva.

The first person I see is Eva.

Shame or comfort, which is more important? Comfort, of course.

I explain my little problem. She laughs, and laughs again. Then she takes me back down the hall from whence I just came, and pushes on the door that I think leads to the storeroom. There it is, right on the door. The symbol for "woman" is etched in the frosted glass.

Can't flush a toilet. Can't find the restroom. May the floor swallow me up and hide me forever more. Amen.

I thank her. I even remember to tell her Vlado's looking for her.

I watch the performers who'd come in for the concerts. They gather their merchandise, tally totals, make sure everything is accounted for. It's the usual after-concert business. They all deal with it in the middle of the camaraderie that goes on with performers—artists sharing CDs, signing CDs for each other, swapping contact info, planning to meet up in a month, a year, telling each other they hope their paths cross again, it's so good to meet, thanks for playing with me. Then they go back to the hotel, catch a train, catch a plane, good-bye good-bye, it's over.

Except for us. Tomorrow Vlado takes off his hat and becomes a regular person again. In the evening we will go to his house for coffee.

Prešeren Square in the middle of the holiday season has a hustle-bustle western feeling about it. Maybe it's the Bing Crosby Christmas songs blaring out into the scurrying crowds. That certainly makes it seem familiar in an "Oh no, you've got it, too" sort of way. Or maybe it's the can-do efficiency of the people walking by. Slovenes are nothing if not efficient. They Get Things Done—like we used to before we got lazy and outsourced everything. Maybe it's because Ljubljana is easy to navigate, what with the castle up there and the river down here and English popping up everywhere—how can I possibly get lost? Most of the buildings are formally ornate and old, but Ljubljana feels as comfortable as a housecoat. Friendly, even, if politely guarded, with a "tell me again why you're here?" bemusement.

Which, since I get that a lot, also feels familiar.

If only it would snow. I would kill for snow.

The last time we were in Ljubljana it had snowed, sometimes off but mostly on, the whole time we were there. We don't get snow this time. We get rain. I have nothing against rain. I've spent many an afternoon doing absolutely nothing except watching a day drip away. But it doesn't have the same magic.

On the other hand, I doubt the house on the hill looks so forlorn in snow.

We've been away from Texas for almost a week now, and I have a major craving for Tex-Mex food. Just off Prešeren Square there's the Cantina Mexicana. Chips and salsa, here we come.

Every table but one is taken. Lucky us. The restaurant is packed with students. They must come here a lot—the restaurant runs student specials all the time. They even have the specials on their website, all in Slovene.

Lucky for us, the waiter, like everyone else here, speaks English. Rick orders an enchilada plate. I go for the salad with grilled chicken and hope the chicken comes out cooked. Nothing big, nothing fancy—just good ol' plain Mexican food. Right?

I'm in trouble. The salad's so big it barely fits in the bowl, with greens and corn, beans and tomatoes, diced avocados, *pico de gallo*, chicken chunks grilled to perfection, and a dressing so spicy it'd make Pancho Villa weep. I'm in a state of bliss, even though my mouth begs for relief. I'm not the least bit interested in Rick's three enchiladas, except for their humongous size. He's ended up with the biggest enchiladas in Europe. They're even bigger than the *chimichangas* back home, and these enchiladas are served up with Mexican rice and beans and Texas fries. Oh, and chips and salsa. Lots of chips and salsa.

We'll never eat all this food. It's good thing we're only having coffee at Vlado and Eva's tonight.

We round a corner on the way back to the Lev and spot a family of Roma playing their hearts out, right there on the sidewalk. The little boy can't be more than six, but he's banging those skins as hard as he can, singing at the top of his lungs. Most people ignore them; a few stand and watch. Even fewer drop a few coins in the box in front of them. The Roma keep on playing, giving it all they've got.

A taxi takes us up to the house on the hill. We dash through the mist for the Kreslins' door. It's not really raining, well, not much, but I still look like a frizzled rat when Vlado lets us in.

As I sit down to pull my shoes off, Eva calls out, "You needn't do that. Really. It's okay."

"Are you sure?"

"I'm sure."

So, still shod, I head into the kitchen where Eva's vigorously blending something at the stove. "It isn't anything special, but if you'd like to eat with us…?"

She doesn't have to ask twice.

The "isn't anything special" turns out to be her awesome pumpkin soup, lamb's lettuce dressed with pumpkinseed oil, and Fettuccini Alfredo. Eva pours the wine, red of course.

"Here." Vlado hands his guitar to me, a black custom-made Martin with mother of pearl inlays. Even his name is written in mother of pearl on the neck.

It's a big guitar, bigger than what I'm used to playing, which is a nice folk classic. Nylon strings, because I'm a sissy. I make a few simple chords, but when I press down on the steel strings it feels like I'm playing on razor wire. Still, passing up a chance to play his guitar because of a little pain is stupid. I make an Em chord, and strum the strings, just to say I got to play Vlado's guitar. I sound muddy. Not enough pressure.

"Hey, you're good," he says. He's kind.

We head back to Vlado's study. Either my memory shifted all sorts of things around, or he's redone it, because it's nothing like I remember. I hope it's the latter and not that my memory has finally gone wonky. A wall has grown an upright grand piano, and the modern desk, which had held his computer, is one of those old wooden desks with heavy drawers down each side. The giraffe-like saz is nowhere to be seen.

One thing is the same, though. The four portraits of the late members of the Beltinška Banda are propped up on the bench seat, still waiting to be hung.

Vlado motions for me to sit down. "This journalist wants to interview you tomorrow. Let me see—" He punches in a phone number on his cell. No one answers. He shrugs. "Anyway, she wants to call you at the hotel."

Interview me?

"Oh, sure. They can't interview Eva or the kids, but you? Haha! They can talk to you."

"A man fell in love with Slovenia because of two words. And Srečko Kosovel, yes."

Ooh, this is nice. The beginning of a story. I shift in my seat, the better to watch Vlado. I wait. Maybe it's a folk tale. Or an allegory. Or even… surely it can't be a true story. Surely. He says nothing more, only this one sentence. It becomes a spider in my mind, weaving a web of a thousand possibilities.

Vlado must be teasing me, but he doesn't look like it. He stares straight ahead, focusing on the wet highway.

I stare at him. I can wait him out. Yes.

We're off on a road trip, Rick and me, with Vlado taking us to Prekmurje. He passes cars right and left. I'm praying we don't hydroplane. Rick's a little pale himself in the back seat. I can't imagine why. Vlado's a good driver. Really he is. The accident of a few days ago doesn't even come to mind. He isn't doing anything Rick wouldn't do. It's just that Vlado is the one doing it, which makes Rick nervous.

I sigh. Vlado wins. "Two words?"

His mouth twitches. He knows he's won. "This man, Ludwig Hartinger, is a writer from Austria. He fell in love with Slovenia because of two words—*tolmun* and *obronek*. And because of those two words, and Sreško Kosovel, of course, he moved here. Lives in Kras, which is the Karst region, down close to Trieste."

Hartinger must be a terribly romantic fellow, falling in love with a country this way. Of course he is. He's a poet. Who better than a poet to be snared by just two words and fall in love? But he gets no points for practicality. Those poor words bear so much responsibility. If those two words made Hartinger fall in love with a country, I wonder what two other words would drive him away.

Romance is something I see, but for the life of me, I do not comprehend. I'm not a poet.

I start writing. *Tolmun* is easy to sound out but *obronek?* I can't hear the consonants. Is it *obronek*? *Odronek*? I ask Vlado to spell it—*tolmun,* too, to make sure I scribble it down right. He does. I still don't hear some of the letters. Not even watching his mouth helps. We toss spellings back and forth a few times. I still don't get it. He motions for me to move the notebook closer. Driving down the highway, he writes the words down in big letters. His handwriting is as bad as mine.

I roll the words around in my mouth, try to get used to the way they feel. If I wait long enough, maybe they will move me the same way they moved this Ludwig Hartinger. Waiting… waiting… Nope, not moved. Maybe if I know what they mean…

"*Obronek* is the edge where the forest comes down to meet the grass," says Vlado, passing another car.

"And *tolmun*?"

"*Tolmun* is a place in the river next to the bank. You know, where it is deep and calm and cool, and fish can hide."

I'm a forest person, but the way *tolmun* caresses my mouth… The word hooks my imagination. A river in the hot sun of a late afternoon, and a still pool in the river under a fallen tree, a deep pool where fish lay in wait. Dragonflies dart here and there, skimming the water, chasing midges. Something splashes, and there's one less dragonfly. The sun burns my shoulders. The water in the *tolmun* is cold, so cold that my teeth chatter when I stick my bare and slender foot in.

Only in my dreams am I so elegant.

"And… Screechko?"

"Srečko Kosovel. Big poet. Very famous. From Karst. Where Ludwig moved to live. "

Take your shoes off when you talk of poets and writers in Slovenia; you're on holy ground. Literature is serious business here. Governments with their attendant officials come and go, but those who weave dreams with words, they remain. Poets and writers here might as well be secular saints, their names come so easily to a Slovene's lips.

Vlado is a musician, yes, and an actor, and being a songwriter and a singer is where his heart is. But deep inside, after you scrape everything away down to his bare soul, he's a poet. Being a poet means he carries on this intimate love affair with words; being a Slovene poet means that love affair is hot enough to scorch the heart, and unrelenting. But being a Slovene poet from Prekmurje? Not only is the love affair hot and unrelenting, it also makes the poet a little wild, a little crazy. Like a lover filled with the scent of his beloved.

So Vlado, this singer-songwriter who is also a poet, writes a poem. It's a good poem, at least he thinks so, and he takes it with him on his way to Murska Sobota to see his friend, Feri Lainšček. They're drinking coffee at Feri's kitchen table. It isn't nearly as poetic as sitting in the moonlight and sipping wine, but what can you do? It's daytime. Vlado has to drive back home. So, no wine for him, but coffee's okay. He's with his friend.

Ever so casually, Vlado pulls out this new poem of his. In a casual way that fools no one, he reads Lainšček his poem, which Vlado calls *Namesto koga roža cveti*.

Lainšček looks at him, blinks. He leans forward and asks Vlado to read it again.

Vlado reads it again. Waits.

Lainšček takes the poem and locks himself up in his house.

Picture this: Vlado in the moonlight, standing outside Lainšček's window, trying to talk over an eerie clicky-clack coming from inside the house.

Vlado calls out: "Feri..."

"I'm writing."

"Feri..."

"I'm writing."

"Feri..."

"Go away. I'm writing."

Of course, that never happened. Vlado knows better than to stand outside Lainšček's house in the moonlight and try to talk to him through a window. Of course he does. He might call him, though. Even writers have to take a break. But Feri Lainšček, completely lost in the story he's writing, would never hear the phone.

Anyway, after a few months—months, mind you, not years like it would be for some writers —Lainšček emerges from exile with a book in his hand, a book based on this very same poem that Vlado read to him over the kitchen table. The book is about the Roma, which is no surprise, because Lainšček writes about the soul of Prekmurje and the Roma. But this book is about one Rom in particular—a man who is writing a poem with his whole life, and the poem is *Namesto koga roža cveti.*

Kakšno noč, ko pri štorkljah prespim
pod visečo meglo
tiho, sam, med njimi stojim
le noge nad vodo.

Ko pa žarek pregrize temo,
prebudimo se iz sanj,
močvirje novih želja
bo odletelo v nebo.

Namesto koga roža cveti,
namesto koga sem jaz,
katera koža najbolj diši,
čigava pesem rabi moj glas?

Če pa trava nad mjo zemljo
bo premogla kak cvet,
enim itho kapljo v oko,
drugim dal bo med.

Namesto koga roža cveti,
namesto koga sem jaz,
katera koža najbolj diši,
čigava pesem rabi moj glas?

Such an honor to have your poem made into a book. But it doesn't stop there. A director, Andrej Mlakar, reads the book and tells Lainšček he wants to make a movie out of it. So the two of them write the screenplay. A movie is made, with Vlado in it. His character sings the song from this same poem he'd written, and then promptly gets killed, although not because of his singing.

Vlado, still teaching me about all things Prekmurje, sends me the movie, now called *Halgato.* "You need to see this," he says. He fears I romanticize Prekmurje too much, and the Roma—the *Cigani*—even more so. That when I write about them my words will be too lyrical. Too romantic.

But, of course, my words would be lyrical and romantic. When the *Cigani* dance around the campfire, their eyes dark and wild with passion, what else would it be— tea and crumpets on dainty napkins, pinkies aloft in fine kid gloves?

I watch *Halgato* all the way to the end in one sitting. Close my laptop. Go outside and sit. Think. I think for a long time.

There is no romance in being shunned. Or begging for clothes and people looking at you in disgust like you're filth because you're *Cigani*. Or living in a shack made of scrounged tin sheeting and broken boards. When you dance around the campfire, you don't dance for joy. You dance to forget. You dance to forget, and you fuck to forget, and you drink to forget. Sometimes when you drink you make a big mistake, and when you do, you die. The *Cigani* will kill you themselves because if they don't, the police will. No one raises a voice in your defense because you're *Cigani*. You die alone in the square, beaten to death by police as people watch with their mouths shut.

People will say, that's the way it used to be, it's not that way now. Tell that to the *Cigani.*

The closer we get to Prekmurje, the less it rains.

"My wife says the lines on my face become softer whenever we cross the Mure Bridge."

The few lines on his face are softer, and his eyes twinkle, but whether it's the river or the cloudy light, who knows?

"I keep mentioning Prekmurje all the time, living my life in 'the Prekmurje state of mind'. Maybe even my kids 'have it too much'. Eva says to Ajdina to collect the dishes, and she says no. Eva says 'You take care. If you do not collect the dishes, you might stay without dinner.' And Ajdina says back, 'You care that you might stay without your daughter, because I will run away from home in the next ten minutes.' Then I take my chance—haha—and get involved. 'If you will run away, you better run to Prekmurje. That is where the people are the most hospitable.' And she explodes, "Prekmurje, your Prekmurje! People are hospitable also in other places, not only Prekmurje. This is *DEMOCRACY*!'" Vlado laughs.

A long expanse of a bridge looms up in front of us. Vlado's song *Joužek* comes on the radio.

"Haha! Look ! We're here!"

The wide and mighty Mura spreads out beneath us. Vlado opens my window and shouts over me, *"Jijijiji!"* Rick and I shout too, waving our arms at the river like children, laughing. Vlado's singing and shouting and laughing all at the same time as we cross over the Mura. He's bringing us to Prekmurje, and Joužek welcomes him home.

Prekmurje means "beyond the Mura", and that's where it is—on the far side of the Mura River, a land apart from the rest of Slovenia. Although a few bridges here and there stitched the banks together, such as the wooden bridge at Radgona by the Austrian border, until the mid-twentieth century the most practical way for people to cross the Mura was by ferry, pushed by the river current.

The Mura made it hard for the Prekmurci to get together with the rest of the country. Ferries are nice, but they're slow. When few people have a car, it's easier to stay home and develop your own culture. So the Prekmurje culture is Slovene, but with its own flavor. Like the Cajuns in Louisiana, they belonged to the nation, but with a few little distinctions. They were different in food, different in culture, different in her people. In the rest of Slovenia, centuries of assimilation have smoothed out some of the more blatant differences. Like in the Midwest of America, a lot of homogenization has gone on. But the Prekmurci are less like the rest of Slovenia. Even the rest of Slovenia thinks the Prekmurci are less like them too.

"So folks in Prekmurje are more like a raucous party of Slovenes."

"'Raucous'? What does that mean?" asks Vlado.

"Noisy and loud. Fun… like a party after midnight, where lots of wine has been drunk and the party is still going strong. Laughing, shouting, music going…"

"Aha, raucous in this way, everyone is raucous in Slovenia from the coast to Beltinci. But we Prekmurci! We are raucous even when we are still!" He laughs. "But the fact is, yes, that we've been 'living on draft', like Miška Baranja said. We lived with Jews, Hungarians, Gypsies; there were Germans and Russians living in Murska Sobota. That makes me imagine that we are open and tolerant, and this makes me proud. Bela krajina has the quite similar 'quality of soul'. They even sing *Vsi so venci vejli*. So perhaps just say Prekmurje people are maybe a little more melancholy, a little more impulsive."

Like Vlado—Prekmurje Man.

It's even different in language, with a dialect so arcane some consider it another tongue. This can cause a little consternation in other parts of Slovenia.

"My father knew a man," says Anda, back when we were at the *gostílna* up in the mountains, "who went to Ljubljana from Prekmurje. Everyone asked him to speak English, because they could not understand his Slovene, so thick was his Prekmurje accent."

Vlado laughs. "My friend Desa Muck—she is a famous author of books for teenagers—when her daughter was four or five-years-old, once said: 'Kreso (that is what close friends call me) is okay; it is only a pity that he doesn't speak Slovene.'

"In the eighties, I had an extra summer job on Radio Slovenia. I was reading the morning radio news for marines. Got a weather forecast at 5.30 a.m. via telegraph from Split, translated it in Slovene, German and English and read it in the air. Then I went to my regular office job.

"End of the summer when I was in Prekmurje, I woke up early in the morning to go fishing and someone else was reading the news. I said to my mama, 'Oh, you know I was reading the news every morning?' 'Yes,' she said, 'I was already wondering where did you learn that good Slovene!'"

So the Prekmurci are a little different, but what would you expect? Prekmurje is the newest region of Slovenia, having belonged barely a hundred years. A few may still remember when Prekmurje belonged not to Slovenia but to Hungary. Only when the Treaty of Trianon was signed did they turn their face from the east to the west and give their allegiance to a new nation, although for the next twenty-five years all sorts of armies tramped through and generally gave them a hell of a time.

These people hail from the poorest region, speak a strange dialect and appear a little more impulsive, a little more melancholy than the rest of the country, like Vlado says. But they do their part to further the success of this young country full of bright hopes. They do this gladly, because if they're anything, the Prekmurci are givers. They give of their work and they give of their friendship and they give of their hospitality, and they are proud and honored to be Slovenes.

But at night? Ah, at night when moonlight slips over the hoar-frosted fields and pale threads of chimney smoke drift across the Mura, that's when the Prekmurci bring out their guitars and their violins. They sing their songs—and maybe they don't sound quite like Vlado. Sometimes it's good to sing just for the joy of singing, even if your fingers are so stiff it hurts to press the strings down and your voice cracks on the high notes. After a long day of work it's okay if you miss a note or two. You're singing with your friends.

It's the old songs they sing, the songs their fathers and mothers sang, and their fathers and mothers before them. When they raise the glass that's full of wine from grapes they nurtured with their bare hands, and when they take to the floor, feet stomping, hands clapping, the men and women spinning around and around, laughing and singing, and kiss and love and shout and weep, they are Prekmurci, and their blood is old and rich and strong, and binding.

It is into this that Vlado was born.

But there's a darker side to Prekmurje. Like many places that have more farms than factories, Prekmurje is depressed. Very high unemployment. The shortest life span in Slovenia. The most suicides.

Vlado nods. "Yes, we have those. But then again, my friends in Bistrica? We really take out the guitar as you say."

We turn south. The land we're passing through looks like a platter—flat in the middle and gently curving up on the horizons. Green fields surround us. Maybe it's winter rye like it would be back home. The sun tries to break through the clouds but they're having none of it.

"*Živijo*," I say. "Zhoo-ee-oh."

"*Živijo*, yes. But that's only said in Ljubljana. Not in Prekmurje. In Prekmurje you say '*Dober den'*."

I glance at Vlado. "When we were getting ready to come here last time, I'd read that Slovenes were formal and reserved. You're not that way at all."

"Not in Prekmurje, no. We don't have time for that. But in Kranjska? They're more formal there. More into numbers. But in Prekmurje we take things easier." He laughs. "In Prekmurje we're on a mission of soul!"

He turns off onto a road that splits a young wood of white-barked trees.

"Now this is the way to a church I want to show you. Štefan and I would come down this road, riding bikes, and we would stop to pick mushrooms."

"Here?"

"Right there," he says, pointing out two clumps of trees. "One day we were discussing it, back and forth. I said we had to get up at four a.m. to pick them; he said three a.m. So of course I said two a.m. Two a.m.! 'Okay'. He wasn't going to cross me." Vlado laughs. "He was the older but he wouldn't cross me. We stayed in this field right here, and went to sleep—it was dark still—and woke up at four a.m. anyway. But we got our mushrooms."

"You could do that? Just go out there and pick mushrooms without someone running you off?"

"Oh, sure. It was the time of socialism, when the woods belonged to all of us. Haha! Joking, but close to the truth."

We pass the sign for the village of Bogojina. Vlado, being a good driver, slows down to navigate a lane. "I want to take you to this church."

Ah, a church. The first time we'd visited the Kreslins he'd showed us a video of a crowd gathered by an ever-flowing stream. Čarna's baptism. In the background was a little church, set back in clearing on a hill. It looked like the same church where he and Eva were married. Maybe that's where we're going?

Houses sit at right angles to the pavement, making triangles of safety that no one uses. Perhaps the safe places are no longer needed here, although having ridden with Vlado I might think twice about that. Women push strollers down the middle of the street, oblivious to Vlado's car creeping towards them.

We head up the hill to a white church with a cylindrical tower. It's not the church in Vlado's video. As we pull into the parking lot a third of the way up, the sun starts shining and washes the building with a blinding whiteness.

A little girl with solemn eyes and a giant pacifier watches us pass, clutching one of her father's fingers.

"Our most famous architect Jože Plečnik built this. He built half of Ljubljana and half of Prague. A student of his built our house in Ljubljana. The architects say it is not bad." He shrugs. "But the priest Iván Baša was Plečnik's friend, and he built this church for him. It is most unusual—the only one like it."

Silently, we slip inside the church.

Tasked with tearing down an old church and building a new one, Plečnik decided to go one better and incorporated the old building within the new. It was done up in Gothic style, although not the tall spindly Gothicism of the British. This is Gothic rich and thick, sturdy like the *bujta repa* that feeds the people during the winter months. Sturdy like Fr. Iván Baša himself.

And heavy. Everything is heavy—heavy with incense, heavy with stone, heavy with wood. The world must have come in and dropped every weight it had carried since the beginning of time, right here in this little church and then gone merrily on its way. Since the weight had nowhere else to go, it seeped into the walls and plinths and lintels of the building. A lesser church would have crumpled under the burden.

The nave with its stark white walls does its best to lighten the mood, but it's so bright and so white that it only makes the shadows darker. The, almost black, wooden ceiling has plates from the nearby Filovci pottery affixed to it. Clay amphorae hang from the baldachin that flanks the altar in the sanctuary, and fat marble pillars line the covered walkways. Ever-present shrines with their blind statues fill alcoves at the front, along the sides, and in the back of the nave.

But this being daytime, the only illumination is the light coming through the windows. Maybe at night when the priest lights candles to chase away the dark, the shadows hide and the whole church glows. Or maybe Plečnik believed when the people come to worship, they should see the dark, a counterpoint to their merry hearts. After all, how will people repent when their hearts are already light?

With this church, Plečnik married the old and the new, the light and the dark. Somehow, he made it work. Strangers from around the world come here, but how many of them know it was also a shrine to his friendship with Iván Baša?

"The priest," says Vlado as we head towards the car, "he was a writer, you know, and a collector of folk songs and such. He even collected the folk song that we recorded. *Igrala Je, Igrala*."

The village of Filovci is next, a few miles down a flat country road. Vlado drives down a lane that passes its church and a group of tidy houses. Each house has an arbor full of grapes. Vlado pulls into the driveway of one with writing over the door. The arbor in front is so woefully laden with grapes it'd be a mercy if someone picked them. Vlado's halfway to the door when a man across the lane hails him. The man waves us over, and we get out of the car and follow Vlado.

Three buildings sit in a row, spread out on a carpet of deep, green grass. Each building is made of two rectangular blocks set at right angles, whitewashed with eaves so deep I could stretch from the wall to the edge and still not touch either end. Straw-thatched roofs top the buildings like mushroom caps. A potter's wheel with a half-formed pot on it waits outside the middle building. That's the building we enter.

Cups and saucers, mugs, baking dishes, cruets, jugs, garlic pots and onion pots, and everyday plain and fancy pots—floor to ceiling and wall-to-wall, the building is stuffed with pots. I cram my hands into my pockets and stand away from the shelves. I sure don't need to snag something with my sleeve and bring everything tumbling down.

Vlado motions me to follow him outside. "You see this house? My mother was born in a house just like this. Here." He reaches up to the arbor over our heads and plucks a bunch of dark grapes, no bigger than the wild mustang grapes back home. He rolls a few around in his mouth, and then holds the bunch out to me. "Try them."

Incredibly tart, incredibly sweet—they taste like blackberry liqueur, and they're stuffed with seeds. Giant seeds.

How am I supposed to get rid of these seeds? I didn't see what Vlado did with his. Spitting them out isn't an option.

I pop more grapes into my mouth as I mull over the problem. What's another grape seed or two? Maybe I could swallow them. Then I remember an old wives' tale about seeds causing appendicitis attacks, but maybe those were pomegranate seeds, not grape seeds. I could just not eat the grapes, but that might offend Vlado. Besides, these grapes are super intensely good. I stick another two in my mouth and decide the best thing for the moment is to ignore the seeds accumulating in my cheeks.

Vlado heads toward the building on the other side of the pottery house, which seems to be painted white on one side and brown on the other. "This is where Beltinška Banda played their first concert. To bring in the people, you know."

"For Štefan's workshop."

He pauses. "Yes." He turns back to the pottery house.

He has lots of memories here—first concert with the Beltinška Banda. Štefan. Vlado is a most haunted man.

I follow after him. I now have a ton of seeds stuffed in my cheeks and my fingers are sticky with juice. Maybe I can find a rest room or a basin or some place to wash my hands in there. Even a faucet outside will do.

A seed pokes between my lips. I push it back in.

We find a room with mugs for sale, including one at the back of a shelf with a man getting a transfusion from a lover's heart. Something's written on it. I reach for it with the hand that held the grapes, and stop.

"Here." Rick holds his handkerchief out, all white and clean and slightly fuzzy.

"Thanks, but that's okay." A gallant offer, but even if I wipe my hands off my fingers will still be sticky. I'll leave fingerprints on the mug. Those prints will collect dirt and attract bugs and grow nasty stuff on it. Everyone will think, 'eh that American woman', and shake their heads. Plus, I still have half a bunch of grapes in my hand. What would I do with them? Put them in my other hand and get it sticky? Better to keep the original hand dirty until I finish the grapes.

Standing on my tiptoes, I reach over stacks of wobbly pottery to pick up the mug with my other hand. I hand it to Vlado and ask him what it says.

Vlado holds the mug out a little bit to read it. "It says, 'You are my lifeline.'" He laughs with delight. "Oh, I want to get this for Eva!"

I pick out another mug for me, and we head back to the main pottery room, my treasure cradled in my unsticky hand. While the men add the mugs to our stash, I contemplate the pots on the shelves, stuffing the last few grapes into my mouth. It wouldn't be right to get in Vlado's car with mushy grapes and sticky hands.

But now my mouth is crammed so full of seeds I can barely make my lips touch. I can't speak even if I want to. The only trashcan is right in front of the men who are talking the schmoozy way men do when they're transacting business.

Quietly, I mosey outside. Check to see if anyone is watching. Lean over the porch railing just like it's the most natural thing to do on a cool autumn morning. Try to spit the seeds out. I can't spit. They're crammed in too tight. So I worm a finger past my lips and flick them out one by one onto the flowerbed below.

I still have sticky fingers, though. I could go searching for a faucet, but what if I can't find it? It's time to go. No time to look. Praying no one is watching me, I do the only thing I can do. I lick my fingers clean.

That's when I turn around and see a door inside the vestibule, the one door that we haven't gone through. The restroom.

I dash inside, wash my hands, and exit just in time to say "goodbye" and "thank you" and "goodbye" again. All is well—my hands aren't sticky at all. Slightly soapy because of the soft as silk water, but soapy I can deal with. Vlado's car is safe.

We all pile in. Vlado turns around and we start to drive away.

"Look," he says, pointing to the arbor. "White grapes." He stops the car, dashes over and jumps, and jumps, and jumps again, trying to grab a bunch. But even though he's tall and can jump really high, the white ones are a smidgen out of reach. He settles for another bunch of red grapes.

"Would you like some?" He hands the dark red, juicy, sticky grapes to me.

"Here we are—take a picture!"

He slows down. I fumble, taking a shot of the "Beltinci" sign and end up getting only half the sign. He backs up so Rick can try. His photo is better. Not good, but better than mine. We can't all be Ansel Adams.

Coming into Beltinci is like driving into almost any town in south Louisiana—gas station on one side, big warehouse-like building on the other, and river land flat as road kill as far as you can see. I half expect flooded fields full of rice and crawfish on the roads but so far, no flooding and no rice. And nary a crawfish to be found.

Vlado points to the warehouse. "I used to get wine here when I was a little boy and we were building a house. Every time I came, the old man who was the keeper opened the tap, and when the wine was going *shhhh* into the ten liter bottle, he would look at me and say, 'Whose boy are you?' And I'd say Kreslin's. And he'd go, 'Ah, your father—he is an honest man.'"

We head down the main street and stop in at a local café. Vlado introduces us around, which means we meet the sole customer and the woman behind the counter. Then he orders coffee I pick the wobbliest stool to perch on. Rick and I drink our coffee, me sipping carefully, while Vlado chats with folks. There's nothing like a café to find out what's going on.

Vlado comes up behind me. Nodding at the building sitting across the way that reminds me of an old masonic temple, he drops his voice to just above a whisper: "You see over there? That was the Hotel Zvezda. The gypsies played there, the ones I wrote about in *Tista črna kitara*. Right there under the chestnut trees. They're all gone now. Smart asses tore them down. Smart asses like to tear down old trees."

I go outside. I don't want to be a tourist but my camera gives me away. I take photos of the Zvezda and where the chestnut trees used to be. The only trees over there now are a couple of skinny junipers and an evergreen covered in Christmas icicles. Still feeling like a tourist, I walk up to the street and check it out.

The day is gray which makes everything else gray but, my word, the town is immaculate. Except for the area right next to the curb where there's a smattering of dead leaves, you could plant your lips on any surface within sight—the street, the sidewalk, the roofs of any building.

A little girl in a red coat who couldn't be more than six years old is handing out flyers. She comes up to me, her face serious, and holds out a flyer. I say, "*Hvala*" and take it. I can't read what the flyer advertises but she grins and runs to her mother. I must have done something right.

Back inside, Vlado talks to the woman behind the counter. "She says so many people came from here to the concert on Monday night. And then they had to drive all the way back afterwards. Because of work the next day, you know. After twenty years of concerts, we can't get a weekend for our three shows in the Cankarjev dom. The Philharmonics get it. And we play Mondays, Tuesdays, and Wednesdays."

We're off again, this time along a street shaded by tall, willowy trees. He pulls up behind Beltinci Castle and parks.

"This is where we filmed the video *V parku za gradom*, with my daughter, Ajdina, and her friend."

"Is it used for anything now?"

"Oh, sure. There's a restaurant inside. I went to school here. Grammar school."

Nothing like putting a building to good practical use, even if it once was a castle.

We hurry along the cloister walk after Vlado, who turns right into a large room. Photos hang like a belt in a straight line all the way around the walls.

"These," says Vlado, about a photo of three young women dressed in the 1900s style, "are the last ones to live in the castle. Three sisters. This one is Maria, the Countess Zichy, and this is her sister Anastasia. The other one… Amalia? My father knows."

Another photo is of a familiar building. "This is the Hotel Zvezda. This photo was taken from our house. Come."

We go down even more steps into the cafe.

One of Vlado's old friends, Martin, sits at a table in the castle *gostílna*, drinking wine with another man. They ask us to join them. With much handshaking amid the introductions, we make sure we say "*Dober dan*" instead of "How are you", although I'm sorely tempted to blurt out "*Comme ça va*?"

Vlado orders wine for us and tea for him. "When Eva's here, I drive there and she drives back, so then I have wine, but not when I drive."

Martin passes Vlado something about the size of a deck of cards. It looks like a circa 1930s package of cigarettes. At one time it may have been tan or maybe it was beige, but whatever the original color it's now gold on its way to dust. Martin then hands Vlado some vintage rolling papers.

"Tobacco," says Vlado, holding it up to the light. "Over fifty years old." He passes the pack to Rick, who turns it this way and that in this fingers, then waves it under his nose.

"No scent," says Rick. "The oils are gone."

I take it from Rick. The printing is blue, in Yugoslav on one side and maybe Russian on the other.

Vlado later tells me: "Not Russian. Serbian, just the writing is the same as Russian—the letters. *Čirilica* the Serbs say. We call it *Cirilica*."

Ah, the Cyrillic alphabet. No wonder it looks Russian.

The glue doesn't stick, and bits of tobacco fall out onto the table. I pick up a few of these with a wet finger. Sniff them. Nothing. Taste them. Nothing.

Vlado heads out to make a phone call. As soon as he leaves, our wine comes, along with a cup of a ruby red liquid. A tea of some kind, although as red as it is, I'm not sure Dracula would turn his nose up at it.

Rick fans some of the fumes towards us. "What *is* that—blueberry?"

Blueberry? The tea's red, darling. Let's try for a red fruit. I keep that to myself. No need to get snarky on the poor fellow.

I breathe in the thick sweet smell. "Could be plum. Maybe cranberry."

Vlado returns and sips his tea.

"Mmmmm," I say. "Your tea smells so good. What is it?"

"Cherry."

Cherry tea? I wonder if it tastes like cherry cough syrup. Hopefully not.

Martin says something, smiling.

"My friend wants to buy our drinks," says Vlado.

"That's awfully sweet," I reply. I turn to Martin, and say: "*Hvala*." I must have said it right because he grins.

Vlado swings into the driveway of a tidy tan house and pulls around to the back. By the time we finish fussing with our coats and squirming out of the car, Vlado's folks have come out to greet us, his dad smiling and waving, his mom with her arms wide open. She calls out "*Dobrodošli! Dobrodošli!*" and hugs me. You'd think we were long-lost family, which is a pretty nice way to be thought of. I hug her back with the traditional two-cheek kiss, and give her my best "*Hvala! Hvala!*" which has to be completely incomprehensible.

Like giggling children, we all bustle into the elder Kreslins' immaculate kitchen. Katarina places a plate of jelly-filled cookies in front of Rick and me, and hands us an album filled with family photos. We flip through the album while I do my best imitation of a prim southern lady nibbling at a cookie. Scattering crumbs on her table would be gauche, and I've already reached my gauche limit for the day with the grape seeds. Milan, pointing at each photo, explains where they were taken and who the people in them are—Vlado and his younger sister Gita as children, Gita's boys, and Čarna, Vlado and Eva's wedding. The subject of driving comes up. Rick mentions his mom is still driving at ninety. Milan grins. He's not ninety yet but it won't be long, and he's still driving, too.

Vlado fetches the original black guitar, the one his father played for the gypsies. He straddles a chair, his long fingers making the chords as he strums the strings. Wonder of wonders, it still sounds good. An icon of Slovene culture playing an icon of Slovene culture while we munch cookies in his parents' kitchen.

I wonder if he knows how astoundingly cool this is.

He looks up at me, and winks.

Chapter Eight

We walk over to the restaurant next door.

Well, well. So this is the building that belonged to Vlado's grandfather, Jože Kreslin—the old Gostílna Central, with the "Boom! Boom!" in the last room of those Saturday and Sunday nights. Where the Kociper brothers played, keeping little Vlado awake.

Jože Kreslin is gone, the Kociper brothers, too. The building that housed the Kreslins is now home to Gostílna Tonček. Vlado says they have authentic Prekmurjian food. I can hardly wait. If I'm lucky they'll even have *Prekmurska gibanica*.

I'm not even close to being a gourmet. Half a tuna fish sandwich for lunch suits me fine most days. But for the last two years I've read about *Prekmurska gibanica*, and I want a taste of it before I leave. One taste—that's all I ask.

Vlado seats all of us—Milan and Katarina on one side, Vlado and me on the other, and Rick at the head of the table. Vlado insists Rick sit there, and then he orders for Rick and me. Or rather, Vlado suggests, and the man who waits on us explains what the suggestions are. He speaks excellent English but the descriptions in the menu are only in Slovene.

I'll eat anything here as long as I don't know what it is. I'm not usually so trusting about my food, but this time I'm happy to let Vlado do the ordering. One day, I will be able to order a complete meal in Slovene but now, all I can say is *Prekmurska gibanica, prosim*. Not the healthiest thing for lunch. If I want something better than sugar to eat, all those lovely syllables that mean nothing to me—*bujta repa, krvacice, bograč, ribe na žaru*— have to tumble out of his mouth.

Vlado orders the main meal for us: *ribe na žaru*—grilled fish for Katarina, *bograč* for Rick, and *bujta repa* and *krvavice* for Milan, Vlado and me. I have no idea what I'm about to eat. Good thing, too, or I would have skipped lunch entirely.

The fish is lovely, long enough to cover the platter, grilled and flaky tender. Rick's *bograč* is a stew made of three different kinds of meat—beef, venison and pork—plus lots of potatoes, onions, garlic and paprika. It's served in a little cauldron, also called a *bograč*, with a table top tripod. Rick grabs the ladle and fills his bowl. The aroma makes my stomach rumble. It smells fabulous, and I'm famished. I need a straw so I can slurp up all the liquid in the *bograč*.

Our meal arrives—a thick orange soup, thicker than pumpkin soup, and a platter of sausages.

Vlado serves me some of the soup. "*Bujta repa*. Traditional Prekmurje meal. Made with turnips and onions and garlic. Meat, of course, and millet."

"*Bujta repa.* Okay." I taste it, and nod. "It's good."

Vlado glances at me. "It's okay?"

I taste it again. "Better than okay."

"Good." He serves me a sausage. "Try this then."

Except for Rick, who's completely absorbed with eating *bograč,* the table seems intent on not watching me.

Of course, it's just my imagination. Watching me eat a sausage isn't that interesting. I slice the sausage up into tiny pieces. It doesn't smell sage-y, thank goodness, but the sausage almost breaks apart once the casing is split. The aroma is savory. My mouth waters.

Vlado's still watching me.

"What is this?" I spear a slice of sausage. I don't want to get stuck eating a huge chunk of it in case it turns out to disagree with me.

"Krvavice."

Krvavice. I take a bite. It crumbles in my mouth. Every piece is filled with all the savory, salty goodness that makes sausage great and nothing that makes it bad. No sage at all.

"Oh, my. That's really good. Really, really good."

Vlado glances at me as if to ask, 'are you sure?' and then nods. "Good."

I devour the *krvavice*. It's the best sausage I've ever eaten. When I finish it, he smiles.

Later I learn what *krvavice* is— blood sausage. Just like Cajun black boudin, with all those hearts and snouts and other ground up body parts, stuffed inside poor old Porky's intestines. They probably got the squeal in there, too. Even though I grew up in Louisiana and didn't think twice about what was in those little packages of ground pork we bought at the grocery store, I avoided eating real blood sausage. You had to be a little wild to eat that, a little dangerous. Like someone who'd run with the wolves.

Definitely not me.

However, *krvavice* is by far the best sausage I've ever had, even though eating blood sausage means… well, eating blood. I didn't even have a chance to waffle about it, just boom! Here's the sausage and here I go, stuffing my mouth with it. Vlado's inducted me into an arcane society of blood eaters. I've been blooded, like in a ritual of some sort. I should feel guilty but *krvavice* tastes too good. If I had a chance to do it over again, I'd be first in line to load my plate up with them.

But now I know why Vlado was so amused watching me stuff myself with *krvavice.*

Full of sausages and stew and a lot of wine, I stand up. My intention is to head straight for the restroom. I made sure to note where it was on the way in. I didn't want a repeat of Wednesday night's search at the after-concert party. We have more sightseeing to do today, and some of it may be in the countryside.

But before I can scurry off in the right direction, Katarina jumps up to show me the way.

Oh, dear. She doesn't have to do this. I shake my head and try to wave her back to her chair.

"Oh no, *prosim*, no. It's okay. I can find it."

She insists. She is indomitable. So, like a duckling, I follow her to my destination. My reputation for not being able to find a restroom has preceded me.

Once again, I am in awe of a Slovenian restroom. This one is outstandingly beautiful with its marbled tiles, elegant fixtures and hundreds of smooth glass stones in the two lavatory sinks. I'm afraid to walk in the room. Even breathing in here might mar its beauty. Which defeats the purpose of having a bathroom. A bathroom is to be used. What to do about the stones in the sinks? Do I simply wash my hands over them? Should I rinse the stones clean when I'm done? Maybe I'm supposed to take them out of one sink and put them in the other sink before I wash my hands.

I peer behind the door. Perhaps there's a more utilitarian sink I'm supposed to use. There isn't.

Feeling guilty, I wash my hands, dripping water and soap over the stones. I rinse the stones. They're still soapy. I rinse them again. I bury the wet stones underneath the dry ones. I pat the stones down to make it seem like no one has used the sink. Then I worry the establishment will l think I didn't wash my hands. Even worse, they'll tell the Kreslins. I run water over all the stones.

I make it back to the table in time to see Vlado heading our way. He carries a box with the holy grail of desserts—two huge pieces of *Prekmurska gibanica*.

"This is the crossroads where we filmed *Joužek*. Five roads come together here."

In the video, the road seemed infinitely longer and deep in the countryside, desolate with only fields and birds and, of course, the crucifix to keep it company. Instead a road runs less than fifty meters away, and on the other side of that lay buildings and edge of town things—other signs of human life.

"This is where Joužek will wait for you," I say. "At the end of the road. With Štefan."

He pauses. "Yes."

With that, we turn right towards *brod*, Vlado steering the car past damp green fields and me thinking morbid, philosophical thoughts.

The area of Prekmurje around Beltinci is flat in the way only prime bottomland can be flat, the air brackish from the river. Fields of cabbages and what appears to be winter ryegrass stretch out on either side of the road. I've read that Prekmurje is the breadbasket of the country with its fields of sunflowers and pumpkins and wheat shimmering in the sunlight, grape vines in rows that run off into the horizon, and bright, painted beehives so big you can walk inside them. Maybe it's that way in early autumn. All I see now are acres and acres of those giant cabbages, like green floppy hats. Not a scrap of paper or soda can or cigarette butt sullies the roadside or the verges or the banks of the Mura. Even the mud is clean.

"They grow some kind of flower there. Gladiolas," says Vlado, as we pass some gargantuan greenhouses set back in a field. "No, no—not gladiolas. Orchids. We grow orchids here in Prekmurje and export them to Europe."

That explains all the winter orchids in Ljubljana.

Vlado turns past a sturdy fence into a driveway and parks in front of a workshop. A huge German shepherd is kenneled next to the drive.

"Milan's dog, Luks. He named him after Tito's dog. The story goes that Tito would have been killed by a grenade if Luks hadn't jumped on it."

I like dogs. Dogs like me—except for the only dog that ever attacked me. A German shepherd.

Milan hops into the backseat with Rick.

Vlado laughs. "You remember Milan, yes?"

I do?

Both men stare at me. "From the concert?"

Milan smiles.

My mind goes blank. He was at the concert? I smile back at the men while I desperately try to remember. Which concert? Not the last one. It had to be the first night, with all the people there… with the wine. "I remember you! You brought the wine!"

"Yes! Haha!" Vlado and Milan both grin at me. I don't know who's more relieved—me or Vlado.

Vlado points to a house across the road from his place. "Štefan's house."

I was wrong. Štefan won't wait for him at the crossroads. He'll wait for Vlado here at his house by the Mura.

Vlado hops out of the car. "Come."

Thus we come, trotting after him as he heads down to the gate to Štefan's house.

Štefan may not live here any more but it looks like someone does. If ever a house is ready and waiting for someone, it's this one. The grass is mown down to a fine crisp carpet, bushes trimmed, house painted and leaves raked. All it needs is someone sitting on the stoop, smoking a pipe and smoke curling up out of the chimney.

I lean over the gate. What I'd like to do is climb the gate and go up to the house itself. Walk around the place. Peep through the windows.

"I want to take your picture," Vlado says.

"Me? In front of Štefan's?"

"Yes, yes."

I stand by the gate. Smile. Not smile? Too late. Vlado snaps the picture. I know better than to look at it. At least Vlado seems happy with it.

He murmurs something to Milan and then, nodding at me, starts singing the chorus to *Odhaja Dan*. He prompts me to join in, and I do. Even if I get the words tangled I can't refuse. We finish the song together, walking up the road to his place, leaving Štefan's house behind.

Vlado's house is simpler, like a new gray shoebox with terra-cotta shingles and nary a shrub within ten feet of the building. The Kreslins' renovation has made it clean and spiffy, with a picnic table under a tree out front, and a chain and strap thingamabob for the kids to swing on.

Milan takes us out to see the woodshed he's been working on. The shed's actually a barn with a wood crib, four stable doors and a brick building with a chimney attached to it. As we walk back to the house I get a bad case of barn envy.

Vlado says of something written on the floor of the porch. "Čarna wrote a poem. Right here." He grins up at me. "See? In the concrete. '*Poleti se ribe rade kopajo.*' 'In summer fish like to swim.' She wrote it when she was four. Good poem, yes?"

I try to make the words out—*Poleti se ribe*— but he's already leading the men into the house.

Poleti se ribe… Ribe means "fish", but I have no idea what *poleti* or *se* mean. The English version clunks along, but in Slovene her poem has a catchy little rhythm. Not knowing what the words mean has never stopped me before from enjoying Slovene, especially when it has a catchy rhythm. I head into the house.

Poleti se ribe…

On the way to the ferry we pass what seems to be a bunch of drawers stacked six or seven deep and at least ten wide, sitting on a wagon just off the road. It's a beehive, as huge as an elephant, with each drawer painted a primary color—red, yellow, blue, white. In its early days it must have been cheery, but what with the humidity picking at it and the cloudy day, it droops like something the circus left behind. The bees probably think it's the spiffiest place in the world to live.

The ferry is spiffy too, waiting at the end of the road under some trees overhanging the Mura. Next to the landing is a river house, or maybe it's just a fishing shack. A small curly-tailed dog struts out of the door, yapping on its way to greet us, followed by an old man. The old man makes his way down to the river, and we all hop onto this raft the size of a garage. A tiny red shed covered in faded playbills sits on one corner. A barricade rings the raft; along one side is a bench. Jutting up behind the bench is a small crucifix with another one of those roofs over it and a fist-sized pot of purple pansies beneath it.

The men exchange the usual small talk, and then the ferryman unhooks the ferry from the bank. We push off, leaving behind his very unhappy dog.

A block and tackle attaches the ferry to a cable over the river. Only the rudder needs to be set and, like a good servant, the Mura does all the work of getting the ferry across. A child can do it, or one aged man who lives by the river. The Mura pushes us on, its current hard and cold.

Rick and I take turns shooting pictures of the Mura, the ferry, the men talking or just standing around not talking, and then Vlado and me sitting on the bench. Even with clouds scuttling overhead and wind whipping around us, it doesn't feel cold. It feels adventurous, like one of those Huckleberry Finn sailing away forever kind of expeditions. Maybe the cable will break, sending us down the Mura, and we can lie on our backs and watch the stars come out, one by one.

We could run away and join the circus.

Vlado says, "Me and my older friend Stanči were fishing on Mura and riding our bicycles through Melinci on the way home that late afternoon when we heard *Satisfaction*. By Rolling Stones. Whoa—what is this? And in the middle of the village there was this circus tent. We stopped.

"When we came closer to the tent, Stanči made a connection with them right away. You know, made friends. They let us in for free. We got in for the first show, and when the magician called for people to come on stage, no one would go. And because no one wanted to go on stage, we went, of course. And then after the show, we were there with them, and they were telling all those stories about traveling the world. I was all ears, of course. Then they called us to the second show. Ha! We were almost assistants now, and when the magician asked for someone to help on stage, we jumped in again, because we wanted to get some tricks to learn how they did them. After the second show they made up our fish and again told more stories.

"About twelve o clock, I said to Stanči maybe we should go home. He said he was staying with them, that tomorrow they go to Prague and he was going with them. I had no light on the bike, and I didn't dare to drive home. There was a cemetery I had to pass. They persuaded me to stay there and sleep in the wagon. In the meantime, there was a frantic search party out looking for us. My parents, police, firemen and fishermen were searching up and down the river for our bodies—for us—thinking we had drowned.

"In the morning when the door to the wagon opened, my mother was standing there in the in early morning light, screaming 'You're alive! You're alive!!' When I rode my bicycle through Beltinci, people were yelling, 'You're alive!' Even the neighbors came to see me when I was sitting in the kitchen, calling out 'You're alive!' Then Štefan came. He winked and elbowed me, saying, 'You really got them good.'"

Or we might drown.

Milan stares at the river and mutters something under his breath.

"A family tried to swim it," says Vlado. "A Czech family—a man, his wife and their children. At Gornja Radgona. They were trying to get to the West. They didn't make it."

Milan says something else.

Vlado points across the river. "Over there, during the war, German soldiers lined people up along the banks and shot them. Twenty one people."

We all stand there silent, facing the soundless shore.

The ferryman resets the rudder, and the Mura pushes us back to the shore and the unhappy dog. Water slaps against the pontoons, making the ferry strain at the cable. So much for being the Tom Sawyer, Huck Finn and Becky Thatcher of the Mura. In light of what I've just heard, that seems silly now.

Vlado pulls into his friend Milan's driveway again. Milan hurries into his workshop, which turns out to be his wine cellar, and comes out, grinning, with a bottle.

Vlado says, "He wants to know if you'd like a glass of wine."

Of course we'd like a glass of wine.

He pours Rick and me each a glass, Vlado abstaining since he's driving. The wine is light and dry, and when we drain our glasses, Milan offers us another. It's a long way back to Ljubljana, though, with few rest stops along the way.

"Pumpkinseed oil—would you like some?" Vlado walks down the driveway towards the street. "Come."

Milan's neighbor has a business extracting and selling pumpkinseed oil. We follow Vlado into a room where they're working with the oil, the flat green seeds swirling and churning in the giant steel hopper. Vlado scoops a few seeds out and passes them to Rick and me for munching. Vlado hands a bottle of oil to me. "It's very, very good."

Katarina hurries out of her house and presses a paper bag into my hands as she kisses my cheeks. "*Adijo! Srečno! Srečno*!" Good-bye! Good luck! Good luck!

"Oh, thank you! *Hvala lepa*!" I reply, kissing her back. Then, not knowing 'good bye' in Slovene, I add: "*Dober dan! Se vidimo*!" Please God, let one of them be right.

I open up the bag on the way to the car. Inside are two *krapci* cookies and a small earthen vase.

We pull out of the driveway and head back down the street.

"There he is!" says Vlado.

Sure enough, his father heads towards us on his bicycle, a loaf of bread in his basket and a beret cocked on his head. Vlado honks and I lean out the window: *"Se vidimo! Se vidimo!"* Milan grins, waves and pedals on home.

Is there any time more marvelous to pass a cemetery than at twilight?

We've been talking about the Kreslins and how his father was Lutheran, which of course made me think Vlado was Lutheran—although later Vlado tells me that he actually is Catholic. Blissfully confused about the religious thing, I go off thinking he was Lutheran, which meant Štefan was Lutheran, too, (which wasn't true either) since they were confirmed together.

Shadows creep in. A lovely building looms in front of us as I think all these churchy thoughts, and I wonder if it's a church or a memorial or even a mausoleum as the shadows grow. It's hard to see Vlado in the car now. He's in shadow, everything's in shadow.

He whispers, "Look over there."

Past the darkened wall flanking the road are jagged stones sticking up. Something moves among them, a trick of the failing light… no, it's nothing, really. Nothing at all.

"Štefan's buried there," Vlado murmurs. "The gravestone itself has waves in it. It symbolizes the Mura. " He strokes his hand through the air. "On his tombstone it is written, 'What is on this side is on the other side, what is on the other side is on this side.'"

Of course that's what a river would say.

It's too dark now to see anything I'd want to see in the graveyard, and soon we're speeding down the deserted road away from Beltinci.

We're heading to Ljubljana, radio going—sound up, sound down, Vlado talking on the phone, Rick in the back and me still mellow from his friend's wine. Vlado flexes his left hand, stretching his long fingers out and curling them in, over and over again. I wonder if his tendons ache from the concert, or if he has arthritis. I say nothing.

On a distant hill a church lights up the black sky.

"That's the first thing I saw in Slovenia," I say. "It's so pretty, like a beacon."

"Yes, I am sure it looks nice," says Vlado, "but something tells me it is friendlier to Mother Earth if the lights are off. Even trees need darkness." Just like that, the church disappears behind a hill. "I like the idea of the Protestant priest in Goričko. A few months ago he turned off the lights at his church. We will see how many will follow."

*

Eva picks us up at the Lev. "The artist we're meeting is very good and a great fan of Vlado's. He's the one who did Vlado's portrait, the one with the glass on his head."

And Vlado?

She smiles. "Vlado is babysitting tonight."

She slips the car into a space the size of a cocktail napkin. It's raining again. We walk through the dark and the rain into a blindingly bright gallery crammed full of people. Dry people, too, from the way the filled wine glasses disappear from the table in the foyer. So many people… A few wine glasses disappear with us, and we move away from the door to let another wave of patrons surge through.

Pictures hang on the wall, beautiful icons set in beautiful frames. A few portraits, too, especially one that is very odd. We're whisked into the back room where a film clip runs of a Greek Orthodox Metropolitan reciting something. A poem, perhaps. It's hard to tell. We sip our wine and watch from the back of the crowd.

Eva introduces us to Roman Uranjek, who created the portrait of Vlado with the wine glass on his head. Uranjek is part of the artist consortium IRWIN, which is responsible for this exhibition called *Was ist Kunst Hugo Ball.* We say hello-how-are-you, and isn't-Vlado's-work-wonderful-and-so-is-this, then squeeze our way through the clumps of people, many of them in passionate debate. Some of it's about the exhibition, but most of the conversations are about politics. Elections are imminent. A former presidential candidate is present, as are various ambassadors and attachés and other high luminaries. It's all very posh and great fun for non-posh me, rubbing elbows with all these people while trying not to spill my wine.

But all journeys must come to an end, even short ones. We finally emerge in front of the very odd portrait.

I wish I were culturally sophisticated. I wish I'd had a better grounding in art beyond "I don't know anything about art but I know what I like". In this I'm woefully deficient.

So is Rick.

"Oven Mitt Man," he declares, grinning at the photograph of the main Dada instigator and poet Hugo Ball, who's wearing a chef's toque and paper claws on his hands as he reads his famous poem *Karawane*. Or maybe that's a bishop's miter and paper vestments. It's confusing.

I wonder how he got his paper pants on without tearing them.

"Shhhh." Oven Mitt Man. I bite my lip to stop my giggles. This is a serious artistic event, dammit, but it's too late. My brain will forever tag it as Oven Mitt Man. I force myself to be urbane and study this stiff man with a solemn face. I decide he's wondering why he is a human lobster with oven mitts for claws. But that might be the wine talking. Ball might be having a ball.

Rick certainly is. He enjoys Oven Mitt Man so much that when he finds a stack of flyers with Hugo Ball dressed in his paper clothes, he pilfers one and stuffs it into his coat.

Eva gathers us up again, this time to meet Darko Pokorn, another IRWIN member. He designed the Pesmarica songbook and a number of CD covers and posters for Vlado. We say hello-how-are-you, isn't-Vlado-great-and-so-is-this. I don't say a word about Oven Mitt Man.

We leave our empty wine glasses on a convenient window ledge. Outside of slipping them into a stranger's coat pocket while he wasn't looking, there's no place else to stash them. Finally unencumbered, we head back out into the rain, this time to rendezvous with Erica and Aleš at a quiet little café. After the churning crowd at the gallery, *quiet* and *little* sound wonderful.

We huddle together in the rain outside the café. A small band, who in the near future will be known as the Deaf Musicians, have blasted the downstairs clear of patrons and now have taken up assaulting the windows and doors with mega-volume wails and bangings.

"Oh, dear," says Eva.

We creep inside to wait.

The music may be great, but at fifty million decibels, who can tell? Eva starts to say something, then shakes her head and motions for us to follow. Creak, creak, creak up the stairs we go. BAM ! BAM! EEEEEK! comes the sound right after us. Chords flail at our ears as we slink around searching for a place where at least we can scream at one another.

Eva yells, "Maybe we should go somewhere else? I don't think we can talk here."

Back into the rain we go. This means passing the band, who are cheerfully blasting noise again. I keep my fingers out of my ears so the band doesn't feel bad. The lead singer, who must be about fifteen, smiles at me. Too bad they all probably have a horrid case of tinnitus by now.

Eva messages Erica to let her know our new destination. "It's okay. She's running a little late." Eva pauses. "Would you like to see the building? It's just around here."

We'd love to see the building. Isn't it old and full of secrets and dreams waiting to be born?

We turn a corner, and there it is. Not too big, not too small. The building looms like a forgotten wedding cake swathed in a fondant of tarp, with a tugboat top and huge round windows facing a small playground. This is the embryonic Mala Ulica, the first family center resource for children in Ljubljana. If ever a building was built for kids, it's this one.

"Of course it will look much different when it is finished." Eva says.

"It's perfect," I whisper. All it needs is a little renovation. And children. Lots of laughing children.

The Zvezda Café at Wolfova 14, deep in the heart of Ljubljana, is lively tonight. We push our way through the patrons to some tiny tables by a doorway. Rick sticks the umbrella under a hat rack as we enter. Actually he sticks it into the hat rack but, as usual with contrary objects, it slips to the floor and wedges itself halfway under the baseboard. I wonder if it'll still be wedged there when we leave, and then I remind myself, this is Slovenia. Things are different here.

Eva, being responsible and mature about watching her weight, orders something lemony-lime and barely caloric. Rick gets cappuccino. And I, because I also have been watching my weight up until I decide it's silly to do so because who knows if I'll ever be in Ljubljana again, order Slovenian Hot Chocolate.

Which is why Eva is very schlank, and I am not.

I thought I'd had great hot chocolate before but I've never had anything like this. Frothy and thick, so thick that I eat it with a spoon, and strong and sweet with whipped cream on top—nothing compares to it. It has to be a thousand calories; I don't care. I may be slurping like a pig as I spoon it into my mouth; I don't care about that either.

So when Erica and Aleš find us in the coffee shop and Eva makes the introductions, I'm blissfully glutted on chocolate. The mature part of me hopes I'm not wearing a chocolate smile. Or chocolate teeth. The saving grace is that our table is tucked back into a dark nook. Erica and Aleš are too charming and polite to notice any errant brown smears. I dab at my lips while they get their coats and wraps situated, and when they look back at me, whatever chocolate I've been wearing is gone.

Now if Vlado was here? I'd grin and roll my eyes and wipe my mouth with my fingers, just like a kid. But he's not here. I feel the need to be proper, all legs crossed at the ankles and fingertip napkins, pinky in the air. Amazing how one person can change everything. I sip my chocolate properly.

I'm cowed by all this fame and fabulosity. Both Erica and Aleš are published, inhabitants of Valhalla for someone like me. I'd read Erica's book, *Forbidden Bread*, long before meeting her. I formed this mental picture of her as a quiet, reserved woman, one of those bony, fainting types who live on tea and crumpets, and stare languidly out of windows on rainy days. Anyone who writes so elegantly has to be quiet and reserved, yes? Erica's about as quiet and reserved as a firecracker. She's the girl everyone invites to a sleepover because she'd make sure it was fun—or else. She crackles with energy. Her eyes open wide as she leans in to ask Rick what he does. Her head bobs and her hands flutter about her face as she describes plans for her upcoming birthday party for Aleš.

Aleš is her perfect foil, spending his words carefully. He's an editor and a professor, an essayist and a poet, with enough awards and honors and published books to dam the Ljubljanica. He got a PhD in sociology of culture at Syracuse University in 1989, and was later a Senior Fulbright fellow at the University of California, Berkeley. And he's sweet. He orders Slovenian hot chocolate and sips it, his dark eyes amused as he watches Erica launch into a tale of another animated adventure.

I watch them as I finish my chocolate. It hits me that I won't see Vlado again this trip. "You must come this summer," he had said, "and we all can go to Dušan's in Piran." Like the chocolate, the invitation is rich and bittersweet.

It's too late for dinner. We haul our weary bodies up to the hotel room and scrape together the few provisions we'd squirreled away in our suitcases. A package of wafer cookies and a few chocolates from France? I don't think so, not after the hot chocolate I just had. Some beef jerky—and then I see it. My holy grail of culinary delights, Slovene style. *Prekmurska gibanica*—the real *gibanica*.

Two pieces sit on the table, their fat gooey goodness taunting me. Each is the size of a bread and butter plate. Each is big enough to fulfill my caloric need for the next week. All mine… err, ours. I glance over at Rick. He's happily munching on cookies. I smile and look back at the *gibanica*. All mine.

I open the box. I reach for a fork… and find nothing. No fork. No spoon. No knife.

Pencils? Pens? I think not. No way should my first taste of *Prekmurska gibanica* to be tainted with graphite or ink.

I want to taste it so bad. Right this instant, just so I can tell Vlado how good it is, how awesomely awesome it is, before we leave.

I poke my finger right into the middle of a cake and pull out a quivering dollop of cheesy apple walnut goodness. It smells rich and sinfully good, as sweet as death. Death by *gibanica*, yes. I shovel the sticky riches into my mouth. Close my eyes and swallow. I sigh, and silently send a thousand thanks to Vlado.

"Come have a bite," I say to Rick, waving in front of his nose the chunk of *gibanica* I'm balancing on my fingers, "before I eat it all."

As if I could eat it all.

Rick takes a bite. "Mmmm."

Five minutes later, all that's left of our first piece of *gibanica* is on our fingers.

We're up before dawn, heading head to the airport. The other piece of *gibanica* rides on my lap.

"You sure you want to take that?" Rick had asked.

"Breakfast," I replied.

Chapter Nine

Once I'm home, Vlado sends me photos, clips of songs, articles and newspaper clippings.

"Here are some photos from our trip this summer," he writes. "Sarajevo. And this is Buric. You should talk to him. Write him." He probably writes to him, too, giving him a heads-up that my email is on its way, and so I do.

Ahmed writes back:

"I met Vlado at some reading/gig at the Festival 'Sarajevska zima'. He had a show in Sarajevo with a friend we had in common, a writer—Miljenko Jergović. Vlado sang and played some of his songs, and the writer read some of his stories. There were not so many people at the performance, around fifty, but he acted like he was in front of thousands of people.

"'A real one', I meant. 'That's how the professionals made their stuff.' But that was not the only impression. This guy has 'something' which is not only a charisma of musician and the poet, someone could say a pop star. He's different, in a way.

"That same night I wrote a poem dedicated to him— *The Sky over Sebilj*."

"In fact, this was not the first time that I saw him in some public space. In 1994, there was a humanitarian concert in Ljubljana for Sarajevo, organized in Hotel Slon. At that time I was a refugee in Slovenia, and Sarajevo was besieged by Serbian troops at the war. I had been working for some small television for refugees and made some story from the concert.

"Some great names from former Yugoslavia performed on that occasion: Kemal Monteno and Davorin Popović, probably the best known singers in ex- Yugoslavia for last few decades came from Sarajevo, Arsen Dedić—great poet and singer from Zagreb was there, even later Hollywood actor Rade Šerbedžija sang and read some poems. The concert was full of emotions, but weird in a way. There is something 'diabolic' in such a kind of being: you always have some bad consciousness when you are 'safe' out of your country when your friends and relatives are suffering, and there are some guilty feelings about that.

"In a corner, there was a guy with the hat, drinking wine. He played some song, and his voice was one of the saddest things that I've ever heard. I don't remember what he did after his performance. It was one of those nights that you cannot remember every detail, because it was more or less a time of no hope, at least for me.

" 'Who is this guy?' I asked.

"'Vlado Kreslin,' somebody answered. 'He is pretty well known here, playing some rock music. But, now he's got a pretty success with the etno band from the village where he was born.'

"'How do you mean?'

"'Yeah, the old guys from bars and tavernas from Prekmurje. Do have a listen to some of that. It's pretty crazy. You could like it.'"

"And I did. It was a complete new and fresh experience. And also changed my life. The song, which Vlado played at the concert, was '*Namesto koga roža cveti* (Instead of Whom Does the Flower Bloom)', a ballad that says we are only drops in this world, 'like a tear in the wind'. I've learned to play that song, and sung that for friends every time when they asked me, 'How was it during wartime in that Slovenija, what did you do there?'"

"Twelve years later it was kind of a satisfaction of some cosmic principles, if they exist, that Vlado and I met in Sarajevo. I've decided to translate his poems and songs into the Bosnian language. Such a small service for someone who has a pretty same look at all the worlds that human beings could find themselves."

Ljubljana, August 2012

Friday afternoon. Ljubljana. The airport is full of people outside the baggage area trapped together like minnows in a net.

Inside the baggage area is the usual mad dash for the restrooms. Some former passengers climb over the luggage in their haste to make it in time. Like Olympic hurdles, only in slow motion and vastly more entertaining. Note the restraint—I'm not describing the restrooms themselves, only the passengers' desperation in reaching them. This is a story about friendship and the discovery of a country, not Slovene Bathrooms I Have Known, although Vlado must have thought my objective was to visit every restroom between Piran and Beltinci. Are they memorable? Do I mention them? If not, then no. I blame the stops on wine.

But that comes later. Right I'm dealing with more mundane issues. Luggage? Check. Husband? Check. Hat? Still on my head. I smile. It looks like everything's here. Now to find Vlado.

I only succeed in finding a lot of backs. A sweaty barricade of brown and sunburnt flesh looms up in front of me. We're all doomed to shuffle out of the door together, but right now we're still at the oozing stage—oozing left, oozing right, like lumps of skinless chicken going nowhere. No way can I break around them to see if Vlado's out there.

This closeness makes me cranky. Longhorn cattle have the right idea, horn-butting anyone who gets in their way. I could use my brim to hat-bump someone. It'd give me a little space and break up the monotony. It might make a gap wide enough so I can see Vlado.

Someone jostles me from behind and we're off, waddling for the exit like a flock of ducks. People bunch up even tighter, bumping each other's carry-ons as they ready themselves to dash off in every direction and trip over each other's feet.

"There he is," cries Rick from somewhere behind me and off to my left.

I peer around the woman in front of me. The crowd splits like Moses-parted waters, and in the middle of this opening sits a very brown and hatless Vlado, holding a giant sunflower. Not quite Moses' staff but it'll do. The only thing out of place on Vlado is the foot long bandage on his leg. It looks like a white neon light against his skin.

He makes his way through the tables and, shaking Rick's hand, grabs me in a hug which smushes my hat. He hands me the sunflower, which is almost as big as my head.

"Stay here. I will get the car." Showing us that his leg doesn't hurt, he trots off, leaving us to guard our luggage in an ever-increasing crush of people.

On the flight over I fretted that it'd rain the whole time we were in Ljubljana. When we've been here before, the city was terminally damp with rain, fog, or drizzle, and sometimes all three.

But, by George, the sun is blazing now. It's hot enough to make your teeth sweat.

"I dropped Naj off at the airport this morning." Vlado eases the car onto the road to Ljubljana. "He's going to Miami with Eva's brother, so this week with you works out really well. Naj is training in basketball, and Miami with LeBron James is for him as Liverpool with the Beatles was for me."

The road he takes runs east, past sun-bleached fields and ditches of lush, green weeds.

"We just got back from holiday on the island Vis, in the Adriatic," says Vlado, "then we went to Sarajevo to see some friends—Ahmed, you've talked with him—and some others. We had a great time there. On our way back we passed Jajce, and since I am connected to this city by my birthday being on the coat of arms of Yugoslavia and on Yugoslav money, I wanted to show my family where Yugoslavia was born, and the famous slopes as well.

"The kids didn't want to get out of the car but when Naj saw the beautiful green water, he wanted to go in, so he and I immediately jumped in. Naj suggested that we go under the waterfall but I said no, you never know what is there, maybe some hole or something. And I was almost proud of myself, how smart and responsible I had become with my ages. My whole life I was the first one to do such a stupid and unthinking thing, you know? And just as soon as this thought went through my mind, I lost the ground under my feet. There was some hole under the water…"

Vlado's cell goes off. "*Jijiji*! I forgot to call Eva!" He answers, and then says to us, "I was supposed to call her when I picked you up!"

Hurried conversation ensues with much apologizing and laughing. "Okay. Anyway, I got this pain in my leg. There was some hole under the water, and the leg looked awful! At first they thought the bone was open broke! And in minutes I was in a hospital. The leg wasn't broken. It just blew up with blood. Haha! It was very romantic. I mean to have such an accident under the waterfalls of AVNOJ. And then the ambulance car and the hospital. Ruth, you first must see some old Yugoslav movies, then I will describe it more."

'Blew up with blood?' 'Romantic?' I bet Eva had a different word for it.

"Ruth!" Eva comes out from the kitchen to give me a hug while I'm pulling my shoes off at the top of the stairs. "You don't have to do that. Really."

I stop in mid-pull. "I don't?"

"No, no. Leave them on. It's okay."

Eva looks great, not a bit frazzled having houseguests, even though she's just back from holiday. "We don't have a guest room; I hope you don't mind being in Naj's room."

Mind? As tired as we are, it's nirvana.

Up to Naj's room we go, hauling luggage and sacks, pralines and chocolates, and a watch for Ajdina. Naj's bed is big and soft. I want to *carpe nappum*, but only after our snack.

Which turns out to be a huge lunch. Pasta with tomatoes and olives, and little crunchy things that may be diced pine nuts or maybe not, lightly dressed with oil, plus salad. To these starving, weary travelers, it's amazingly good.

After we've eaten and put our stuff away, Vlado sets up the video of their recent holiday and fast-forwards to where they're heading to Jajce.

Rick and I settle in to watch while Vlado heads to the dining room. You want to know why he's so slim? He's always moving. Always.

"Too bad Eva didn't get Naj and me in the water," he calls over his shoulder.

A waterfall comes up on the screen. We see Vlado and Naj walking on the banks of a natural swimming pool at the base of the fall.

"Are you sure?" I say. "That looks like you right there. The water's green, right?"

Vlado comes back to watch.

Sure enough, that's Vlado in the green water, waving at the camera. And oops, suddenly he's two feet shorter.

"Hah! Look! Eva got it after all! Naj was waving his hands—see? Trying to get her attention to get help. She thought he was telling her to keep taking pictures. Haha! But the ambulance came to take me to the hospital, so it was okay."

"But what's Jajce?"

"Oh. Eh, the Partisans were allied with AVNOJ. The Anti-Fascist Council of the People's

Liberation of Yugoslavia."

"Partisans?"

"Partisans were anti-fascists fighting the Alliance in the war—you know, the Fascists. You see," and here Vlado leans forward, his face intent, "what became new Yugoslavia had been divided and given to all these different countries—Italy, Germany, Hungary, others. And Jajce is the town where Tito and the leaders of the Partisans got together on November 29 to make plans about the post-war future."

"Your birthdate."

"Jajce was earlier, in 1943, but yes, on the same date."

Jajce. Tito. AVNOJ. Partisans. My eyes glaze over. Except for Tito, I've heard of none of these before—well, Partisan, yes, I've heard the word but I doubt Partisans here are anything close to the partisan politics we have back home. But Jajce and AVNOJ? That's new to me.

History needs to be discussed deeply over time, preferably late on a winter's night in front of a blazing fire with lots of wine, but if that won't work, then at a tavern with friends. Wherever the discussion, it must be led by a dreamy-voiced raconteur. All we have now is the raconteur, and he's moved the conversation on to something else. Do I care about this Jajce and Partisans? If it helps me understand Vlado and his background, of course I do. But so many questions. I don't know where to begin asking. With Vlado laughing now about the happenings at the hospital, history will have to wait.

His leg, though — that's here and now. It must have hurt something awful when he fell in the hole.

"Your leg's better now? It doesn't hurt?" I glance at the bandage, half expecting to see something thickly red and oozy seeping from under it. The kid in me wants to see it in all its awful glory. Would he show it to me if I asked?

"Hurt? Oh no." With a wince he lays an ice pack on it.

Later I look up all these strange and weighty words--AVNOJ, Jajce, and the Partisans, rabid anti-Fascists of whom some were Communist and some were not. The AVNOJ meetings, which brought about the birth of Yugoslavia as midwifed by Tito, were convened to discuss the future constitution of the state made up of all these different nations. And things like the Mura River Massacre, where the Germans simply lined up the people and shot them so the bodies fell in the water—stuff like that can put you right off Fascism so, yes, I can see this.

Not a fun time for anyone.

To top it off, they neglected to inform Stalin, who had more than a little interest in the new country. After all, he was guiding them in the communist way. Kindly, genial Uncle Joe. If it weren't for him, who knows where they'd be? He thought he should be privy to such meetings. He wasn't. This pissed him off. As if they cared.

All this happened at Jajce with Tito and the Partisans, this putting together of a country that later came apart. So Vlado took his children there, to see where some of their history was made. The jumping in the water, falling down the hole and cutting the leg was pure lagniappe. Poor Vlado.

Ljubljana on a summer's evening. We're headed to a restaurant down by the river when a young woman breaks away from a crowd and runs up to Vlado. I expect her to ask for a photo with him, or at least an autograph, but she wants is talk. He stops to talk, so three of us stop, too.

Eva sighs. "It happens more and more these days, people coming up when we're out in public. She's saying they sang together ten years ago …" Her voice trails off.

"Do you think she did?"

"Maybe."

Butchers' Bridge (*Mesarski Most*) is a new bridge with glass walkways on the edges. I can see right through the bridge to the river beneath. It's a clear view too, which makes me glad I didn't wear a skirt. With horizontal steel cables making up the railings on either side, it sounds austere but it's not; people have covered the cables with "love locks". Lovers write their names on the locks and fasten them to the bridge, like barnacles of love, proclaiming their undying devotion—at least for that day.

In the middle of the span are beautiful grotesque sculptures by Jakov Brdar. They tower over us, their bodies twisted in agony. Or maybe ecstasy; it's hard to tell. Scattered on the bridge are smaller grotesques, something cuddly left over from a Maurice Sendak story.

An older man with a wild grizzled beard flying in the air hurries up to Vlado. It's Jakov Brdar. Vlado makes the introductions, then we move away so the two men can have their conversation in peace. As they talk, I look first at Brdar, then at the sculptures, and wonder what the landscape of his mind really is

"Sorry, sorry." Vlado rushes to join us as Brdar hurries away. "He doesn't speak English and he hears very bad…" Vlado shrugs.

At the end of Butchers' Bridge is the Restaurant Most. We're to meet a friend of the Kreslins there, Damjan Kozole, for dinner. On this summer night tables are spread under trees by the river. There's not much of a breeze, though. I wonder if we'll swat mosquitoes all dinner long. The other customers aren't flailing their hands about. Maybe they don't have mosquitoes here.

"Oh, yes, we do," says Damjan, sitting off to my left. "My place gets them all the time."

"We didn't even have them at the country house last year," adds Eva.

No mosquitoes at a river? This I've got to see.

“You will,” says Vlado. “We’re going there in a few days. After Piran.”

The wines are wonderful. Damjan and Vlado have the white and the rest of us the red. It’s just dry enough to let me know it’s not a teenage vintage dressed up in its mother’s bottle.

The talk is light, mostly about our different projects and how we each got to meet Vlado. I mention the book we’re doing. Damjan, a director of some renown, talks about going to Houston; his film *Slovenka* is up for an award. Eva’s work with Mala Ulica is progressing well. Even Rick is relaxed, especially after his second glass of wine.

And Vlado is Vlado, telling stories and making us laugh, and sometimes checking his Blackberry when there’s a lull in the conversation.

The food comes.

Each time a plate is set down we exclaim over the presentation and how wonderful the food smells. I’m having prawns, after being talked out three other things. But prawns won, a nice safe choice. Damjan has something similar, Rick’s is a robust meat and Eva, being smart, ordered something small and slimming.

Vlado’s plate is last to arrive. It’s covered with tiny little squiggly things.

We all weigh in on it. “Octopus.” “Oh yes, definitely octopus.” “Are you sure?” “Sure, sure. It’s good.”

Tiny little heads, tiny suckers. Babies. He’s got pasta, too, in a garlic sauce that smells wonderful, but it’s the octopus I see, all those wee little tentacles curling up.

“Here—have some.” Vlado waves his fork at his plate. I can’t, not octopus. I taste his pasta, and it’s very good. I hope he forgives me for not noshing down on the squiggly things.

The next morning, we tootle off in Vlado’s car, heading into Ljubljana for a calm day of people watching before the concert tonight in Bled. Prešeren Square is as good a place as any to sit and watch the world go by, although I’m not sure if we’re the watchers or the watchees.

But before we get to Prešeren Square, Vlado’s got something he wants to show us. He parks, and sets out on a path that takes us through a tree-lined promenade. It’s a lovely street, flanked by official looking buildings and stately trees. Vlado leads; Rick follows close behind; I dawdle. There are things to see, dammit. I want to see them.

“Who are these?” I ask. We’re passing a row of black busts propped up on tall gray pillars.

“Eh? Oh, they’re famous composers.”

Famous composers? I was hoping for something more specific. I try to work out the name on the run but either my eyes or my brain isn’t fast enough. Vlado’s already halfway down the street. Maybe I can ask him on the way back.

He takes us down Vegova Ulica to the Križanke stage. This is the outdoor venue where Vlado plays every August, redesigned in the fifties by Ljubljana's favorite architect Jože Plečnik. It's part of an old monstery complex of the Teutonic knights, which means there's an old church around here somewhere but we never see it. It's the performance venue we're going to see.

We wander in. It's easy to believe it was once part of a monastery. It's like a sanctuary with the stage below us and the seats climbing up to the sound booth above and behind us. Above, Vlado tells us, is a retractable roof. The complex is respectably sized, and surrounded by trees. Peaceful. It's the kind of place that makes you want to break into an aria, just to see how good you can sound. Notice I said "you". Not me.

Then Rick or Vlado—I don't remember who—says something. The words crack out, sharp and clean.

"Wow." My soft "wow" is stripped of fuzz. It sounds magnificent. I'm tempted to sing to see if that sounds good, too. I understand why Vlado likes performing here.

We head to Kavarna Pločnik, a café-bar right on Prešeren Square next to Tromostovje. If you want to watch people, it's the only place to be on a Saturday morn in late summer. Anything you want to drink is here, the wait staff speaks enough English for a tourist to get along, and somewhere there will be restrooms. We are going for coffee, after all. But with a beautiful day, beautiful friends and beautiful restrooms, what else could you want?

A spare euro comes to mind for the attendant. But that comes later.

"Ah," says Vlado, and grabs a table. Another man joins us, and Vlado jumps up to greet him, a huge grin on his face

"Cola! This is my friend Cola-Ciril. One day we put on this performance out in the road. In the summer we hitchhiked to the seacoast, and as we were waiting too long for a lift, we made a 'happening'. I took out the flute, which was always with me, started playing, and he was standing on his head for quite some time. For a kilometer of a car row. Haha! We stop traffic right there, with me on a flute and Cola standing on his head. We were in Gimnasium together. Actually he is one year older."

"In the road? Really?"

"Oh, sure." Vlado laughs again, and Cola shakes his head.

Later Vlado tells me: "Cola was a great provocateur. In the third year of Gimnasium, he attended a concert in Ljubljana in Hala Tivoli—Brian Auger and the Trinity. This was back in 1970. Cola undressed, and only in a G-string he climbed on stage under the piano. He could do this because, as you remember, there were no safety lines and no safeguards as it is now. Cola opened the violin box and started eating, like he was camping. I mean a real conceptualism. In 1970! I have to tell Ulay! Next day he was on a front cover of a magazine and almost got thrown out of school."

Vlado and Cola strike up a conversation in Slovene. Folks drift by, say hello and keep on going.

I sip my well-sugared, almost white coffee, which is what you get with three teaspoons of sugar and enough milk to turn it creamy. Since we're here to do some serious people watching I'd better look around.

It's more fun to watch Vlado, though. Now he's telling Cola a joke he told us yesterday. The cadence of his speech, the way he shakes his head as he raises his eyebrows, the places he stops to laugh—all the same. He leans towards Cola, laughing, and Cola laughs with him. Vlado then says to me: "It's the joke, you know—the one with the two guys. You remember."

Prešeren Square has her best face on, all gussied up and wearing her finest clothes, like it's the set for a movie called Perfect Day in Ljubljana. And it is a perfect day, if you go for warm sunshine and hazy blue skies. Buskers are all over the place. Behind Vlado, a juggler keeps five clubs in the air for the amusement of a handful of people. A man dressed in buckskins and a feathered headdress plays a flute and hawks CDs on the other side of the square. Across the river a singer in a hat and an ersatz Roma costume serenades—in English—a crowd standing around him. He's not actually in the square, but his music is very much so, thanks to his PA system.

American song, Native American flute—both in a Slovenian square. It's not what I expected.

I eye my coffee and furtively glance around for the nearest restroom. Since we're with Vlado, there's no telling when we'll get back to the house. I spy the sign for the restrooms, down the steps at the bridge. That'll do nicely.

Time for a walk.

The joys of European public toilets. Traditionally, you have to pay. The trade-off is they're clean, well stocked and safe. These days, when it comes to paying, it's not every toilet, not all the time, but this one? I have to have a coin. Not for the stall door but for the attendant. I'm fresh out of coins. But the attendant, a male—and isn't it curious there's a male attendant in the women's restroom? —takes pity on my stricken tourist face and waves me on in.

Bless him. The bathroom is clean.

But my conscience isn't. So I trot back to the café, dodging a man in an old time postal uniform who pedals by on an antique tricycle, courtesy of the Ljubljana Tourist Office. All that's missing out here are some clowns and a few acrobats.

I slip up next to Rick. If I whisper just right I can get a euro off him without drawing attention to myself.

"We were worried about you," says Rick in a low voice. "Vlado wondered if you were okay."

"I was having an adventure."

"In the loo?"

Over the bridge and down the stairs, tra-la-la back to the restroom I go. I skip through the door and drop the coin into the tray. There's a different attendant here now, still male. My actions mystify him but why should he care if a loony tourist wants to dump coins in his tray? I don't feel guilty any more.

Halfway up the stairs I start feeling odd. Not full-blown crawly-skin and swimmy-stomach odd, but off enough that food doesn't appeal at all. Curious.

Eva shows up, and off we go to get me a swimsuit, she cheerfully and me reluctantly. Rick trails behind us. He's coming along for the novelty since I buy a swimsuit as often as my dog whistles. He's also paying, a minor but important detail. The adventure goes about as expected. Many suits are tried, most of them outright rejecting me, but I find one that doesn't mind me wearing it as long as no one sees it on me.

Other folks have joined Vlado's table. Vladimir, the ambassador and another friend from Gimnasium Murska Sobota—almost the complete "bad company", as Vlado says they were called—and Cola's wife. Vlado's got a bona fide regular salon here. The conversation flits like a dragonfly from literary—Vladimir's mother has a book coming out soon—to the Olympics and finally, inevitably, to politics.

Slovenes love to talk about politics, even more than Americans do football. Vlado, not wanting us to feel left out, breaks away every few minutes to explain what they're discussing. He's like a pearl diver coming up for air. After a minute he's back in the water, churning with the best of them.

Then suddenly everyone stands, settles checks and disappears.

Eva and Vlado lead us, trek-like, to Sofrica. We find a table and settle back to relax in the sun. Not Vlado. He jumps up to say hello to someone at this table, a few someones at that table. When he comes back, another friend of his, Tomo, drops by, and gives Rick and me an autographed copy of his book, *Slovene Olympians*.

Vlado says, "He has a birthday on 29 November, same as me. If I party somewhere in town, Eva picks me up afterwards and takes me to Sofra where he has a party every year. Great guy!"

Vlado orders for all of us—*čevapčiči*, savory minced meat like a kebob, and *lepinja,* a flatbread that's a puffy naan with a pita-like pocket. It's so good, but I can only eat half. I want to return and have some more.

Then it's back to the house for the afternoon. Eva needs to pack for Savudrija, and the men need their beauty rest.

"Now tomorrow, you and Vlado will come down to Savudrija, and then you will have some time by yourself. Is that okay?"

Eva and I are in the kitchen, going over last minute details before she leaves.

"Oh, sure. That's great." I can do alone like nobody's business.

"You're sure?" She looks worried, but I'll be fine. Really I will.

She smiles then, and with one last flurry of making sure she has everything she needs, she heads out the door.

It's rest time. Vlado is big on afternoon rests. They're not long, maybe thirty minutes, but he attends them religiously—as does Rick. When we get back from the Ljubljana excursion, Rick goes upstairs for a quick nap. I never nap. I curl up with my laptop on the couch. Vlado hands me a couple of magazines in case I'd rather read, and he follows Rick up the stairs.

Chapter Ten

Hurry, hurry, dash around, grab up everything. Guitar? Guitar picks? Jacket, no jacket, yes—jacket for me, shoes, shoes… Hats, playlist, harmonica, shirt for performance in Bled.

Tires crunch on the gravel outside.

"Driver's here!"

Driver?

We clatter down the stairs, all of us burdened as if we're off on an expedition.

Vlado introduces us to Marjan, a small dark man who speaks excellent English and loves to practice it. But instead of getting into the driver's seat, he gets in on the passenger's side. Hmm, he's a designated driver who isn't driving. Vlado takes the wheel, turns left at the street and whips into a small driveway. More of Vlado's team is here, loading musical paraphernalia into a trailer.

We jump out, Marjan chattering away in front of me. He plows past these giant plants that arch over my head with swollen yellow blossoms. Goldenrod. It's got to be goldenrod.

I stop. My nose isn't tickling yet. But if I follow Marjan… Oh, well, even with my luck, what are the chances I'll get smacked in the face— *Whap!* Like a drunken bobble-head doll, a stalk bounces back in Marjan's wake and slaps me hard on the head. Pollen flies everywhere, including up my nose, and covers me in sticky yellow dust. How lucky can I be?

Marjan looks back, horrified, but I laugh and shake my hair out.

"It's okay. No problems."

"You've met the most of the guys but we have a few new ones." Vlado makes the introductions and we shake hands, old guys and new. We're just part of the gang, at least for tonight.

The musicians are almost finished cramming instruments, cords, and other concert things into a clamshell trailer. I don't see how they've shoehorned all their stuff in there, but what do I know? I have trouble packing suitcases.

We pile back into Vlado's car with Marjan in the driver's seat. We're all caravanning to Bled—"The Vlado Kreslin and Mali Bogovi (Plus Two Tagalongs) Cross Country Expedition!"

Vlado rides shotgun now. His seat pushed back, his long legs are stretched in front of him with his feet up on the dash with his hat, the better to take the pressure off his injured leg. He won't be diving into the audience tonight.

The guys with the overstuffed trailer pull out behind us. Anyone passing our caravan would think we're headed for a camping trip. Low key—that's Vlado.

"Now Leon... let me tell you about Leon. He has a restaurant in Bled, called Okarina. Great

Indian food. One day Leon is there alone, and he hears this knock-knock-knock on the front door, which is slightly ajar. Someone calls out in this British accent 'Are you open?' Is he open? He's there by himself, no staff at all, so of course he's closed. Eh, yeah, yeah, oh, sure.

"But Leon has a kind heart. He goes to the door, opens it and says, 'Paul!' And standing there—right there—is Paul McCartney. He was there incognito with his fiancée, who had a summerhouse in Bohinj. Haha! So, yes, I'd say he was open!"

As soon as we get into Bled, Marjan pulls into a gas station. Vlado jumps out and strolls in, a man on a mission. Marjan says Vlado wants to buy a blank cassette for his camera. Alas, no blank cassettes can be found.

Marjan threads the car between the tourists sauntering down the street and parks us by the lake. The concert tonight is outside. Chairs are stacked, ready to be put out for those who don't want to stand. The rest of the band is already here, scurrying across the stage with cords and stands, positioning speakers and testing equipment. Overhead, the sky is grumpy. The breeze feels wet. I cross my fingers that the storm blows over.

Vlado and Marjan go one way to get ready for the concert; Rick and I go the other direction to explore the area around the lake. Bled Castle sits far above us, looming over the lake from its perch on the cliff. Now that tempts me—I'm a sucker for a castle—but how do we get up there? Walking would take too much time. I don't want to miss the concert.

Instead of another grand adventure exploring a castle, we settle for strolling around the lake, making our way towards the casino. We poke around inside tourist shops and, to kill time, make up crazy stories as to why the door to the women's public restroom beyond the horse-and-carriage stand is jammed. This interests me since food and I aren't on speaking terms yet.

Ah, Bled. Everyone loves Bled. Even the little town where I live in Texas is taken with it, so much so that it wrangled a sister city arrangement with Bled for several years. Lack of funds on our side squashed that arrangement.

Bled is postcard perfect (except for the jammed restroom door). The Assumption of Mary Pilgrimage Church waits on its tiny island out in the lake. Bled Castle looms high above. Steep streets wind down between chalk white buildings with black roofs. Trees decked out in thick, rich greens crowd the road. Stick-skinny fire hydrants like praying mantises perch next to the sidewalks. Tourist shops and cafés line the street that curves around the lake, and people behind the counters smile at the customers who come in the door looking lost. It's a lovely place, cool even in August. Thank God I brought a jacket.

So we walk. From the concert grounds to the casino, from the casino to the concert grounds—back and forth we go on our promenade. But there are only so many times we can pass the restroom-cum-carriage stop without the carriage drivers giving us a jaundiced eye. Maybe they think we want a ride. Maybe they're wrong. For the last time, we turn back towards the lake and make a beeline for the concert grounds.

Bees do not fly in a straight line, thank god.

I glance over at the restroom. Someone's gotten the door unstuck. With just five minutes left for the facility to be open—irony is alive and well in Bled—desperate patrons hold the door open for the next person in line. Bless them.

"The song Vlado is playing now— Hungarian song. *Forget-Me-Nots*." Milan Kreslin nods at his son who's up on stage, doing sound check.

I like Vlado's folks a lot. I'd adopt them but I'm too old for that, and they're already taken. They're fun to be with, whether at their house or just hanging out next to a sound stage, waiting for their time to go up for sound check. Milan is amazingly encyclopedic when it comes to knowing about the music of this part of the world.

It's still an hour before the concert. People stop. Watch the stage. Look for a place to settle. Someone's lining up the chairs now, back by the sound booth, which is a tent set out in the lawn. A kid comes by on his tiny bike, trying to ride through the pea gravel on the pathway.

Milan and Katarina head off for their sound checks. Rick and I stroll down to some chairs on the back row. Other people take a seat, evidently thinking the concert has started. I can see why—the sound checks seem flawless.

Then everyone leaves the stage.

Vlado had mentioned something about dinner at his friend Leon's Okarina Restaurant, but where is it?

"Vlado wanted me to let you know the band is getting something to eat if you'd like dinner." Luka, the guy from the band who wears the hat with pheasant feathers, is behind us. Food? Rick's eyes light up. We scramble out of the chairs and start to follow our Pied Piper to gustatory bliss. But Luka doesn't come. Instead, he points the way to the band. We tag along with them to Leon's place.

At least I think it's the band. Maybe we're following a random group of strangers to the casino. Wouldn't that be a mess, ending up somewhere we're not supposed to be with no idea how to get where we are supposed to be, and no way to call Vlado? But there's Milan and Katarina. We're following the right group.

The path to Okarina winds up hills and through trees, giving the merry band of music makers and their two tagalongs a knights-on-a-quest ambiance. Just when I'm convinced Okarina is set deep in the woods, our path opens onto a street. We march single file into the place, Rick and I sandwiching ourselves in between band members so the staff know we're with the band.

Mushroom soup. I'm not ill enough to say no to mushroom soup—creamy and smooth and full of mushrooms. I consider stealing Rick's as well but that would be rude. I don't want to make Vlado regret bringing me here. I leave my husband's bowl unmolested. My body happily says thank you for the soup. It also says, eat nothing else.

Since ours is a most symbiotic relationship, I comply.

Vlado makes it to the table as the entrée is served. Soon after comes his friend Leon, the owner of Okarina. He's a gregarious fellow, which helps if one has a restaurant, with straight silver hair cut like a monk's and a quick grin. Vlado introduces him to the newcomers and brings out his camera for some photos.

Back at the concert grounds there must be over three thousand people—young people, old people, people-in-the-middle people, couples, singles, friends, families—all standing on this patch of grass. Over by the sound booth Rick and I claim a meter that's empty. Vlado's friend Leon opens the concert. He's the Program Director of this Okarina Etno Festival in Bled.

Then Vlado takes over and weaves his magic all over again.

A young woman in front of me stretches up on her tiptoes to kiss her boyfriend. People get starry-eyed when Vlado sings, even if it is cold. It's damp, too. No one cares about the cold and damp. Even the older folks sitting in the chairs huddle together and keep right on listening.

An August night in Bled, under racing clouds and crystal stars, listening to Vlado… it doesn't get any better than this.

The concert winds down amid applause and whistles. Vlado and the band slowly file off the stage. Couples go off, holding hands. Parents grab children; elders make their way to the parking area. The rest of the throng surges forward. All I see of Vlado is his hat above the crowd and soon, not even that.

The crowd that rushed up to talk with Vlado drifts away. Rick and I wander up to the stage. Some of the band does road crew chores; others hang out with Vlado, sipping wine and talking about the show.

"Ruth! Rick! Have some wine!" Vlado pours us a glass.

Nothing beats backstage camaraderie, when everyone is chilling while still on that performance high. Luka, the feathered hat guy, and Rick get into a detailed discussion about woodworking; Vlado's talking with Miro, Gal and the other Luka who is the bass player. And me? I look around and sip my wine, happy as a pig in mud.

"Leon!" Vlado waves.

Leon heads our way. The subject of Rick and me being from Texas comes up, and Leon's eyes dance.

"I visited Texas as part of a sister city delegation. Bled was a sister city for a while to a city close to Fort Worth. Benbrook… do you know it?"

Imagine that. Here we are in Slovenia, in Bled, meeting Leon, this friend of Vlado's who owns this awesome restaurant, and this very friend has ridden down our hometown streets and breathed our air, and seen just what a fine state of things Benbrook is in, and, of course, Fort Worth as well. Because, let's face it, there's not a whole lot to do in Benbrook unless you're into checking out municipal dams and reservoir lakes.

What are the odds?

Later in the car, I rush to tell Vlado about it, my words tumbling over themselves. He laughs. "I knew you should meet Leon! Haha!"

Vlado breaks off a chunk of bread and sets it on a wooden cutting board. Next he places a big square of butter wrapped in paper on the board. Then come strips of ham, thin and stringy like prosciutto. He slices a tomato and fans the slices out. Next to those he places the knife. All this and two plates he carries to the table. The wine is brought out with a couple of glasses. One last time he goes back to the kitchen, fetching the ice pack for his leg.

Finally he eases into a chair and, stretching his leg in front of him, centers the ice pack over his bandage.

"Have something to eat," he says.

I tuck my bare feet under my chair, and layer butter, ham and tomato onto a fist-sized piece of bread.

"This woman came backstage tonight— did you see her?" he asks.

I shake my head, my mouth too full to speak.

He nods, leaning back in his chair. "She said, 'I was privileged to sing with you.' And I ask 'Where?' because I did not remember her. She said in Polje Institution, where I had played a long time ago. And I said, 'oh?' And she says yes. Now at this institution, one of the patients thought he was Shakespeare—he was reading his Complete Works. Another thought he was director of the Vienna Philharmonic, and that one conducted music like so while I played." Vlado waves his arms. "Both 'Shakespeare' and the 'director of the Philharmonic' accompanied me. The 'director' was very enthusiastic so I pointed over the window, and said, do you see all those people? He said yes. Can you conduct them? And he did so, while I performed the concert. So I wondered about this woman. She saw me looking at her, maybe wondering. After a slight pause she said, 'But I wasn't a patient there. I was a doctor.' Haha!"

"People just come backstage like that?"

"Oh, sure. One man came up and said Beltinška Banda played for his wedding back in 1938. 1938! And Janez forgot his bow! He played the violin—you remember. And so he forgot his bow and the band never let him forget it, haha! I remember how Joužek was teasing him for this forgetting the bow, even fifty years later when I played with them. I always wondered if that really happened to him because he was so full of care for his violin. Never let her out of his hands. Here…"

Vlado jumps up and fetches a book—*Venci*. He flips through the pages and then, with his glasses perched at the end of his nose, he reads:

Violina

Nikdar nisem videl Jančija
odložiti violine kar tako,
zmeraj jo je imel v rokah,
bolje rečeno,
v naročju jo je zibal
kot zelo ljubega dojenčka,
edinčka.

Celo avtobusno pot v Lyon,
v avionu na olimpijado
ali na biciklinu,
razen tistega poznega popoldneva.
Pripeljala sva se
iz Sobote od Miške,
opevali smo
travico zeleno.

Janči je bil zelo kavalirski
zadnja leta,
po vsej sili je hotel plačevati pijačo.
ideva k Viliji v Lipovce
če si poznal lastnika gostilne,
bi ga zatajil,
če bi šel kar mimo
samo deci novoga vina!

Bil je konec oktobra,
vino pa noro
dajva še en deci,
viš, viš,
gda va se pá naslednjič srečala
res nekak čudež
tistih par dni vretja,
kot da ti ni nič,
vseeno pa si nekam
čudno munjen.

In potem, ko sem bil že
za hišnim vogalom,
mu je violina padla iz rok
v ograček,
tik pred pragom.

Baje ga še niso videli
tako obupanega
kot zjutraj.

Ge je violina?
Prespala je na vrtu med zeljem.

In nikdar tako srečnega,
ko so mu jo prinesli.

I take a sip of wine. "The band member who wears the pheasant feathers in his hat—Luka?"

"Ah, yes. Tonight he was wearing a hat with the feathers of a vulture, raven, peacock and four feathers of a buzzard. He can talk to birds. We need such a one in the band." Vlado grins. "I love to talk with people after the gigs. They come, we have a drink, we talk… eh, I could write a sequel to the book *Venci* with stories people tell me about how they met the musicians of Beltinška Banda years ago. So, on one of those days, a pilot told me that in the sixties they were training parachute jumpers in Prekmurje at the sports airport Rakičan. One day they picked up Miška Baranja, his brother Elemir and the rest of the band, and put them in the jump plane—the big one without doors, you know—and they played while the guys jumped out of the plane, haha!"

Upstairs in bed. Everyone's asleep, even the house itself is asleep. Well, not quite everyone. I'm awake.

Some time ago Vlado had written me:

"Ruth- I met a guy in Budapest- English Journalist (*Financial Times*). He was at our house in Prekmurje last weekend. Nice guy. Writes about me for his paper. He knows quite a lot about Slovenia/Yugoslavia and I asked him if he would answer some questions for you. He says yes. What do you say?"

Before I could send my answer, Vlado wrote again: "This is the guy-he lives in Budapest. An Englishman-charming one: Kester Eddy"

So I wrote to Kester, asking how he'd met Vlado. He wrote back:

"It was one of those times that only later do you realize some of life's great events hang by the thinnest thread of a decision.

"It was mid-April, I didn't feel very good, and I had an invitation to some art event at the Slovene embassy. Somewhat out of duty—the ambassador had been very kind to me over the years—I hauled myself off to the embassy, three miles distant up the hills in Buda.

"It was an authors' book reading. The official bits went on long, what with the Slovene original being translated into Hungarian. Standing at the back of a large, well filled, hot room I could barely understand a word of anything. This was, perhaps, an evening to forget.

"Fortunately, there was this Slovene singer-guitarist there, who played between each reading. I barely understood any of the lyrics. I managed to get 'This black guitar' to one song, but not much else. I can't say I was wowed, but he was the saviour of the event for me.

"The readings over, everyone gathered for food and drinks. The singer guy was standing with nobody talking to him, so I said, "Thanks for the music." He seemed happy to talk, especially after I told him I knew his home area in Slovenia.

"Who was his musical hero? 'Oh, Dylan, of course.' We discussed the age and phenomenon that was the Beatles, and others like Neil Young. We must have talked for twenty minutes or more, then Vlado stood up and gave an impromptu concert to the remaining crowd of perhaps thirty people.

"The audience, now almost entirely Slovene, lit up, and were singing along with the refrains. This was especially true with *Od Višine*.

“I was sitting next to the ambassador – a great admirer of Vlado, I later found out. I said something about people being so radiantly happy, and pointed to one young lady across the room. The ambassador said: "You know, she's a Hungarian, who's learned Slovene. She works at the embassy. I've never seen her so happy."

“At one point Vlado said, in English ‘I suppose you are waiting for a Neil Young song, right?’ at which point he launched into a passable version of *Down by the River* - but we both forget the words, to much audience amusement. To make up, he then said: ‘This is a song in the mood of Neil Young,’ and played Tisoč Let.

“When I got home I looked him up on the net and realized that as far as Slovene artists go, this guy Vlado is as big as they get. Little wonder the Slovenes were so happy at the impromptu concert. Imagine the Beatles, Dylan or your personal teenage hero playing for thirty of you in a single room.

“What was unusual was that I liked his videos. I find most rock videos crass. But I watched *Tisoč Let* and adored the potter, and the way Vlado brought in the Muratextile factory at Murska Sobota. I felt Vlado and I share similar values. As a journalist I love to get ordinary people from the streets of small towns or villages into my stories, to give them a voice – or in Vlado's case, a picture - into the big world.

“It didn't matter that I mostly didn't understand the words, though I did search for translations. His phrasing and tone still brought things to life.

“What really struck me was Vlado's willingness to go the extra mile - or sixty - to please folks who show an interest in his music.”

Sitting here in Vlado’s house, at his son’s desk, I’d say that’s an understatement.

“For me,” continues Kester, “some of the most beautiful renditions of his songs are from the night he played with pupils and teachers at Slovenska Bistrica Secondary School, just before Christmas in 2008. The choir's singing and harmonies – especially in Tisoč Let – well, I think the spirit of Mozart must have been flown in from Salzburg that night.

“I assumed that Vlado had gone along that evening because he knew the teacher or somebody involved – but no, not at all. The teacher had just phoned him out of the blue, and Vlado turned up for the show.

“That knocked me out. ‘You just get a feeling, people are ok, and you just do it,’ Vlado told me later.

“But I was not the only person to be surprised.

"'If I'm honest, I had no idea what he would say about our collaboration or if he would be interested to perform with us. But he accepted our invitation, without even knowing who we were. It still amazes me how positively he reacted,' Nadja, the teacher involved, told me. 'I cannot forget the first time Vlado appeared in front of us on rehearsal. I remember some of the singers had tears in their eyes.'"

Kester asked me later: "What is it about Vlado? He sang a solo acoustic version of '*Se je čas*' (There's still time)—the old Martin Krpan hit. I could not stop tears running down the side of my face. Why?"

Chapter Eleven

"Why do you sing *Lili Marlene*?" I ask Vlado.

We're heading to Piran Vlado's driving. He doesn't say anything for a few minutes and then he nods.

"*Lili Marlene* and *Gloomy Sunday*. Two songs. Both songs were repressed. *Gloomy Sunday*, you know, is a Hungarian song that was first recorded in the thirties. People would listen to it and then kill themselves, jump off bridges… When they were found, they'd have a paper with the lyrics on it stuffed in their pockets. Even the author Rezso Seress committed suicide in 1968. They say that is why the Hungarian authorities banned public performances of the song. The cursed song has the similar fate in the Balkans. It was banned on the BBC when different versions emerged all over Europe, and in 1941 even Billie Holliday's version in the US. But even that version was softened with more optimistic additional chorus. "

"But you sang it. You were the first to perform it again."

"In Slovenia. Actually I am not sure, gypsies from Beltinci played it. They were probably not the only ones, but we recorded it and made it popular with Beltinška Banda because I thought the old guys should have the legacy… they should have the right to perform it."

"And *Lili Marlene*? Yugoslavia was occupied by Germans, so why sing *Lili Marlene*?"

"*Lili Marlene*. Eh, it's a love song.

"Let me tell you a story. A seven-year-old boy heard our version and asked his mother, who was my friend, if this Lili Marlene was beautiful. She asked why, and he answered, because the singer sings as if she was. Great compliment!

"When Germans invaded, they set up a radio station in Belgrade and asked their troops in Vienna to send them some music. Among other records there was this song, perfectly unknown. So on the Belgrade German radio station they put it on the air and soon it became a hit among the soldiers—Germans, Allies, Partisans, even Russians. Everyone had his own version with its own lyrics. Later in Yugoslavia it was forbidden as a 'German war anthem'. My friend had some problems on TV Slovenia where he worked as a producer of pop music programs when he put Milva singing *Lili Marlene* on the program. This was at the end of the eighties.

"Actually we played and recorded those two songs because my whole youth, local 'gypsies came to our house to play'—you know, 'That Black Guitar'. After some time my father would ask in a little lower voice, 'And now play those two.' And they would move inside of the house and play *Gloomy Sunday* and *Lili Marlene*. That was Yugoslavia. It was nowhere written that they are forbidden but they were just not around. Socialistic self-censorship."

"But you recorded it."

"Yes, but it was much later."

Vlado zips past cars, checks his messages, plays radio roulette with the stations. Talk radio, news, advertisements—oh, wait, there's a song. Vigorous polka music, full of accordions and *oomph pa pas*, red-cheeked girls and richly costumed men all dancing and singing in a jubilant mess—it fills the car with so much commotion I have to put the window down to let some of it out.

Vlado nods. "Avsenik. You know him? His influence on polka in Germanic world is immense, and also in the United States. He is like a god there, he and Lojze Slak."

"He's Slovene?"

"Oh, sure. Both Slovene. Very big. Very respected. Many people in America think their polka—*gorenjska* polka—is the only authentic Slovene music."

"So much for Prekmurje and her bittersweet songs. And your guitar."

Vlado shrugs. "Remind me to show you something when we get back home."

Vlado's friend Dušan is sitting at the head of our table, facing the boardwalk. With the steady stream of people coming by to say hello, he could be the local Vito Corleone except he's thrilled to see them all. Vlado explains that Dušan is the unofficial mayor of Piran. The official mayor, Peter Bossman from Ghana, is the first black mayor in Slovenia, something which both Dušan and Vlado think is really cool. If he is a good mayor, as Vlado adds.

We sit at a table with Andrej and Anna, friends of theirs who are on their way back to Moscow after a long holiday. Deeply tanned and gorgeous as a model, Anna chats with me about Vlado's music and the delights of Piran. She speaks excellent English. The only thing I know in Russian is unrepeatable.

Eva and the girls join us for lunch, which quickly turns into a massive sharing affair. I end up with not only my scallops that are swimming garlic and olive oil, but some of Vlado's little fish, Ajdina's calamari and Čarna's dessert.

"Perhaps you can stay at the country house a few days and do some writing," Eva had said. Back then, it sounded like a great idea. But that was early on in the planning stage, back when we talked about me driving alone to Beltinci, and easily agreed to.

Soon they'll head off to Istrija, for tonight and tomorrow. I'll stay behind in Piran, in my room at Dušan's mother-in-law's house. What sounded peachy in theory suddenly terrifies me.

It's not that I don't understand the why of it. Understanding is the easy part. They need their time together as a family. It's their holiday. The kids are busy during the week when Vlado is free. The kids are free on the weekends when Vlado is busy. So, any time when they can be together is precious. I understand. At least the part of me deep inside that sounds like my Victorian grandmother as she archly intones "Let's be adult about this" understands. The little kid being intoned to, though? Not so much.

My inner boat is listing. Except for the wonky sensation of staring through the wrong end of a telescope I feel fine. It's probably just the wine and the heat, and maybe Ajdina's calamari.

We taxi up to Dušan's place high above Piran, stopping only long enough so Vlado can take me to buy a bottle of wine. I left the one I'd brought in Naj's bedroom, and I'm determined to show I'm up on all the protocols on how to be a proper guest—witty, charming and bearing good wine.

Well, I got the wine part down pat, at least.

Curled up in a chair, I listen to them talk. Polona, who is Dušan's lovely wife, and Eva chat as Čarna and Ajdina watch the Olympics. Vlado and Dušan pore over old photos, which Vlado passes on to me. They are of Dušan's former cult club, Maona ~~M~~, where Vlado performed a lot. English emerges from time to time, but I'm too out of it to do much except smile. Wit and Charm have deserted me. Instead I watch the conversations and get metaphysical with the wine. It smells like chocolate.

It's time to go.

"We'll meet you at six tomorrow evening," says Eva. "That will give you a whole day to do whatever you want. Walk around the city, have some time alone…"

"That's great. Sure." Twenty-four hours alone? Little fingers of panic pluck at me. What will I do for twenty-four hours? Staring at the ceiling comes to mind. "Which way to the steps?"

Eva points to a skinny path threading between ancient stone walls. "Right through there. The steps go all the way down, and then you just follow by the sea." She studies me, a fretful, motherly look in her eyes. "Are you sure? Dušan can drive you down…"

"Of course I'm sure. Walking's good. I'll be fine. It's okay." I try to think of something else to reassure her, but my mind is off doing its own thing. Thinking of Ophelia. Thinking of the Lady of Shallot. If I'm going to be alone, it's time to lift my chin and find a song to whistle. Standing around talking about it feels like I'm slowly pulling a bandage off a wound.

With a wave, I start my trek. I make it about five feet, then, standing in the road like a puppy, I glance back at the SUV. I wave again as Dušan drives away with the Kreslins, to make sure they know I'm doing fine, thank-you-very much. The windows of his SUV are dark, though. They're already gone.

I walk down the steps from Dušan's, all the way down to the sea.

Folks who come here talk about how beautiful Piran is. It's got everything an ancient town needs to win a beauty contest—crumbly old buildings with faded Mediterranean colors and terra cotta tiles, a promenade along the water's edge, gulls and boats, a tower out on the very tip of the point.

A few boats skitter between here and Savudrija, but most have wearied of the heat and gone home. Happy sunburned people down below mill about like ants full of wine, laughing and planning for the nighttime. Together. Everyone's together with someone.

I have never felt so lonely in my life.

*

Vlado later writes me: "Ruth, but I must tell you I really thought that you wanted to be alone a day or two in Piran—I even thought that maybe in Logarnica. I thought that you like to be alone, and thought it also is the best way to objectively observe the place and people. I mean, it wasn't that we want to be alone with the family"

I read everything wrong. And I am ashamed. Mea culpa, my friends, mea culpa.

*

I *clop-clop* down the hundred or so steps to the sea. Why this loneliness? True, I'm by myself in a strange country, but Vlado and Eva are maybe half an hour away. I've got email. I've got a phone. People do this all the time. Seriously, what's the big deal?

A migraine greets me at the bottom of the steps, and suddenly it all makes sense.

How many miles is it to where I'm staying? A hundred thousand miles or… maybe three. I don't know. I'm in pain; ergo, distance is irrelevant. I fixate on putting one foot down in front of the other. Life has suddenly become a narrow-threaded walk through pain.

I make it up to the garret apartment, gobble down a headache pill, and push open the door to the terrace. What am I—five floors up? Enough to make a juicy splat if I fall, smearing a few walls on the way down. Hmmm. I look out over the roofs to see if the iron-colored sea is there, rolling and heaving—it is; imagine that—then I run back inside because the light hurts my eyes.

An email is waiting for me.

"If there's any problem or question, call or send an email. Eva."

I should call Eva. If I were smart I'd call, just to make sure I can get through. Instead, I take the easy way out. I write back: *"I will. Don't worry. Thanks."*

Time to find something to eat. I take the stairs down to join the people out on Prešeren Quay.

Piran on a summer's evening—is anything more romantic than walking hand in hand with your love by the sea as the sun washes the world in a peachy glow? Gulls skim the waves, mothers gather their naked children from the boulders along the promenade, and old people shuffle along in their own little world. And the lovers… young, old, fat and thin, they stroll shoulder to shoulder, stealing kisses as they go. Whatever else it has been today, tonight Piran is for lovers.

Behind me looms a tower set right on the end of Rt Madona, the point that juts into the sea.

You'd think with it being so tall that it'd be the Punta lighthouse but no, it's the bell tower to a thirteenth century church. But the lighthouse is right there too, crowding up next to the church. The church, once known as St Clement, is now called Our Lady of Health. It seems the sainted pope fell out of favor four hundred years ago after the church was built. Then a nasty plague swept through Istrija and Piran, and the faithful determined the Blessed Virgin Mary had been a bigger help than the saint. The church itself is a sturdy building that looks like a giant bread loaf, but the bell tower is tall and cylindrical and quite handsome in its own way. The modest lighthouse is there too, not tall and not old, but functional for its job.

Once there was a castle here in Piran. Its ruined walls sit high above the city. They're not as massive as the ones at Ljubljana, but this castle still had been impressive. It's a lovely ruin—all square towers with crenallations and walls that march up and down and over the hill. Trees watch from within the walls, their gray finger-roots creeping over the stones. So far, the towers are winning against the arboral sentries but it's only a matter of time.

Something I had for lunch definitely is not happy in my stomach. I can't tell whether it's my scallops, or Ajdina's calamari, or the 'small fish' I stole from Vlado's plate. What are small fish anyway—sardines? Minnows? Really tiny herrings? Maybe all three are ganging up on me. I should be careful, eating things I don't know, but Vlado would never steer me wrong, and he didn't get green around the gills.

Then I remember—it's not the seafood. It's part of migraine's little gift to me. My head's numb but a migraine gives more than a skull-exploding headache, much more. Slipping into one of these restaurants for a leisurely meal would be really futile with the way I feel. Maybe I can find something to take back to the room.

In one of the outdoor cafés I spy a case with beautiful strawberries and blueberries and kiwi, which makes my mouth prickle, and bananas. Now fruit I can take back up with me and munch tonight and tomorrow for breakfast. I start choosing containers of fruit.

"*Ne, ne, ne, ne*! No!"

A flustered young man rushes towards me, hands waving at me. "English? You speak English?"

It must be written on my forehead, along with "stupid" and "guess who doesn't know what to do here". Plus my forehead burns. No doubt it's flushed along with the rest of my face. A slow throbbing starts in the top of my neck. "Ye-es. I speak English."

"I am sorry but this is for our customers. For ice cream."

"Oh." I carefully place the containers back in the case and back away. "Sorry."

"Would you like an ice cream?" He holds out a menu for me.

Actually I wouldn't like an ice cream. Shame is such an appetite squelcher. On the other hand, I'd better have something to eat or my migraine will return to impale an eye with its icepick pain. I study the menu, hoping to find a simple fruit cup without any ice cream at all. No such luck. But there is a mixed fruit something glued together with more ice cream than I can eat in a week. I can always wash the ice cream off once I get to my room.

"This?" I point to it.

The young man beams. All is well. He's made a sale and saved his fruit. We should all be so happy.

"Which ice cream would you like?"

Oh good grief, it's not pre-chosen? Dang. I look over the frozen offerings in the other case. I don't know what any of them are beyond the brown one being chocolate, the pink strawberry—or maybe it's cherry—and one of the ivory ones may be vanilla. They've got to all be enormously sweet and incredibly fattening.

That's when I see one little container of yogurt. I smile. "That one."

Joy suffuses the man's face. He's going to make me the most expensive dessert he offers.

If it gets me through breakfast without any pain, it's worth it.

He passes me a towering concoction of blueberries and strawberries, kiwis and bananas, peaches and grapes and even some pineapple, all stuck together with a quivering mass of yogurt, with a jaunty paper parasol on top. The dessert must be eight inches tall. If I get it back to my room with dropping it, it'll be a miracle.

Balancing my monstrous mixed fruit and yogurt dinner which I've gotten all the way up the stairs without dumping the whole thing down my front, I back my way inside the apartment, bump the door shut with my hip and check my emails.

"I don't feel very well about you in Piran," Eva writes, "because I don't know if you enjoy being alone there or not. Then again I do not want to hang around you all the time not giving you time to
breathe and look around in your own tempo. PLEASE tell us what is better for you and your needs…"

Aw, shoot. Now Eva feels bad. I don't want her to feel bad. I don't feel bad. In fact, I feel really good right now except for guilt because Eva feels bad. I'm finally pain free. No more throbbing in the back of my head. I can conquer the world, or at least this little corner of Piran.

I suck the yogurt off a strawberry, pop it into my mouth, and write back: "You really are very kind. Okay, yes, I felt a little lost but it's okay…"

So, after much emailing back and forth, we decide Vlado will pick me up at the Hotel Slovenia in the morning in Portorož. That's the next town over, since old town Piran has a no vehicle policy.

Everyone here has to park in the municipal garage and take a bus to the square, or pay a 200-euro fine. But Portorož is really not far at all, Eva says. Only about a forty-minute walk down by the sea. I can't miss it.

Ha. It's amazing what I can miss.

"You just go a little way down by the sea, pass the casino and the ugly gray buildings, and you'll find the Hotel Slovenia."

That's what Eva said. Eva knows. She's done this before. I keep telling myself this.

How thoughtful of Portorož to put itself so close to Piran. On such a beautiful morning, it'll be an easy walk. I hope. Eva once told me that you can walk anywhere in Ljubljana. Maybe if you're used to it. Americans aren't so keen on walking, especially if they're from the South and especially if it's summer. God forbid we have to walk any farther than from an air-conditioned building to our car. Otherwise we collapse with heat stroke and turn into fat puddles on the ground. It's that hot in Texas.

It's not that hot in Piran, but it's hotter than I figured it'd be. That's why I have these doubts about the walk, the heat and how far I can lug all my stuff for this day trip. Still, I'm by the sea and where there's the sea, there's a sea breeze, and where there's a sea breeze it's cool. At least it should be. I turn my head to see if I can find a breeze. Maybe there's a little one, a very little one, so small that it's more a lack of perfectly still air than anything actually blowing on my skin. Today Piran is in the doldrums.

I head out along the promenade and turn my face to the sun. After a few seconds of squinting, I pull my hat down to my nose and navigate by watching the ground. That's how I miss the Mermaid Statue. I've read that it's a petite little thing sitting primly on the rocks next to the sea. All I see is the concrete below my feet. When I glance at the water off to my right to keep my bearings, because god knows I can't walk a straight line to save my soul, I catch sight of a few swimmers bobbing up and down with the waves.

Locals say the key is to swim before the tourists wake up and crowd the sea. A few non-swimmers are out, drinking coffee and watching the handful of walkers on the quay but most of the action is in the water. And by "most of the action", I mean maybe ten white-haired swimmers treading water in a half mile stretch.

I'm nervous. I shouldn't be. Yes, I'm heading off with no idea of where I'm going, but so what? Lots of folks do that. They throw all caution to the wind and set out totally clueless about what they're getting into. Me? I obsess about checking how to get to an appointment before I get there. That's not an option here. I've got one chance to make it right.

"Follow the sea to Portorož until you get to the Hotel Slovenia." How hard can that be? I've got my spiffy new swimsuit from NAMA—"Bring your swimming costume," Eva said, so I tossed it into the tote, even though I'm leery about swimming in front of people. I can see the headline now—"Beluga Whale Sighted in Bay of Piran" but hey, I'll be among friends, and no one else will ever know who I am. I've got my passport and purse, and I've got my phone so I can call Vlado if there's a problem.

My path veers left. I've made it up to the little sailboats tied up across from Tartini Square, a huge expanse that's paved with creamy marble. Right in the middle of the square is a monument to composer and violinist Giuseppe Tartini who was born in Piran. As monuments go it's not that old—it was erected in 1892 to mark the 200th anniversary of Tartini's birth—but it's a bigger than life bronze statue high on a pedestal conveniently in the middle of everything. You can't miss it, especially if it's late at night and you're drunk, steering a motorbike.

Right under the surface of the water is a little ledge, just right for me to step on and cool my feet off. My feet beg me to do it but if my sandals get wet, they'll make blisters on my feet. That would be bad. Especially if I have miles to go before I sleep. But when I get to Savudrija…

I turn away from the water and almost walk into a car. I'm no longer in the auto-free zone. The driver glowers, waving his hands at me. I stumble back, and the car speeds on as much as any car can here, which means it's tearing up the road at ten kmh.

The bus to the municipal garage sits by the square. It tempts me with its seats, and whispers I won't have to walk all those kilometers if I dash across the street and get on. It's free. It's easy. I want to take the bus back to the station, I really do. It'd get me farther down the road. Less walking. Less time. The driver's looking right at me, but I can't do it. Taking the bus is what people expect a lazy American to do. So… no. I'm going to walk this, all the way to the Hotel Slovenia, wherever it is in Portorož.

The bus pulls away without me. That's when the fear hits me—I've made a grave mistake.

But it's too late. The bus is gone. Nothing I can do about it now. Besides, this is about having an adventure, and learning how to get around in a country I don't know (and failing), and especially making it to the Hotel Slovenia to rendezvous with Vlado. I hoist both the tote and my purse to my shoulder, squish my hat down on my head, and hie off again for Portorož.

The problem with walking to Portorož is it keeps moving away. I'm already weary, and I've only made it to the bus station. Folks stand there, clumping together like barnacles on a hull, waiting to be shuttled back to Tartini Square. Once I get to the Hotel Bernardin Casino complex, which is on the edge of Portorož, it'll take no time for me to get to the Hotel Slovenia.

Fifteen minutes later, I stop. Nothing looks like a casino here or even a hot sheet motel. I'm sweaty. My shoulder hurts. I lean up against a stone wall that's holding back some bushes and slip the tote to the ground.

A black cat, crouching under a row of privet, stares at me with wide yellow eyes. Somebody cares for him. There's dry kibble in a pile on the stone wall. Watching the cat's eyes, I slowly stretch my finger out to touch a piece of his kibble. For the longest time he doesn't move, and then *whap!* he slaps at me and hits the kibble, sending it and him flying into the bushes.

I walk on. In twenty minutes or so I travel from Piran to Portorož. I've made it to the Hotel Bernardin Casino complex, and let me tell you, it is definitely complex. I pass rooms and restaurants and spas, and people enjoying themselves in the sun. I'm an intruder in my shirt and jeans. If I wasn't walking as close to the sea as possible, I'd get lost.

I get lost anyway.

I now have only fifteen minutes to get through the complex, pass the two ugly gray buildings and find the Hotel Slovenia. Unfortunately, there's no path around the boat slips to the other side. Swimming the ten meters across is not an option.

So I backtrack, looking for a big sign with a big arrow that says “EXIT” or a trail of crumbs through the complex—something, anything. Halfway to where I came in, I see metal medallions in the sidewalk, designating the bicycle path that leads to an outside road. Where a bike can go, I can go. I pick up the pace and pray it doesn't lead me too far away from the sea.

Right on the other side of a boutique shopping arcade is the exit to the Hotel Bernardin Casino complex. I almost burst into tears, but I don't have enough time to cry. I must be horridly late and if he drives off without me…

I pull out my phone to find it's turned itself off. I turn it back on. The screen won't stay lit. I frantically swipe my fingers across the screen. For a full three seconds the screen lights up, then it defaults to a setting too dim to see.

I walk on, finally making it to the two gray buildings. Eva is right—they are desperately ugly. But they cast enough shade that if I squint hard enough I can see my phone screen. I punch in Vlado's number. The call doesn't go through. I punch it in again. Nothing.

Good thing I'm not close to the sea now, or I'd fling the stupid phone into the water. Beating my forehead to a bloody pulp against the wall won't do any good. In tears, I leave the dim shade of the ugly gray buildings and head on into Portorož.

Hotel after hotel after hotel line the boulevard, ornate early baroque mansions shoved hip to hip with modern steel and glass buildings. They face the sea with their bright and shiny faces, all on a tree-lined boulevard. It's lovely in a Las Vegas meets 1940s Beverly Hills way, but the charms of Portorož are lost on me. I'm hot, frustrated and so thirsty that I'm swallowing spit just so I can keep on walking.

There it is—the Hotel Slovenia, tucked between two other larger hotels. I trip over a ledge into two ladies having a genteel cup of coffee. I apologize, gather my things and dash inside. There must be another road on the other side of the building where Vlado would pick me up.

Wrong.

I run back to the boulevard, giving the two ladies a wide berth. I find a bench to sit on, and wait. And wait.

A black SUV with a carrier on top slowly makes it way down the street.

"You're the most beautiful person I've seen all day," I say, getting into the car. I launch into my frustration with my phone and the casino complex. I stop.

He looks at me as if I've grown a third eye.

Chapter Twelve

Vlado steers the SUV through the clot of cars and motorbikes and people that make up normal traffic in Portorož. “The line was backed up getting into Slovenia. I tried to leave you a message.”

“Sorry. The phone was giving me problems.”

He nods. “You have your passport, right?’

“Always.”

We leave Portorož, skirting the sea as we travel up the hills. The conversation is light and easy, the sun warm and the wind cool. I ran out of spit to swallow an hour ago but it’s okay. Everything’s wonderful now.

Except my phone.

Vlado pulls into a gas station. “Want anything?”

God bless the man. “Water. I’d love some water. Please.”

“Sure,” and he heads into the station.

I pull out my phone and dial my number back home. My answering machine picks up. Of course.

Vlado gets back in and hands me the water.

“Thanks.” I drain the bottle dry.

A couple of lanky youths, brimming with hormones and *joie de vivre*, crawl out of the car next to us. They go stand in front of the gas station door. One of them holds up a cardboard sign that in big block letters says where they want to go. It’s nowhere I’ve ever heard of, but that takes in most places in Slovenia, and Croatia as well, which is only a few kilometers up the road.

Vlado nods at them as we pull out of the station. “Hitchhikers. I haven’t seen them in a long time. We had a lot of them years ago and then they disappeared. I don’t know why. But it’s good to see them again.”

“Is it safe?”

“Yes, I think so.”

Safe hitchhiking. Slovenia must be low on nut jobs.

We pull out, heading for Croatia ourselves. “In my hitchhiking days, back in the seventies you could take one hundred deutschmarks and hit the European roads for a month. Most of the ways went through Amsterdam, that most liberal of cities, when there was actually a hitchhiking culture.”

“The only time I ever hitchhiked I was picked up by an ambulance transporting a body. It was a man who’d been at the state insane asylum so long the paperwork on him had been lost. Every time the ambulance hit a bump, the sheet on the body slipped down a little further. I could see his hair, then a little of his forehead, then an ear. Until we hit a huge bump and the sheet slid sideways…"

"I need your passport."

Vlado pulls up to the border control. The kiosks are like the ones at DFW airport. The guard waves us through. That takes care of getting out of Slovenia. A hundred feet down the road and we do it all again—hold up the documents, bored guard waves us through, we drive on into Croatia.

The road winds up a scrubby hill. Dušan had said they had so little rain last year that Piran had to turn the water off in the afternoons. You couldn't draw enough for a small cup of water until evening, let alone flush a toilet. Of course, that was Piran and this is Savudrija— different town, different country-- but as dry as it is here, I wouldn't be surprised if they had water restrictions too.

But maybe the countryside is always this way in summer.

We go west, passing vineyards and olive groves. It's greener now, the vegetation no longer tinder.

Vlado turns into an enclave of villas, all facing the sea, and navigates a maze so arcane that it's a wonder anyone ever leaves this place. After a dozen or so turns, he pulls into a driveway.

"Over this way," he says, leading the way to the back of the house.

The deep blue Bay of Piran stretches out beneath us. Boats bob toy-like in the waves and the terra-cotta roofs of Piran sleep in the distance. It's beautiful and peaceful, and I shouldn't be here at all.

"Oh, Ruth, I was so worried about you!" Eva emerges from the kitchen to give me a hug. "If you like, you can go down to the water and swim a while. Ajdina can show you how to get there. She doesn't mind at all."

Ajdina smiles at me. She still has her watch on.

I change into my suit and the two of us head down to the sea.

I pity the person who gets tipsy and tries to head down these steps. Each step has its own idea about how much pitch it should have, which is different from the step before it. The whole flight of stairs is steep. Ajdina's like a mountain goat, scampering without a care. I do well to keep her in sight, although I suspect she's going slowly for me. She leads me safely to the water and then skips back up the stairs.

Well. I've made it down here to the sea. I'm even in my swimsuit. If I work this right, no one I know will ever see me in it. I pull off my T-shirt and head for the gently rolling waves. There's no sand here. Skinny jetties with ladders stick out into the bay so swimmers can hoist themselves out of the water when they've tired of fighting the drift.

My feet go *slap-slap-slap* on this particular jetty, right up until a ferocious green crab, no bigger than a sand dollar, blocks my passage. He scurries a few inches across the stone, and then cowers while I bend over to study him. A few seconds later, he finds his courage and waves his arms at me. Satisfied that he's shown me he's the boss, he scurries a few more inches, then stops and waves his arms again. Eventually he crawls over the edge and glares at me, backing into the water, one claw open and ready to pinch me if I get too close.

I wave a finger back at him. Don't worry, little one. I know my place.

Eva's folks have a kiwi arbor. Under here is a table with chairs and a bench seat. This is where we have lunch—Eva and Vlado, Čarna and Ajdina, and me. We're all either about to get wet or about to get wet again, but first we're going to do some serious damage to the lasagna and salad Eva's bringing out.

Slovenes really eat. All that *gósti*...I'd settle for a half a sandwich but lunch here is a proper meal. At least when they have guests. Maybe when everyone else is gone they only have water and salad. I'd be happy to have water and salad; I'm an easy keeper. But the lasagna is awfully good and the salad just right. Čarna's apple strudel is waiting for when we're not so stuffed from lunch.

But now it's time to rest.

"Stretch out," says Vlado, pointing to the pillows on the bench as he heads inside. "Move them around and take a nap."

I eye the bench. It would take several non-graceful acrobatic moves to get over there. Very entertaining for those watching, but not so much for me. Besides, I'm already stretched out in my chair. I'm too relaxed to move.

"Oh, I'm not going to sleep," I say. "I'll just sit here and enjoy the breeze."

A Tiger Swallowtail flits through the garden over the oleanders. Some other insect, a cross between a hummingbird and a bee, checks out the geraniums. The afternoon buzz grows faint...

Someone's watching me. I can feel it. I open one eye. Sure enough, Vlado's got his head poking out of the doorway, watching me.

"Hey..."

Vlado sits on the bench and stretches his leg out. Eva's stretched out on the trampoline in the sun. Čarna passes by on her way to join her mother.

I nod at Čarna. "You're lucky she still wants to hang out with you. Is that a Slovene thing?"

Vlado scowls. "Oh, no. Most of them don't want to be with their parents at all, not even on holiday. But our kids seem to enjoy being with us. Some think it's strange our kids want to be with us. Like there's something wrong with them." He points to the now vacant trampoline. "I'm going to get some sun."

Eva settles down in a chair under the arbor. "I really thought you were going to ask us questions the whole time but you've hardly asked anything."

True, and I feel guilty about this. I should have tons of questions—all the questions that any stranger can ask. It's the only proper way to play journalist. Even though I'm not one, I should act like one. I don't want to waste their time. But watching them be a family, living their life in front of me—what question can take the place of that? My stomach is in knots at the thought of asking something. Still, a few questions come to mind. "Okay. How did you and Vlado meet?"

"Oh, that." She laughs. "I didn't want to meet him. Everyone was into Vlado. I wasn't interested. I had established MOST—Service Civil International Slovenia in 1990; the activity was held since 1986 under Youth organization, I joined in 1988 and then I established the non-profit organization."

"MOST means 'bridge', right?"

"Yes. We originally organized international work camps where volunteers from all over the world worked in non-profit projects—ecology, work with physical and mentally handicapped young people, renovations of cultural/heritage buildings. Things of that sort. And Vlado performed at some work camps every year. I never attended those concerts, because I'd rather come here to my parents' summerhouse."

"So Vlado would come and perform at concerts for the volunteers?"

"Oh, yes. Then in the summer of 1991, war broke out in Slovenia and the borders were closed. As you know, the summerhouse is here in Croatia, so I couldn't come here. And I thought, well, if I can't go to the summerhouse, I might as well go to the concert for the volunteers, and that's when I met Vlado."

Eva's smile lights up her face.

"But with MOST… you also worked with refugees."

"Ah, yes. The first refugees came to Slovenia in the beginning of 1992, first from Croatia, a year later from Bosnia. At that time many refugee camps were established. Our volunteers worked with them—psychosocial help, work with children, teaching Slovenian and English. Anything to help them, even to finding some way for them to help in some way. When you are displaced, it helps if you can do something so you feel like you are contributing."

I thought of the young people singing with Vlado by the river. "The group Vali—they were refugees, then."

"Yes. Vali was established by Bosnian teenage refugees. I got in contact with them through my work with refugees, they found out I knew Vlado and they asked me if he would sing a song with them. And the rest is history."

"So it was through the concerts that you met Vlado."

"Yes."

"I see. Hmmm. That's a little different from what he said."

"Oh, really? What did he say?"

"Something about you and your group of volunteers out working with Štefan and him, clearing the spring… Črnec? at Copekov mill in the mud with all those kids."

Eva tips her head back, setting her dark hair dancing about her shoulders, and laughs again. "Oh, tell that story! It's much better!"

Ulay is staying with his wife Lena in their summerhouse, a tower at the heart of Piran, a tower so tall and narrow that only one room is off any landing. Above the tower terraces, which are planted with all sorts of fruit trees, is the Cathedral of St. George. Tonight, the cathedral is lit up for a festival. What the patrons don't know is they are about to be treated to a concert that will be performed around the dining table at Ulay and Lena's home.

Ulay is an internationally renowned performance artist, and freshly married. Tonight Vlado has a gift for them.

"You read the book I lent you, yes?" Vlado asked as he and Eva and I headed back to Piran earlier that evening.

I did read it, late into the night when Rick and I first arrived in Ljubljana—*Marina Abramovic and Ulay Together & Apart*, by Thomas McEvilley. I'd made it through how Marina and Ulay divorced each other by walking the Great Wall of China. I'd gotten a few pages into the interview with Ulay, who came across as a very intense person. Then we'd packed up and drove to Piran, and I left the book behind.

Intense people make me wary. I never know how to keep them from blowing up.

So who is this gentle soul meeting us in Tartini Square? Thin as a prophet, with a soft voice and kind eyes, Ulay has come to take us to his aerie above the sea. We follow him through a canyon of alleys, the buildings so close together that I doubt even a bicycle could pass by us. He slips inside a door and leads us up a steep, turning flight of stairs.

Ulay's wife, Lena, welcomes us with open arms and introduces us to her mother who is leaving for Mass. The rest of us trickle out to the kitchen terrace where a dining table sits, laden with candles and cake. Lena commandeers the end closest to the kitchen. She's on hostess duty, bringing out wine and plates for all of us. I'm on the far end, same side. The Kreslins have the opposite side of the table.

"Do you mind if I sit by you? I don't speak Slovene either." Ulay crawls between Lena and me. I'm charmed. Tonight our mutual lack makes us conspirators.

As does the muzzle jabbing my hand. A giant black dog pushes a wet rock between my fingers. I skip the rock across the terrace floor, and he bounds after it, tail a-wagging, pounces and brings it back. He pushes it against my hand. I toss the rock a few more times and then hold it, wet slimy thing that it is.

"He's chasing rocks." I usually don't state the obvious but Ulay is watching, and I feel like I should say something.

Ulay nods. "He also chews them until they break. He's had six teeth pulled."

So much for rock throwing.

The plan is for us to go down to a boat and have fish later on. Whether we have to catch our fish or not isn't discussed, but I'm game for night fishing if everyone else is. When in Piran, do as the Piranese do, although I'm not sure that's what the inhabitants are called.

Vlado brings out his guitar and starts to sing. Time and food are soon forgotten. What with the songs and laughter, songs and wine, songs and stories—because Vlado always has a story with his songs—it's too late for the boat. No matter. Lena brings out salads and cheeses and breads and meats, butter and olives and spreads, most of them akin to foods back home but some of them very new and a little strange.

"You must try this." Ulay says to me as he reaches for a bowl in front of Vlado and Eva. "It's a Russian salad and very good." I try it, and it is very good although I have no idea what it's made of beyond something creamy white and cold and crunchy.

So we eat, and as we eat sometimes Vlado talks and sometimes he sings, but whatever happens is perfect. Eva beams at him, and the looks that pass between them are very sweet. Ulay and Lena smile, too, and huddle together. At some point Lena's mother comes in from Mass and joins us. Vlado asks her what she'd like to hear. She softly says, "Ah, '*Spominčice', prosim*. (Forget-Me-Nots, please.)" Vlado serenades her with "*Spominčice*". As he sings, the years fall from her face and she sways to the music, her eyes closed.

A moth drops into my wine. It's a wee thing, fluttering on its back in the ruby liquid. I lift it out with my fork and coax it onto the edge of my plate where it stumbles around, flapping its wings.

"Are you Buddhist?" asks Ulay, watching the moth struggle on the fork. He sounds surprised.

I shake my head. "I just hate to watch something die if I can help it."

Vlado sings another song. When he finishes, wild applause breaks out above us. A crowd stands around outside the Cathedral of St George several terraces up. I'm not sure if it's Vlado or someone else they're cheering but it's certainly a propos for the song.

"It's the festival," says Ulay. "Tonight is the eve of the 500th anniversary of the visitation of Mary in Strunjan, and the churches are celebrating."

Maybe the people up above can't hear Vlado. Maybe the clapping is for something we can't see. But every time Vlado sings, the people at St George grow quiet, and when he stops, applause rains down on him.

We gather our things and say goodbye. Ulay turns the traditional kiss-kiss into a three-kiss farewell—"That's how we do it where I come from"—and we leave for our respective places, the Kreslins to the taxi that will take them to the municipal garage, and me to my garret.

It's midnight, but the night is young in Piran. Tartini Square is filled with people hanging out, enjoying the night. On top of a building on the corner, a band plays light jazz and the music fills whole square. The circle of new-old streetlights in the square makes the marble expanse glow with rich amber light.

Eva, looking sad and gives me a hug. "I won't see you again this trip. I'm staying here in Savudrija for a few more days with the kids while you go on with Vlado."

"November then? In the US?"

She shrugs. "I don't know if I can make it then. We'll see."

One last time we go over the instructions for when I meet Vlado in the morning—at the vehicle barrier by the sea at ten-thirty. I can be dense about these things. I don't want to end up at the wrong place with a phone that refuses to call his number.

We say our farewells one last time, Vlado giving me a cheery send-off that gets lost in a burst of musical cacophony. I wave back at him. I'm sure whatever he said was absolutely delightful.

A taxi ferries the Kreslins off to their car. I start off on my midnight jaunt down the half-dark sleepy quay and pray no muggers follow me.

On my last morning in Piran, I arise this bright sunshiny day to find my email dead. I try my cell. It's still boycotting all Slovenian numbers. Great.

I toss my things together and go down to pay Polona's mom. I rap on her door. Nothing. I knock louder. Nothing. Maybe I have the wrong door. I go up a flight, but the door there doesn't look right.

Hmmm.

A gangly young man tromps down the stairs towards me. I ask if he speaks English, and he does. I then ask if this is the door to Polona's mom's apartment. It is. Now we're getting somewhere. He knocks. No response. He says maybe she is swimming.

Oh, yes. She does swim early, doesn't she?

Ah, well. I thank him and watch him walk away.

I can't stay. I have a ride to catch. I drop the keys into the letterbox, say a prayer that she finds the keys, and hurry out into the morning sun.

I get into Vlado's car, slinging my computer bag and the tote in the back. "I tried to pay Polona's mother but no one was home so I dropped the keys in the mailbox. I hope that's okay. I can give you the money, and you can give it to Dušan. I sent a message to Eva. Did she get it?" I don't sound cool. I need to sound cool, in control. Mature. Vlado's going to think every time he picks me up I have a crisis.

Vlado mutters something and punches in a number. It doesn't go through. "Eh, I will take you to his office in Portorož. You can pay there."

That works for me. I just want to pay someone so they know I'm not skipping out on them. Piran is nice; I'd like to come back without a guilty conscience.

The traffic still creeps along in Portorož. Since the hotels are conveniently on one side of the street and all the shops are on the other, I know where to look for Dušan's office, but not what to look for.

"When we find it," says Vlado, "you get out and I will go around. Because of parking."

"Okay, but what's the office called?"

"Maona."

Maona. Okay. I can look for… "There it is!"

Before the car even stops I'm on the ground, running for the door. Finally I'm in control of something even if it's only my feet.

I explain to the lovely girl behind the desk my predicament, my wallet already in my hands so I can pay. She's perplexed. I explain it again. She asks why didn't I pay in Piran? I didn't know there was an office in Piran. For a moment I think she's going to pat my hand and say, "There, there." Instead she says for me to wait while she calls Dušan. Another phone rings while she makes the call. She takes the second call instead, smiles, and then turns to me.

"It is taken care of. No charge."

"No charge? Are you sure?"

"Yes. That was Dušan. He said no charge for you."

I'm touched, really touched that Dušan would do that for me. All I can say is thank you, which I do. In both languages, maybe even three.

Vlado's still parked in the same place, but now he's leaning out the window, talking with someone—Dušan's wife, Polona. The serendipity gods must be working overtime to give me this chance to thank her too, probably too profusely. I'm still stunned by their kindness.

Vlado smiles. I wonder who is really the serendipity god here.

Polona and I shake hands, wave, and wish each other good luck and take care. Vlado pulls away from the curb and points the car towards Ljubljana.

The white chapel of Sv Vid sits in a clearing deep in the forest close to Bukovnica Lake, not far from Plečnik's church in Bogojina. From the back of the chapel, a planked path leads through the cool dark woods to a healing stream. Vlado says the whole area is covered with energy points. Long before Sv Vid was born, people would come to these waters to be healed.

"When we were young," Vlado says, "Štefan and I used to pilgrim here, because we heard it was an old pagan magic spring from before Christ. The water is good for the eyes. And later in 1995 I washed my eyes when Štefan gave me the water at my wedding."

Vlado drives on, silence filling the car. It makes me antsy.

"Why wait so long to get married?"

"Eh, I was never keen to get married. But Štefan promised to make it a whole ethnological study of Prekmurje. Haha, at five o'clock in the morning, when the last band Šukar arrived to Žižki—"

I shake my head. "Šukar?"

"I was very much into gypsy music in the eighties. We even formed a trio—Zoran Predin, Boris Cavacca and me. Unfortunately, we never performed publically. Just in Boris' kitchen—haha. His wife Mojca was singing along and cooking these great meals for us 'til the early hours of the morn'. I even remember once me and Zoran so fell in the mood of the movie *I Even Met Happy Gypsies* (*Skupljaci perja*)' that we were breaking wine glasses by raising our hands high and smashing them down on top of the glasses."

"Yee-ouch! Didn't it cut your hands? "

"Oh, sometimes, but not bad. Zoran was unlucky this time. He cut himself seriously. We had to rush to Izola hospital where they sewed his hand. He needed six stitches but we only had enough money for two. The doctor was kind, though, and gave him some extra stitches.

"So I needed a gypsy band to record *Namesto koga roža cveti*. I found some guys in Folklorna skupina Emona, and we recorded the song and made concerts. After some time I said, 'Now you need a name', and they became Šukar.

"When they arrived for the wedding and glasses started to fly, Štefan was standing in the middle of the *gostílna* with a beer in his hand and murmuring, 'Oh god, I have to get this wedding back into ethnololgical context." Vlado pauses and then says, "Did I show you the video of our marriage?"

Ah, the video, where Eva is fashionable and confident, and fully able to take care of Vlado no matter what. And Vlado? Well, Vlado looks like he needs taking care of. He's going back and forth between fidgeting like kid wanting to go outside and desperately trying to be serious. Then there are all the different bands, Vlado talking with the *pozvačin*…

Now there's a character for you. The *pozvačin* is a quick-witted fellow dressed in a thousand ribbons and flowers from his head to this feet, covering him so much you barely see his face. This wild crazy fellow, carrying a staff with a hedgehog's skin on it, jumps and dances and spins around as he leads people to the wedding.

And there's Eva, trying to break an earthen jug that mightily resists its shattering. The walk down to the stream where yet another band plays, the horses and carriages, and Štefan…

The work on the book continues. We email back and forth, me asking questions about something Vlado or did that connects with what I'm writing now, and him answering. He always answers. I'm embarrassed, asking so much.

"What about your early days? Before Mali Bogovi?"

Vlado sends me a photo of him as a young soldier. He's down on one knee in the grass, his smile a little crooked as he stares straight at the camera. A flight caps sits smartly on his head but you can tell his hair is already starting to go. He holds the leash of a German shepherd.

Chills run down my back. I don't know this man. I don't know him at all.

Guard duty, in the wind and cold and snow. Guns. Rat-a-tat-tat and all that. Did he shoot at anyone? Would he have shot at me?

Vlado says, "Once, in the winter, we were by the Danube patrolling the Yugo-Hungarian border and some Czechs swam down the river. They were trying to cross the border into Yugo and then planned a run to the west. We fished them out and gave them blankets and hot tea."

We've yet to talk about politics, since politics is one of the four verboten things you don't talk about in polite society. Our friendship is still too new to poke around in forbidden territory. But I wonder if he could even be a soldier in a communist country without being a communist. British soldier, German soldier, communist soldier. Such a small segue from nationality to philosophy. The fear of communism was so ingrained in me as a child that it trumped everything, even nationality.

Vlado makes a good-looking soldier. Happy. Confident. The idea of him shooting at the border doesn't bother me. That's what border guards do. But this communism thing? It never occurred to me he might be communist. We laugh together, drink wine, tell stories, trade pictures. We Get Along. I've fallen into the trap of thinking since We Get Along that We're Just Alike. Which would mean our philosophies are probably Just Alike, and if not, then not that far apart. How naïve of me. Different cultures, different backgrounds—of course our philosophies aren't alike. Still, he's my friend, and his country isn't communist any more, although communists live in Slovenia. Besides, even if he's a communist, we can be friends.

But old childhood fears rush back. I remember crouching head down in a dim hallway at school during a bomb drill, back in the early sixties. Our teachers said all communists were bad, they wanted to destroy us, that children in communist countries were desperately sad and desperately oppressed and wanted nothing more than to come to America, the bright and shining land of the free and home of the brave. The only reason a child in a communist country smiled was because someone off-camera was pointing a gun at him.

And the communist leaders, Mao and Tito and Khrushchev? As far as our teachers were concerned, they were all out to take us over. If that didn't work, they would bomb us into oblivion. Thus the bomb drills. I filed into the hallway on a regular basis and hunkered down on the floor next to the wall. At six years old I learned two things—communism was out to get me, and when the bomb hits, the wall will save me.

But fears are ephemeral ghostly things. Vlado is solid, and he's my friend.

"The photo of you in the military, where you're with the dog—was that your first post?"

We're traveling from Piran to Ljubljana, heading for a doctor's appointment for Vlado's leg, and then on to Beltinci in the afternoon.

"Oh, no. In the photo I was in Beli Manastir, close to the Hungarian border. No, my first post was Banjaluka. A city."

"That must have been nice."

Vlado makes a face. "Strange. I don't think any place where you had to be in the army could be nice. But yes, the town was very nice and the girls, too. It still is nice. I took my family to Banjaluka few years ago to meet a dear friend from the army—Milorad. He has great kids. Naj did not want to go home."

"Kester Eddy said something happened with you in the military, that you had to audition."

Vlado drives past the Koper shipyard, his face unreadable.

"For years I'd had ulcers, been on medication, that sort of thing. I knew people who had them and they didn't serve. So I wasn't worried, but they chose me anyway, and I had to go. They said, 'You are half-capable. You won't carry a gun', and there I was in Banjaluka with the biggest gun, a machine gun, on my shoulder. So from October 1980 to April 1981 I was in Banjaluka."

"What about the audition?"

"Ivo—who was eighteen; I was twenty-seven…"

"Twenty-seven? How'd they let you wait so long?"

"Twenty seven was the limit for students. Ivo was a big brother for me though he was much younger. He was in charge of a warehouse, which was great. You could hide there. Most of the soldiers were eighteen; they called me 'Papa'. Ivo helped me much. He was 'the old soldier'. He was already there when I came, and he left before me. He forced me in Banjaluka to go for an audition with a soldier's band.

"I didn't want to go but he persuaded me, saying, 'Are you crazy? Two days ago you won *Slovenska popevka*. You are great musician, and besides, you will have easier life here.'

"When at last I went to the audition, they played some folks songs that were totally strange for me. I was standing in front of the band made up of old soldiers with all their nonchalance and superiority deriving from the simple fact that they came to this 'planet' just some months—maybe even weeks—before I did. A Croat on keyboards, drummer from Sarajevo, accordion player from south Serbia, guitar player from Montenegro. Great film cast. Of course, I did not know any of their songs. I was getting more and more red, swearing at that little blond guy from Kranj who pushed me into this shame.

"They stopped playing, grinning among themselves, like—'We knew it, soldier, Slovene guy.' You know, a little discriminating. 'Okay, maybe next time.' They were just giggling cynically. I turned around and headed to the door. Thank God it was a big hall. While walking, for the first time in my life that the thought struck me, 'Oh, shit, they are really walking over me! I should fight for myself.'

"Right before I reached the door I turned around and asked the guitar man to please give me a guitar. Grinning, the man gave me the instrument. I played a recent hit song *It's a Heartache*—very popular song those days, which I thought they knew. The smiles suddenly died out. I afforded myself another one: *Darling*. The slightly shocked keyboard player murmured: 'We will let you know!' As I was walking to the door I heard: 'Look at him, a Slovene, and he even can sing in English!' So I sang in a band. Ivo helped very much."

I wait for his laugh to let me know the story's over. He doesn't laugh. There must be more, but he's not going to offer it up unless I ask.

"That's how you spent your military service?"

"No. One of the soldiers asked me one morning if I would 'get organized.'"

"'Organized'?"

"First I said 'I don't understand what you mean—'get organized'.' And I really did not. That must have made them pissed. They thought I was joking with them.

"'Join the communist party.' That's what they meant when they said 'get organized.' I would be able to sing if I got 'organized'. I could stay in Banjaluka, which would be very easy on me. I would move to Dom JLA. Life there was great. All my colleagues from the band lived at Dom JLA, but I had to toil in the barracks. Usually if you played Dom JLA you lived there. You didn't train. But I lived in the barracks and had to train as well. At that point I slept in barracks with other soldiers, woke up early with them, trained with them—life there was much harsher than what they would provide. We trained in snow. And I had to carry a machine gun, even though I had a duodenal ulcer. Boys who had ulcers usually did not even go into the army."

"But you survived."

"Oh, sure."

"And the organizing?"

"Of course I said no. So, because of that and because I had a "1"—the worst mark—in the political lessons, they sent me to the Hungarian border. Beli Manastir. Guard duty. We ran off into vineyards, and I played guitar there for peasants and people in the vineyards. They gave us wine. Ah, it was great. It felt very much like Prekmurje. You know, Prekmurje is on the Hungarian border with the music and food, very Prekmurje-like. And then of all the places in Yugoslavia they want to punish me and put me there.

"Ah. Just like Br'er Rabbit," I say.

"Who is Br'er Rabbit?"

And so I told him the old Joel Chandler Harris tale of the wily rabbit and the tar baby trap he get into, and how Br'er Fox thought he was finally going to rough Br'er Rabbit up before he put him in a stew, and how Br'er Rabbit said he could do anything—barbecue him, drown him, skin him alive but please, please, please don't throw him in that brier patch—which of course is exactly what Br'er Fox did, and it was exactly what Br'er Rabbit wanted him to do, because he was born and bred in that very brier patch and knew it like that back of his hand.

Vlado continues, "This is from *Pojezije:*

Hvala bogu,
De capetan Radović ni znal latinsko
Kar ni za vole je sa Prekmurce.
'Qout licet iovi
Non licet bovi. ' "

"What does it mean?"

"'Thank God Captain Radović did not understand Latin because *'Qout licet iovi non licet bovi'* means 'Which is not for steers is for Prekmurci'.' "

"When you got out," I ask, "you came back and joined Martin Krpan, yes?"

"Eh, not quite. Before that I started a band with Žan Zmazek and recorded a few songs."

"But after that you joined Martin Krpan."

He laughs. "Yes, after that I joined Martin Krpan."

Vlado may have won the Festival *Slovenska popevka* but he really had his breakthrough with this rock group called Martin Krpan. Soon, he was in role of frontman.

But who was Martin Krpan?

If you see a picture of a man carrying his mare over his shoulder, that man is Martin Krpan.

Inner Carniola, down by Postojna, was always part of Slovenia, but at one time it was also part of the Habsburg Empire. This was something the Habsburgs enjoyed, and the Slovenes less so. Legends grew up about different local folk heroes, strong men with attitude and a healthy disdain for authority, especially when that authority oppressed the little people. A hundred years ago, writer Fran Levstik took those stories, mixed them together and came out with a man of incredible strength—Martin Krpan from Vrh, a poor farmer and sometime trader in illegal salt from England, because even back then farming wasn't the most lucrative of businesses. Levstik made sure Martin Krpan was a thorn in the side of the emperor, who, of course, was a Habsburg.

Which made Martin Krpan the perfect name for a rock group.

Large swaths of me are melting. Time to roll down a window. I'd leave it down all the time but if we're talking, I can't hear Vlado. Who would I rather listen to—road noise or Vlado? Hearing him wins by a country mile. If I start passing out from the heat, I'll change my mind.

So I scoot over closer to the window, the better to toss my hair in the breeze, and pray my scalp dries. This works so well I angle my arm just the right way. Now the air can blow up my sleeve and chill my back.

Vlado looks as cool as a popsicle.

Shall I be a wimp and leave the window down, or roll it up and prove I can take the heat as well as he can? Not withstanding the fact that he's acclimated to no air conditioning, unlike one fragile delicate flower who will go unnamed.

I roll up the window and slump back in my seat. I have questions and the road can't answer them. Bye-bye, breeze.

"Can I ask something?" I ask.

"Yes, yes. You can ask me anything. Anything at all."

When I was a girl, there were four subjects one never inquired about in polite society—sex, money, politics and religion. Sex I can't ask, money I won't ask, and politics—well, that would be a fine mess I'd be getting myself into. So… religion wins.

"You go to church?"

He grimaces. "Eh, I was in Ljubljana *Stolnica*—cathedral—last month as godfather to Valentina's son Viljem, Štefan's grandchild. But speaking truly, I was more often in a church in the old times of socialism, when a lot of those who are filling the churches now were still members of the communist party."

"Wait a minute. I thought you were Lutheran."

"My father is Lutheran but my mother is Catholic, so I am Catholic."

"Then Štefan was Catholic."

"Very much so."

I work on digesting this chunk of information. Vlado's not much for chit-chat while he drives. It makes the miles very quiet for great stretches of time. Time to roll down the window.

"My father was the one of the very rare Lutherans in Beltinci," he says.

I crank the window back up in a hurry.

"He was great friends with the Catholic priest there, though he never went to church, not even to the Lutheran church as far as I know. He was such good friends with the priest, in fact, he wanted Milan to be with him when he was making out his last will and testament."

The road slips by faster now. Vlado checks the radio, punching through the channels. Nothing appeals. He searches through the CDs—not this one, not this one… Ah. He picks one out and puts it on.

Ooh, music. This should be good. "What is that?"

Vlado shrugs. "I don't know. Someone sent it to me yesterday."

"People send you CDs?"

"They do, yes. Demos, poems, love songs…"

We ride like that for a while, listening to the CD, me with my head back, letting the atonal wailing roll over me. I glance at Vlado. Nothing's rolling over him. He studies the tones; he grabs every note and beat, parsing the song right down to the first spark of creativity.

Halfway through the third wailing track, Vlado murmurs to the singer, "Sorry. I don't understand you." He hits the eject button.

Ah, sweet relief. Bless him. "That makes two of us."

Vlado tries not to smile.

"So," I venture before he tries another CD, "how do you have a family life with all this rock'n'roll?" Vlado's family is so normal. I know he works at keeping them that way. And he looks so normal. Like the man next door.

"Haha, Croat singer Oliver Dragojevič and I were once backstage at a double bill concert, and as he poured us Jack Daniels, he said, 'It is not difficult for us; not for us, but for our women'.

"Well, there really was a lot of partying along this musical way of mine. But if music is true it has to be. I never pretended to be a saint. Sometimes when people come to me and remind me of the past years, I have a feeling I had a drink with almost every Slovenian. I was lucky compared to a lot of my buddies who are not around anymore. And I am lucky to have people with a good sense of humor around."

Chapter Thirteen

We're off to see Valentina, Štefan's daughter.

I'm glad Vlado is still in contact with Štefan's family. Not that he'd have any reason not to be, but you never know about these things. You can think you're as close as glue to some folks, and then when the friend dies, the relationship gets tossed in the can like yesterday's memories. So good for Vlado for being close enough to be a godfather.

Vlado pulls into a parking lot. Evidently, while Vlado goes to see the doctor for his leg, I'm to visit with Valentina over coffee and cookies, or something like that. I hope she speaks English, or we're going to have a most amusing time.

We hurry over to a building, or rather Vlado walks and I hurry. If I had to follow him every day, I'd be stick thin. But I keep up, and we both enter the foyer at the same time.

"Nejca..." he says on the intercom.

Who on earth is 'Nejca'? I thought we were seeing Valentina. Maybe Nejca's his doctor. If so, he's on chummy terms with her. My mother was chummy with all of her doctors, some more than others and some more than they liked, so it's not beyond thinking that Vlado would be friends with his doctor. Especially since he's Vlado.

Nejca comes on the intercom and, after they have a good chuckle over something, Vlado winks at me and we get buzzed through.

Up the stairs we go, and Nejca lets us in. Except Nejca is Valentina. I've got to ask Vlado what *'nejca'* means. Vlado stays long enough to make sure I'm safely perched on a chair at her kitchen table, and off he goes to get his leg looked at.

I see Štefan in Valentina—the same eyes, the same cheekbones. She's lovely and, thank goodness, completely fluent in English. She's busy making something as we talk, saying the chicken is almost done and now she's going to make apple strudel.

We're eating lunch here? That's news to me, but it's a great idea. It's past lunchtime anyway and the chicken smells out of this world. Valentina has to be an awesome cook.

She's got a lovely kitchen, with a big blue range and a huge refrigerator. Cooking must be very important to Valentina. Me? I boil water, but I'm good at appreciating the culinary arts of other people.

So we talk food and cooking, how my youngest loves to cook, how we have a place in France that we're trying to redo. She mentions how she and her husband Luka love Provence and try to go there once a year. I tell her my favorite story is by Maja Novak—*The Fall of the House of Pirnat*, and Valentina says Maja Novak is Luka's cousin and that she'll be sure to tell her the next time she sees her. That's when I realize she's married to Luka Novak, the author. After all this do I learn that Valentina is a celebrity in her own right, with her own cooking show on television and published cookbooks and everything.

Oh, boy. It would have been nice to know about this ahead of time. But, no, Vlado's thrown me into the pond to see if I can swim on my own. I file away this quirk of his to remember when we meet the next set of people.

Soon our conversation turns to Vlado and Štefan. I mention how much they remind me of Tom Sawyer and Huck Finn from Mark Twain's books. "Ah," she says, "but who was Tom Sawyer and who was Huck Finn?"

"Good point!" I chirp.

She nods. "Oh, yes, and Vlado? He never grows up." We laugh.

But even as I laugh, I wonder. Maybe it's not that he never grew up but that he wants to go back and walk the Prekmurje roads again with Štefan.

Valentina works on the apple strudel. She grates apples into the biggest mound of shredded fruit I've ever seen. All this goes onto a sheet of waxed paper. After that's done, she clears the kitchen table to make the dough. She flours the tabletop, making little clouds of white powder in the air. Then she rolls the dough out until it covers the surface. It even hangs over the edges.

She's exuberant in her cooking, fast and precise but still having a glorious time doing it. As she cooks, her oldest daughter comes out to say hello. Valentina tells me she's learning English and loves all sorts of things about America. Her daughter looks at me and gives me a shy smile. I tell the girl I'm from Texas, and her eyes light up.

Just as Valentina pops the strudel into the oven, Vlado appears, his appointment over but still with the bandage on his leg. Our luncheon is about ready. Valentina shoos us over to the table set in the alcove by the windows. Her daughter heads downstairs to fetch Valentina's mother and the new baby, and while the younger Novak watches her brother, the four of us feast on this finger-licking delicious meal.

Afterwards, when we're so full we can barely move, Valentina announces the strudel is finally ready. We have to stay for a bite of that, but only one bite, even though Vlado is not a sweets person. As she pulls the very hot strudel out and cuts a slice for each of us, Vlado starts telling the story of how he got instruments for his first band, Apollo.

"We didn't have our own instruments and no one had any money to buy them," he says.

"Didn't go you door to door?" says Valentina as she passes him some strudel.

I stop my fork in mid-air. "That was gutsy. I couldn't have done it."

We say goodbye to Valentina, hugs and kisses all around and lots of well wishes. I trot after Vlado, who's heading as fast as he can for the car.

"You didn't tell me she was Luka Novak's wife." Novak is a prominent novelist in Slovenia.

"I know." He smiles. "I wanted you to find out on your own."

Later, back at his house, I ask him, "How *did* you do it?"

Vlado leans back in his chair across from me and stretches his legs out. "How did I do what?"

"Follow your dream. Become a folk-rock singer. Communism and rock 'n' roll don't exactly play well together, you know."

"Ah." He thinks for a minute, a finger touching his lip. "Did I tell you when I was in my first band Apollo, we went door to door for money?"

"Valentina said something about it."

Vlado nods. "We had to get permission from the local government, but sure."

"So you went door to door in Beltinci—"

"No, we went to five villages around Beltinci, knocking on doors. A little here, a little there. People helped out where they could."

"That was awfully brave. But why'd you do it?"

"I needed a drum set. I would borrow some from the town crier to practice and then when we had a gig, I used the full set from the School of Music. I even used the Army's once. But…" He shrugs.

"Yes, having your own drums would be helpful, especially for those late night practice sessions."

Vlado gives me a look.

"Practice must've been a pain," I say, "having to borrow drums all the time."

"Oh, no. We had a mentor, a sax player, studying in Austria and Berlin. He taught me, saying, 'No problem if you don't have drums, you play and act as if you had, work with your hands and feet. I am watching you.' Haha!"

Ah. Table top drumming. The bane of family dinners everywhere. "But still, how'd you even know about rock and roll?"

"Oh, the radio, of course. It was the middle sixties. We heard everything. Beatles. Stones. I was shocked. I thought, 'This is my world out there.'"

I guess singing *Clementine* in Professor Hradil's class was not quite the same thing as belting out *I Can't Get No Satisfaction*. "And here I thought nothing could get in except maybe Voice of America. We were told people huddled around the radio late at night to 'hear the sound of freedom'."

Vlado smiles at my naiveté.

"So your first group was called Apollo…"

"Yes. We named ourselves after the Apollo 11 moon landing. I even wrote to Dr. Werner von Braun at NASA to see if they wanted to sponsor us. "He laughs. "Of course I never heard from him."

"That would've been awesome. So then you formed a group. And did… what? Practiced? Played gigs? Cut a record that went platinum?"

"Oh, we did more than practice. After we got permission from the local authorities, like I said, we asked for money, getting a dinar here and there. We even got some from the priest. Haha! We were connecting both the local government and the Catholic Church. We were progressive even then."

"But you did play some gigs, right?"

"Here." Vlado pulls some photos out of an accordion file and lays them out on the table.

Sure enough, there he is, playing the drums at an outdoor venue and people crowded around him. "This is a folklore festival in Beltinci, and this one," he says, pointing to the photo of them in the room, "is where we won the first prize in a talent show on my birthday! It was a national holiday known as Republic Day. We even got to play for the bishop, because of the priest who helped us."

Vlado with thick hair, looking all of twelve years old, sits at the drums, while in the foreground, the judges' numbers lay on the table.

"The five villages you went to when you were trying to get instruments for Apollo—did anyone ever come up to you after you were famous and said they had given to you 'way back then?"

"No one. Never."

"Ruth! Where are you?"

Vlado's in his study, turning on the computer, rummaging through papers on his desk and generally doing all the getting-ready-to-work stuff one has to do before really working. I lean against the doorway.

A familiar figurine of a girl with a parasol is set not far from his desk.

"The girl there—is she from your video?"

He glances back at me. "Ah. There you are." He hands me the figurine. "Yes, this is from *Rulet*. Šajeta gave it to me when we finished filming."

Rulet, the beginning of all this for me.

I study her face, rendered in milk white china. She's a pretty little thing. "You won the fair maiden after all."

"And this hat—I got this from Jan Akkerman, one of the biggest guitar players in the seventies. " Vlado reaches up for a hat. "Played for one of my favorite bands—Focus. From Holland, you know. I saw them on their first appearance in England at the Reading Festival in 1972. And forty years later I met him when he played in Ljubljana. Just a few years ago. We talked about the Reading gig, and Akkerman mentioned how he was hit by electricity in the guitar. 'And we thought you were performing some strange kind of dance,' I said to him. He got hit to the ground. I know the feeling. It hit me a few times too. A very interesting guy.

"Akkerman told me about Focus being in the same hotel in Toronto when the famous Toronto drug bust happened in 1977, when Keith Richards got busted for possession of heroin. He laughed and said, 'It was good luck police did not check our rooms.'"

Vlado hands me a dark gray gimme cap with "J.A." on it. Not too stiff, with an earthy man-smell to it.

"And these…" he holds out some drumsticks, "are from the drummer with Bob Dylan's band. The sound engineer gave them to Čarna when they were last here."

I stick the hat on my head while I observe the drumsticks from afar. He almost touched him, his holy grail. So close…

He suddenly smiles and takes the hat off my head. "You go rest now. I need to do a little work."

The aroma of coffee wakes me from my nap on the couch. Vlado sets a cup down on the table.

"Did you see these?" he asks.

Vlado walks over to the entertainment center and reaches up to the shelf high above the television. He teases out what looks like a wooden pod from the arrangement lurking behind all the other memorabilia. He holds it for a moment, and then hands it to me. "From Štefan."

The pod has dried to a deep copper color. To make sure I don't break it, I cradle it in my palm.

"What is it?"

"It's a poppy pod," says Vlado. "Štefan gave them to Čarna, when she was born. As a rattle toy."

I wonder if Štefan even got to see Čarna.

"And this…" he takes the poppy pod from me and replaces it with a carved wooden elephant, "is from Tomaž Humar. He was a mountain climber, an extraordinary man. One of many Slovenian mountaineers who stayed in Himalaya. Forever. Ajdina's kindergarten was going to see him. Eh, she didn't want to go see him, and so I told her, 'You must go, you must. He is a great guy and you will like him. And he is a friend of mine.' So she went, and came back totally charmed with him. He gave her this elephant for me. I never saw him after that."

"He died?"

"Up in the mountains—yes." He picks up an aboriginal sculpture. "This is from my late friend Marko Zorko. A beautiful man. He was a publicist and an *enfant terrible*."

He then reaches up and pulls out an old violin. "Janči."

My fingers skim the surface, touch the head. I bend over it and smell the wood. Old music still lives here. Janči, with his eyes closed, his ancient fingers pressing the strings, the bow making the violin sing one more time…

Vlado takes down an old bow, longer than one for a violin. He doesn't have to say a word. I know whose bow this was.

"Jožek," I whisper.

"Yes."

I hold the bow by the pad and slowly stroke a finger down the still rosined hair. How many songs did this bow bring forth, how many eyes wept when Joužek played his contrabass? "Wow."

In silence I hand the bow to Vlado. He carefully places it back, and then heads down the entrance stairs. "Have you seen these?"

Along one wall of the entry stairway is a photo collection of Čarna, Naj and Ajdina as toddlers. I see a few smiles, a few tears, but in most of them they're solemn-faced, facing the camera. In each photo, a different man poses with one of the children, usually holding the babe but not always—a few show them playing a guitar, and in one the man and the baby are eating pasta together. Brave man.

Vlado touches each photo as he names his friends. "These are some excellent Slovene writers—the poets Milan Jesih, Peter Božič, Evald Flisar, Jaša Zlobec, Jure Potokar, and Aleš Debeljak—you met him, yes?"

"When I was here last year. At the Zvezda with Erica." And the wonderful hot chocolate.

"Of course," he murmurs, and I touch my lip in memory of that night's dark goodness.

He moves on to another section of photos. "Musicians Halid Bešlić—that's Naj eating pasta with him. Drago Mlinarec playing guitar with Naj, Vlatko Stefanovski—a friend who recorded on my CD *Generalcija.* Singers—Dino Merlin and Saša Lošič, Rade Šerbedžija—"

"He was in Stanley Kubrick's film *Eyes Wide Shut* a few years back. My daughter thinks he's great."

"Ha! Yes," he says, "and this is Radko Polič and Enes Kiševič. Here with Čarna is the American poet Charles Simič, and then Australian writer Richard Flanagan, rockers Peter Lovšin... and this man. " He taps a photo. "This man is a legendary diplomat from Prekmuje, Anton Vratuša, with Ajdina."

His eyes crinkle. We're little children, sitting on the stoop in the late summer sunlight. Vlado opens up his box and, one by one, shows me his treasures: Here's my family, my friends, my life.

"When we were in the car going to Piran, you said you would show me something. I think we were talking about… Avsensik?"

"Ah, yes. Come!"

Vlado has me sit at his desk, and he pulls up a page on his computer.

""'You know when I first came to perform in Cleveland for our community—and I love to meet Slovenes all over the world, my folks from Prekmurje, especially from three Bistricas who are just everywhere and I know hundreds of their stories—how they moved, why they moved, how they ran over the border—the audience was a little skeptical towards my black guitar. They are crazy about polka and accordion and have the museum about it and polka awards and the King of Polka, and all that."

"What is this?"

It's an article from *Glas Naroda*, dated April 2, 2009. A review of his concert at St Mary's in Collinwood, a suburb of Cleveland, said: "A few more similar performances and Cleveland Slovenians may soon use Kreslin's name in the same sentence as Avsenik and Slak."

"Avsenik and Slak, ha?" Vlado wears a huge grin.

Something else catches my eyes but Vlado, suddenly bashful, jumps up and turns off the computer, once again in a hurry. "We must go soon."

Last minute preparations for going to Beltinci: Baskets of clothes. The tote I'm using. My computer. My hat. We cart all this down the stairs. Shoes, too, because we go barefoot in the house—even me, finally.

"Did you get your ice packs?" I call out.

"Oh!" Vlado stands on a stool, grabbing them out of the freezer. Camera and guitar, hats, glasses—all go into the car. A couple of golden red plums from his orchard he puts in the cubbyhole on the dashboard.

"Have you seen my bag?" he asks.

I dig around in the car. "It's not here."

He dashes back in to find it. I make one last trip to the restroom. It's a long way to Beltinci.

On the way out he introduces me to his downstairs neighbor, an older neighbor who's busy in his workshop. I wish I knew how to say, 'It's nice to meet you'. But alas, I'm not quick-witted enough to ask Vlado to translate. If I ever make it back here some day, hopefully he won't need to.

"I'm working on this song. I want it to be a duet with my father, just the two of us. I don't know why I haven't done this before."

Vlado looks earnest, resolute even, as he drives us over to Prekmurje. It's so hot in here I think my hair's melting, but if I put the window down, the road noise drowns out Vlado's voice. The window stays up. I tell myself sweating's good for me as I wipe it off the back of my neck.

"But you've sung with your father, many times."

"But not a duet just for us, for him and me. So we will work on it."

"Maybe you can put it in the concert in December."

"I don't know. If it's ready. Sure. Why not?"

We turn south, away from Murska Sobota, and zip down the road towards Beltinci. Vlado's cell rings. He talks, listens, and then he asks in a low voice, "Are you hungry?"

Now that's a loaded question. Vlado's thumb covers the speaker on his cell. The look on his face is awfully Zen. "Who's cooking?"

"My mother."

"I'm hungry." I'm still full from Valentina's feast, but with his mother cooking, of course I say I'm hungry. If I'm lucky, I will be hungry when we sit down to Mama Kreslin's dinner.

We pull into the Kreslins' driveway. His folks greet us with exuberant "*Dober dens!*" and wide-open arms. I feel like a little kid going to see the grandparents, complete with riding over the river and through the woods to get to their house where there's cookies and milk and home cooking.

I say hello to his folks in between hugs, muddling up the little Slovene I know. Thankfully, they don't seem to mind. Vlado unloads baskets, bags, papers, more baskets, his guitar, the video camera—all the overnight stuff and then some. Ah. So he's going to stay here and drop me off at the country house. Okay, that's cool. If I can handle Piran by myself, the country house should be easy.

I stand off to the side with his folks, staying out of the way of all this unburdening of the car, but no, Vlado doesn't let me get away with that. He pulls out another bag and hands it to me. The overnight things go back into the car. Hmm, maybe I'm to stay with his folks then while he stays at the country house, but he leaves my things in the car, too.

Milan leads us through his workshop, past his garden where he shows me the vegetables ready for harvesting. A table with four chairs is set out under a fruit tree.

Vlado hands me the camera. "Tape us while we work on the song."

He wants me to tape? Poor man. He knows nothing about my talent for killing electronics. Having me tape is a disaster waiting to happen. I cross my fingers and say a prayer that I don't screw this up. "How do I turn it on?"

"Here." Vlado touches the record button and shows me how to pause it.

How cool is this? The screen captivates me. I can see the world without my glasses.

"And don't forget the most important thing," he says.

I look up from the screen. He reaches over and removes the lens cap.

This is how Vlado and Milan work: Vlado has the lyrics and the basic chords written on a piece of paper. He places this front of Milan. While his dad follows along, Vlado sings the melody. They then discuss the song. Milan makes notes on the paper. Vlado sings it again, this time with Milan joining in. After a line or two, they talk about whether the harmony should go up or down on a particular word. They try out the harmony, and when that's settled, they sing it line by line, singing the same line over and over until Vlado's satisfied with the way it sounds. Again, they sing the song, this time Milan taking the melody and Vlado the harmony. He doesn't have the final title of the song, but mostly likely it's *Tisti bejli grm.* The White Bush.

Then it's time for dinner—chicken, seasoned well with little if any breading and fried to perfection; mashed potatoes with butter, cheese and cream; and green bell peppers, sliced thin, dressed with vinaigrette. And, of course, white wine. Three of us take our places at the table while Katarina fries more of her perfect chicken.

Vlado translates for us all. Milan speaks some English but Katarina speaks none, and what Slovene I know is made incomprehensible by my southern drawl. Yet the conversation flows, thanks to Vlado's translation services. Vlado even gets to eat.

Katarina starts to serve us pie that looks like a cross between a coconut pie and tapioca pudding but Vlado says we have to go, that he has an appointment for me. No problem. She cuts the pie into perfect quarters and then, folding it on top of itself, wraps it up and puts in it a bag for us to take with us. Then it's thank you and good-bye, and with lots of waving off we go down the road.

"You go to Bojan's for an hour, and then I will come get you. Okay?" We pass the sign for the village of Lipa, a few kilometers from Beltinci.

Bojan I know. We'd met the first time I came to Ljubljana, when he'd interviewed us at the Slon Hotel, and I'd resolved to never again give an interview after drinking a bottle of wine. This time will be better. I've had only one glass and that with dinner.

Bojan greets us on the patio. His hair is lighter than I remember but he still hums with energy, even when he just stands there.

Wine comes out, along with glasses and cake and napkins. We all take a seat, even Vlado who doesn't seem to be in any hurry to go. He chats with Bojan and then his parents who've come out to say hello. He takes a sip of wine, has a bite of cake and brushes the crumbs from his lips. Maybe he's changed his mind about leaving.

Then up he bolts out of his chair, promising to return in an hour, and dashes off to wherever, leaving me in Bojan's care.

Bojan offers me cake again. "Vlado is an idol here. He's so big, so famous, and yet so down to earth. I've heard his music all my life, from my parents, and now I know him too. Great singer, great family, and his parents are wonderful."

The cake turns out to be very good.

That's when his mom comes to tell us goodbye, when my mouth is full of cake. I swallow my bite and choke out a very dry good-bye and thank you. I pray I'm not spilling crumbs all down my shirt. She waves as she bicycles off to Mass with bunches of flowers in her basket. Tomorrow is the Feast of the Assumption, and Catholics here take their festivals seriously.

"You really should go," Bojan says. "It's a very beautiful Mass, very moving. Vlado knows about this church. Ask him to take you. Even if you stay only for ten minutes, it is so meaningful."

True, but I don't think Vlado wants to take me to church this evening. I'm not sure I want to go.

The mosquitoes come out, and we go in. Bojan is eager to show me his research on the history of the Jews in Prekmurje, and especially Beltinci. I want to find out what he knows about the Kreslins and Gostílna Central, and what really happened at the Mura River Massacre.

"This," says Bojan, opening up his book of photographs, "is a picture of Joužek Kociper when he was a little boy in school."

Gaggles of children are lined up, staring at the camera, and after fifty years everything is sepia-toned. This photo has to be about a hundred years old. Right in the middle of a bunch of boys is where Bojan puts his finger.

"I think this one is Joužek Kociper. No, this one is." He points to another boy in the back, "may be a brother. I'm not sure."

A dark-eyed boy stares up at the camera.

"I got this photo in New York from a Jewish woman. She was Joužek's mate in school. She lived in Manhattan and died last year at 105 years old. There are still some old Jews from Beltinci and their offspring in Manhattan."

We explore the Jewish history of Prekmurje and talk somewhat about the Countess Zichy and even less somewhat about the Gostílna Central and the Kreslins. Then we move outside to his vine-draped balcony that overlooks the village of Lipa.

Neat houses line the street. Tidy yards, and in each lies a garden bursting with pendulous vegetables and the bright purples and pinks of late summer flowers. A few houses have window boxes stuffed with a riot of scarlet blossoms and wild vines springing out in every direction. Over all this bounty wafts a fragrance only a gardener could love—the vaguely overripe, rotting, shoe-checking scent of organic fertilizer. Manure tea, if I were a betting man.

Bojan asks if I'd like to see his garden.

Herbs and vegetables and flowers are crammed into huge borders, with wooden planks laid out across each perfectly weeded bed. Everything's mulched and fertilized, and in the middle of the borders is a patch of green grass.

Bojan plucks a plant from a bed and holds it out to me. "My mother adds this to water to make a fertilizer for plants."

It's an innocuous little plant, delicate with leaves that look like mint. Bojan holds it by the roots, which should have told me something, but as usual I don't pay attention. I gently brush my thumb against its stem. The plant stings me. It's a nasty sting, too.

"Ouch! That's nettle!" I squeeze my thumb, which now hurts like it's been stung by a scorpion.

Bojan nods. "It's very good."

Maybe for his garden. Not for me.

We complete the circuit of his garden, although I have to admit the bloom is off the rose now.

I follow Bojan back to the house, rubbing my thumb the whole time, as Vlado drives up. Bojan takes a few photos of Vlado and me. We say goodbye, Bojan promising to send me more information.

Vlado and I drive off.

"Everything okay?" he asks.

"The nettle got me. But yes, everything's okay.

Chapter Fourteen

Vlado pulls into the driveway of his friend Martin. In less than a minute we're sitting out under the eaves next to the rose border, and Martin's bringing out wine. I'm in the middle chair between the two of them. It's the best place to be when you want to be in a conversation without having to say anything.

The men talk and drink, and talk some more. Their Prekmurski words fly over my head as they solve the problems of the world, *mano a mano*.

Lulled by their voices, I watch the dark drift in. By ones and twos, the stars wink in the evening sky. Somewhere close a dove calls, and in the distance the long, thin wail of a train welcomes the night. Like a slow-stroked string of the master's violin, on and on the mournful note sings, threading past homes and fields and rivers. One clear, sweet note… The train is the bow in Janči Kociper's hand, and the very Mura his string.

I think of Vlado's poem. A song, really, and sweet, one he wrote for Miška, Janči, Joužek and Tonek, musicians from Beltinška Banda, and how the late musicians, sometimes, at twilight, descend from heaven and play in the mist over the river. He says you can hear them when the wind blows from the south, up from Veržej. *"Tam v meglicah nad mursko vodo."* There, in the Mist by the Mura River…

Spomnijo se še stari ljudje,
da se je rado hodilo v goste.
Da si se ustavil, pobaral al' gre,
nazdravil še kakšno besedo al' dve.

Včasih pa, ko je sonce zašlo
spod' goric tja v mursko vodo
zaslišal se je tisti cimbalski glas
pobožal je loke, pobožal je vas.

Da si znal srečati štiri može
z violino in brki
in kar zraven gre.
In če si ženil si hčerko al' dve
gosli in bajs so ti zbrusli pete.

Včasih pa, ko se zvečeri
in zapiha z veržejske strani,
baje se jih sliši igrati glasno,
tam v meglicah nad mursko vodo.

"You okay?" Vlado looks at me.

I breathe in the rose-scented air, and smile. "Very okay."

We're at his friend Milan's house now. He pours me an aperitif, no more than a sip or two. We've already had a glass of his wine and gone over the finer points of the fish he'd caught earlier in the day out on the Mura. Big fish, too. Sometimes Vlado joins him.

This aperitif is something else. It's a good thing I'm sitting down while I drink it. Vlado scratches the head of a cat that's taken possession of his leg. Luks, the dog, is in his kennel, none too happy that a cat is flirting with his Milan and Vlado.

Vlado and Milan also work on the problems of the world. I watch the cat. Every time the dog barks she closes her eyes and smiles.

Milan looks like a happy man. He's happy to see Vlado. He even seems happy to see me. He takes us into the room where his wine casks are and shows me an old picture of his mother meeting Tito in Radenci in 1963. I've never met the leader of my country so I think it's a very cool thing that she met Tito. I ask Vlado to tell Milan that for me. He smiles even more so when Vlado tells him.

Vlado turns the car towards his house. "A good night with good friends."

It sure gets dark in the deep country. Vlado drives through Logarnica's gate, and ignoring the house, rushes out in the murky darkness to his garden.

Well, dang. What do I do now—stay in the car? Follow him? If he's left the keys I can turn the headlights on for him. I feel up and down the steering column and around the dash—all the places the keys might be. No keys.

I don't want to go creeping out after him in the dark. No telling what's out there—holes to twist an ankle in, roots to trip over, snakes creeping though the grass and giant spider webs with humongous spiders. We're close to the river, and the closer to water, the bigger the spider.

But if I cower in the car, I'm bound to miss something.

Besides, he didn't yell. Surely he'd yell if he crashed through a spider web.

I stumble after him into the night. Please God, no surprises.

"*Pička mata*," he says. "I can't see a thing."

"Turn your phone on."

He does and chortles: "Look at this!"

I lean over to get a better look. Yep, they're tomatoes, big and juicy and a lovely dark red, each of them a pendulous ovary bursting with sweet fecundity, if you can call seeds 'sweet fecundity', which sadly I think I can. I blame it on the wine.

"What tomatoes, eh? *Jijiji!* Just look at this!" He goes from plant to plant, fondling each vegetable in delight.

He breaks for the house. "Come!"

Well, I'd like to come, I really would, but I can't see the ground. I can't see anything except an oval shadow that I hope is his head and a vague lump in the distance that must be the house. But the ground has totally disappeared.

Where's the moon when you need her?

"Vlado, wait." I take a few steps. The world spins forward. Better it than me. I am not dizzy. This is not vertigo. "Please."

He stops.

"I can't see." Hands out in front of me like a blind man, I creep up to him. "Let me hold on to you so you can lead me."

My fingers tremble touching him. Only his thin summer shirt separates my skin from his skin. The muscles next to his spine tighten. Damn. I should have stayed out here in the dark while he went on to the house; it's not like anything would get me out here, not with all the noise we're making. Is he offended? He's got to be. Why didn't I grab his shirt instead? That would be better. Yes. Less… oh, what's the word? Where's my brain? Less… intimate. That's it. But my fingers won't bend, and he's already walking away. I have to follow, touching him, or I'll be left out here, night blind, as the world falls away in front of me.

So with my fingers skimming his back and me a neurotic mess, he leads me to the house.

As soon as I make out difference between the ground and the porch I snatch my hand away. He hurries up the steps while I stay on the ground, and suddenly the darkness is flooded with blessed, beautiful light.

"Come in," he says, and I do, right into the warm terra-cotta-tiled hall.

Then it's right back out to get the food, camera, clothes, guitar—all the important stuff. And my laptop. I can't leave that in the car because I never know when the muse—or guilt—may hit.

Vlado shuts the door. Here we are, just the two of us, alone in the country house.

Oh, dear.

Up until now, I convinced myself that Vlado would lock me in and then head to his parents' house for the night. Back home, it's eyebrow-raising for two married people who are not married to each other to spend the night together alone. No one believes they're not groping and panting all night long. Protestations only fuel the idea that major hanky panky is going on. But Vlado firmly locks the door with him on the inside with me. We'll be here unsupervised. Well, of course we will. But we're adults. And, maybe this is normal in Slovenia. Still, there were those ooh-la-la looks that his friend Milan gave us. Hmm. Maybe not so normal after all.

How will I ever explain this to the folks back home?

Perhaps no one here thinks twice about situations such as this. When in Slovenia, do as the Slovenes do, right? Since Vlado is Slovenia to me, if he isn't bothered about this, if Eva isn't bothered by this, if his parents aren't bothered by this, then I won't be either. Much.

But Vlado is a man of honor, and not only honor but integrity as well. From the time he locks the door until we awake across the house from each other the next morning, he's careful to stay several feet away from me. He's so careful that I slip away to the bathroom's mirror to see if I've been hit with the ugly stick.

Not that I want anything to happen, not at all. I love my husband, and Vlado is besotted with Eva. But still, a woman likes to see a twinkle in the eye of a man, even if it's followed with regret. '*Ljubézen*, I am so sorry. I would if I could but I belong to another and so…' A shrug. A smile. Not only is there no twinkle in his eye, he barely looks me at me.

His courtliness is most endearing. I feel safe with him. But I fear he doesn't feel quite as easy as I do. My easiness isn't exactly out there being the life of the party, but I don't I need reassuring. Vlado, on the other hand… well, I'd pat him on the top of his head if I could reach it, and whisper, "There, there. It's okay." But I'm too short and it might only discombobulate him further.

This situation was never covered in "How to Be a Guest in Slovenia 101".

Vlado shows me the way to the children's room. I immediately claim the bed off to the side of the bunk beds. Top bunk I might fall off; bottom bunk I'd hit my head getting back in if I go wandering in the night. I'm more a sleep screamer than a sleepwalker, but in a strange environment, who knows what will happen?

"*Jijiji!* Where are the mosquitoes coming from?" Vlado swats the air about his head.

"A hole in the screen?"

"*Ne, ne, ne*. There is no hole." He bats at the air on his way out of the room.

The best thing is to turn the light off.

I close the door. Maybe I should lock it against my sleepwalking and other misadventures. Would that be insulting? On the other hand, it might reassure him that I won't run screaming out the door at some ungodly hour and attack him. Should I ask? 'Vlado, would it bother you if I locked the bedroom door?' As a child I always locked the interior doors against beasties that roamed the house. But I'm not in the house of my childhood, and I am not a child.

I leave the door unlocked and crawl into bed.

The shutters on the bedroom windows have little cutouts—hearts or diamonds, I can't remember which, but whatever they are they let enough sunlight in to disturb my dreams. Sleep has scrubbed away the misapprehensions from the night before. My soul is shriven clean.

Or maybe I'm forgetful. It's hard to tell.

I slip into my clothes, and after a fight with the front doors—I win, but not without creaks and groans on their part, and a few choice words on mine—I head for the road.

Freedom. I stand in the middle of the road and breathe it in. I can go anywhere, do anything. I can run with the wind if I want to. At least I could if there was any wind, which is iffy right now. Sultry is more like it, even at seven a.m. We're in for a scorcher of a day. Still, I'm outside in the Prekmurje sunlight, hazy though it is. I'm soaking up the atmosphere, walking down past Štefan's house. The road beyond crooks her finger at me, undulating, whispering, "I've got something to show you…" Hazy, sultry, windless—I don't care. No way am I passing up this chance to go walking by the river. Huck Finn would do it.

But I'm not the only one soaking something up. My arm itches like crazy. Mosquitoes, and please note the plural, have turned my arm into a welt-fest. Where are these little buggers coming from anyway? Oh, yes, the river. Where, in a fit of romance, I wanted to go walking.

Now a whole gang of them swoops up under my hat brim, whining with joy. Stupid little vampires. They dive-bomb my face, my arms, my ankles—anywhere they find open skin. I yank my hat off and, right here in the road, slap at my head like a crazy woman with the herky-jerks. It's worse than a Louisiana swamp out here. If mosquitoes are this bad on a country road, what's it like down by the water? The birds must be going crazy on this feast.

I stop slapping.

Where are the birds?

All I hear is the bloodsucker's whine. Nothing else. Not a peep, not a chirp, not a song. This place should be filled with birdsong. But there are no birds. No spiders. No insects. Just mosquitoes.

Forget the river. I walk the other way, down to the cornfield, ringed by six-foot high weeds that are uncomfortably familiar. This preternatural silence unsettles me. Everything watches, waits. No hawk flies overhead; nothing shakes the corn; grasses sleep. It's as still as death.

Back in the house, I leave my shoes in the foyer. Maybe I'll lie down for a while. Not to sleep…

Someone's stirring, far too big to be a mouse. I fall out of bed.

"Would you like coffee?" Vlado putters about the kitchen, pulling the butter and prosciutto out of thc fridgc.

The coffeepot is a stovetop deal. How do I get this thing work? Coffee making is not my best skill, and I've never used one of these before. But no, he's got everything under control, especially since the coffee turns out to be instant. Instant I can do.

I put my requisite three spoonfuls of sugar in my coffee and search for the milk.

"I threw out the milk," he calls out. "It was…how do you say it?"

"Sour?"

"That's it. Sour."

Coffee without milk. Okay, when in doubt, add more sugar. I add four more spoonfuls of sugar and take a sip. Not bad. I can drink this.

The sliding glass door to the back is open. Vlado must be out on the patio. I go over to see if he wants his coffee brought out to him.

Swish.

Vlado's barefoot, wet grass splattered halfway up to his knees. The mosquitoes leave him alone today, at least so far. He's scything down the weeds between his yard and the cornfield beyond, his arms moving in an easy rhythm—swing-swish, swing-swish.

It's hypnotic—the waltz of the man-scythe, the *swish-snick* of the blade and the hazy August sun shining down on his back through the trees. River, sun, the cornfield beyond and a barefoot man with his scythe…

I want to scythe.

Gas fueled weed-whackers give me asthma. Using one is like wrestling with a calf. A scythe looks light and easy to use. Soft in the hand, and deadly to weeds and other small things.

"Can you teach me?"

To my consternation, I'm nervous about asking but I may never have another chance to learn. Carpe diem, and all that jazz.

"Eh?"

"Can you teach me?" I ask, a little louder this time. "Please?"

I put down my coffee and slip up next to him like a supplicant. I'm so close that the end of the snath hits me in the chest on his back swing. Not hard. I'm still breathing but it gets his attention.

"Can you teach me how to scythe?" I ask. "I'd like to learn."

"Oh, sure. Okay, make sure you swing it out away from you. That way you won't cut yourself.

You'll get the rhythm. Like this." He first shows me, then waves me over and passes me the scythe. "It helps when the grass is wet, you know?"

Cutting weeds in the cool of the morning when they're covered with dew instead of waiting until the heat of the day when they're dry? That sounds like my kind of mowing.

The scythe in my hands is perfectly balanced, light as balsa wood. I swing it once, checking how it works. Like a giant scalpel the scythe floats through the air.

"While you do this, I can go water." He walks off towards his garden, and then turns around. "Be careful of the trees."

Trees? But I can't cut a tree down with— Oh, wait. In the high weeds are saplings about as tall as I am, caged in fine mesh wire. Deer deterrents. Probably good scythe deterrents, too.

I settle into a rhythm. Lo, the weeds bow down before me, sliced off a scant inch above the ground. This is ever so much more fun than weed whacking. Before long, I've made it down one side of the yard and halfway across the back. It's so quiet I could hear the birds sing, if there were any birds singing.

Someone's watching me, just like he did in Savudrija. I straighten up and slowly turn around.

Vlado's laughing. He stands in the doorway of the house holding his video camera up to his eye, and he's looking right at me.

Vlado pulls out of the driveway onto the road, but he only goes a few yards to the cornfield before slamming on his brakes.

"*Jijijij!* Look at that!"

Look at what? The road? The sky?

"This… this plant! Ambrosia! We have to get rid of it. It's horrible, and bad for Ajdina and Eva, too!"

"It looks like ragweed to me."

He jumps out of the car and immediately starts yanking up some of the stalks.

Wow. Either the field belongs to Vlado or he's got some really nice neighbors. Back home I'd be shot for pulling weeds in someone else's cornfield.

Should I pull the car off the road? If we're going to be here a while someone's bound to come up behind us. But maybe it's better to let Vlado take care of that little detail.

I open the door to go pull ragweed as well. If he pulls weeds, then I'll pull weeds. I pray I don't break out in welts.

But I don't even get my foot down on the ground before Vlado gets back in the car.

"The government can fine the owner of the field if he doesn't get rid of it," he says.

"Really?" Wow, what a way to get people involved in eradicating ragweed.

"Yes."

"It's not your field?"

He shakes his head. "I don't know who it belongs to."

"If we did that back home, we'd either be arrested or shot."

We drive off, but instead of heading for Beltinci he turns towards the river. "Milan was going fishing this morning."

Fishing I can go for, although isn't it too late for that? The sun's been up for hours. No respectable fish would bite now, unless there's something really different about Mura fish.

We bounce down the dirt road, past the circus-colored beehive. Maybe it's the sunlight or someone painted it, but the beehive looks clean and spiffy now, and the air around it is thick with bees. Vlado drives up to the ferry. Sure enough, friend Milan is there, grinning at Vlado's car.

"He is who he is, you know? What you see is how he is. I like that," says Vlado.

We all need friends like that.

While Vlado and Milan talk, I wander down to the river's edge. The ferry is too busy bumping up against the far shore to take any notice of me. Its few passengers mill about on its platform, jockeying for the best place to jump off and go… where? Down the road? Across the field? What is over there, anyway…?

"Ruth! This is how high the waters were this year." Vlado calls out, pulling my attention back to this side of the river. He waves at a bench that has a watermark halfway up its back.

"Because of the ice?" Ack, what a stupid question. As if the ice had come up all this way. I don't think so, Einstein. The Mura froze hard this past winter, unusual for a fast flowing river, but for some reason I figured the ice was to blame. Err, that would be no. Obviously I'm not wise to the ways of a river. *Because of the ice…* Where's my dunce cap?

"That," he says kindly, answering my naff question, "and the floods."

Flooding. Of course. Which makes such lovely breeding grounds for mosquitoes.

I wonder how the ferryman's shack fares when the floods come.

Vlado's eyes crinkle. "That's not his house. It's just a bar made of mud and wood. Like the house of Johnny B. Goode—haha! The ferryman lives in another village."

Oh, okay. But still, losing the bar wouldn't be good.

Vlado and Milan walk back towards the car. I pass them and keep going. It's my last chance to get a picture of the beehive.

"Did Milan go fishing this morning?" I ask Vlado, once we're in the car.

"Oh, no. It was too late."

I think back to the night before, with Milan and Vlado and the rod and reel. "Do you fish a lot?"

Vlado smiles. "My fishing is like the legendary Slovenia climber Nejc Zaplotnik wrote: 'Important is the way and not the goal.'"

"I see. It's the journey and not the destination."

"Ah, yes!"

"The fish don't like you, eh?"

"I love to fish but hardly ever catch any." Vlado sounds awfully cheerful for a man who doesn't catch many fish.

"But you took Naj fishing on the Mura."

"Oh, sure. And once after fishing, Naj said, 'What good luck we didn't catch any.' "How do you mean that?' I said, and Naj replied, 'Because I don't like to eat them.'"

We go back to his parents' house. Vlado and his father have more work to do on the duet. This time they're under the covered porch by Katarina's flower garden. Beyond the men is a cleome, a large multi-flowered annual that my mother used to grow. Vlado passes the camera to me again. I open up the viewfinder and start. Well, almost.

"I think you've forgotten something," says Vlado.

"I have?"

He smiles and takes the lens cap off.

Five men, sitting outside a café. They could be anywhere in the world that serves both coffee and wine at ten in the morning, but these guys are in Beltinci. Vlado introduces me to everyone—Martin, who came over from the Kreslins' on his old-timer motorcycle, I already know; Vili, Vlado's cousin, with the awesome moustache and wide grin; Bada, brother to the late Štefan; and an old friend called Pele. I wedge myself in between Bada and Pele, across from Vlado.

They all talk—well, mostly Vlado talks. The other men nod, say a word or two, settle back in their chairs and take a drag off their cigarettes while listening to Vlado and watching the world go by. Once in a while Bada looks over at Vlado. Something hangs in the air between them like a long thin thread of grief.

Vlado tells his joke du jour. The men chuckle, even Martin who's heard it before. Martin says something to Vlado, who translates for me: "He feels bad that we're talking in Slovene and you don't understand."

Aww. "That's very sweet of him. Please tell him thank you and not to worry. I promise I will ask if I have questions." But how would I even know what to ask?

Vlado translates back to Martin.

I say, "*Hvala*" to Martin, too. I hope I've got it right. It takes a special person to mess up "*hvala*" but I can do it. He smiles back at me anyway and nods, which doesn't fool me one bit— my accent is atrocious—but he is a sweet man.

Then Vlado tells the motorcycle story, first in Slovene and then in English.

"I was speeding through town on my motorcycle, a BMW. And this policeman had been trying to catch me on it for the longest. So I speed right past him, and here he comes after me.

"Well, I head for Vili's house. He's my cousin, you know. His mother always told me if I was in trouble with my parents I could stay there, so sometimes I stayed there a lot—haha! So off to Vili's house I go. While the policeman was coming to the front door, Vili's dad and I were hiding the motorcycle in the barn." Vlado motions over our heads. "And here comes the police and he says, fuck this, I know that motorcycle is here. He looks around, and he looks around, but he doesn't look in the barn. Haha!"

Vili squirms in his chair, looking at Vlado, then me with a glint in his eyes. Finally, he grins.

More coffee, more wine for those who are drinking it, more solving of problems, and then it's time to go.

Our entourage heads for the castle, except for Bada. He stays behind at the table, lost in thought and a cloud of smoke. Half way across the parking lot, I turn back to him and wave. "Bada!" He smiles his sad smile and raises his wine glass to me.

Pele walks ahead. Vlado nods in his friend's direction and leans close to my ear. "He was the greatest soccer player of our generation here. Amazing player."

We cross a modern footbridge to get to the castle grounds, which is only on the other side of the café parking lot.

"Did I tell you about the time I caught minnows here?" Vlado says.

"In this stream?" The slow dark water didn't look deep enough to grow anything but mosquitoes.

"Yes, yes, right here. We were right down here, catching minnows. I'd caught a big one, the biggest one. I stood up, excited, and threw my head back and hit it on the bridge. It knocked me out. The taxi took me to the hospital in Murska Sobota, and my taxi driver was the brother of the taxi driver who drove the architect Jože Plečnik all over Prekmurje when he was building the church in Bogojina."

"Ouch. You got a concussion?"

Vlado nods. "And I had to wear a swaddling bandage on my head. For three weeks!"

A man with intense blue eyes and wearing an intense blue shirt hails us from where he sits alone at one of the bistro tables that line the castle's cloister walk. With a moustache and some teeth he'd be distinguished. As it is he's merely memorable. Someone in the entourage must know him because we stroll over and claim a chair around his table.

Unless it's a Prekmurje thing to hail strangers and ask them to sit at your table? I steal a glance at Vlado. He's cool with it.

The waiter, Bobi, calls out to Vlado. "*Piré pa tebé*!"

Vlado peers at me under my hat brim and smiles. Raises an eyebrow.

I whisper to Vlado, "Okay. What is *pi-ré pa te-bé*?" I speak the words very slowly, hoping he can figure out what I'm saying.

Vlado grins. "A year ago, I came here with the kids for a meal. Naj and Čarna love *bograč*. Traditional Prekmurje food—very hot. But Ajdina does not. She orders Wiener schnitzel and *pouree*. You know, potatoes."

Actually I don't. I've never had Wiener schnitzel, but I nod like I'm a veteran schnitzel eater.

"And then I joke, 'Why don't you love traditional Prekmurje food? What a shame! What do you love then?' In that second Bobi brings her meat and *pouree*, and she looks at it and says, '*Pouree pa tebé*.' Potatooo and you!'"

Vlado orders wine for me and wine for himself. "A sweet wine for you, is that okay? Eva likes it very much."

Sweet wine sounds wonderful. It's lovely and fruity, flirty on the tongue and chilled just right, although right now I'd be happy with a jar of rotgut or even nothing at all. I settle back and, like before, listen to Vlado and watch the conversation.

So five of us crowd around this little table and sip wine here at Count Zichy's castle. This is where the count raised his three lovely daughters who never learned Slovene. The daughters liked Vienna so at least they weren't Rapunzels, trapped in these towers with no escape. One of them even died in Vienna, working at the tuberculosis sanatorium until she herself was stricken. Yet all the Zichys—Count August and his wife Hedvika, and their three daughters—Maria, Anastasia, and Amalia—are buried here in their crypt underneath Mary's Chapel.

The Zichy crypt… This makes me think of the cemetery close by where Štefan sleeps, under a gravestone with the song of the Mura River.

And Vlado, will he be buried in this ground, too?

Vlado scoots his chair back, and we're off. I leave behind my half empty glass of wine and slightly morbid thoughts, and dutifully trot after him.

But not too far. Crunching gravel under my feet, I almost step on a little purple and red flower, shaped like a honeysuckle blossom. I pick it up and twirl it between my fingers. "Vlado."

But Vlado keeps right on walking, getting farther and farther away. His legs are long; he covers a lot of ground in a stride.

"Vlado!" I shout, but my shout isn't loud enough to get his attention. He wouldn't ignore me so he must not hear me.

"Vlado!" I rush up next to him and hold up the flower. "Do you know what this is?"

He slows down to glance at it and then shakes his head. "Eh? Oh, no. Sorry."

"Hmm." I cradle the flower in one hand and poke at it with a finger. "I bet if it was a vegetable you'd know."

He laughs. "Probably."

We walk on a ways, and then I say, "Did you really hide a motorcycle in the barn while the policeman was looking for it?"

"I did."

"But why was the policeman after you? Was it contraband?"

"Contraband? Eh, not so much. Unlicensed, though. And I was underage, too young to ride it. And speeding! They were always trying to get me. Haha!"

Lunch is soup at his parents' house. I haven't a clue what it is outside of being orange, but it's awfully good. Pumpkin maybe? And green peppers dressed with vinaigrette. Wine. Yum.

A napkin trips me up, etiquette-wise. In Slovenia one leaves the napkin on the table. I don't pick up on this, so in my imitation of a well- mannered guest, I place mine in my lap. This is not the thing to do. Vlado's father Milan notices my napkin is missing, and with a 'tut' he jumps up to get me another. Oh, dear. I thank him and, noting everyone else has their napkin next to their plate, make sure I leave this one on the table.

I still have the red-purple blossom. I show it to Vlado's mom. She grows flowers; maybe she knows what it is. She gasps, then leads me out to her garden. Sure enough, right here on the patio is a window box filled with the same red- purple flowers. Begonias? Columbines? Bleeding hearts? Maybe, maybe not.

I see the cleomes again, purple and white, and as tall as me.

Vlado loads up the car while I head for them. They're my favorite summer flower, so of course they won't grow for me. But my mother had a bed full of cleomes, tall and spidery, bobbing and bowing in the lightest breeze. Those hot humid summer days when I was little, and my mother in her scarf and sunglasses, outside in the garden…

"Cleoma," Katarina says. "Cleoma."

Of course. "Cleoma," I reply. " We call them cleome."

Chapter Fifteen

Vlado paces. It's really time to say goodbye now. We all hug and wish each other well. Then Vlado and I ride back to the country house.

"*Jijiji!!!* Look at that!"

Vlado slams on his brakes by the cornfield and jumps out of the car.

"This is horrible."

This time, I jump out, too. I figure we can be shot together. We spend the next five minutes pulling up ragweed, although with the field this full of it, it's futile. At least it's easy work, but I'm not sure about how wise it is to pull this stuff barehanded. Contact allergies and all that. But if Vlado's pulling, I don't want to be a slacker.

"Time to take a nap," he says as soon as we get into the house. He stretches out on the sofa. I turn my laptop in the children's room. Sleeping would be a disaster, but writing is good.

But first I want to check something.

I pull up the page Vlado had shown me in his study, the article from *Glas Naroda.* Next to the Zakelj quote is another one by Johnny Srsen. It, too, is about Vlado. "Overall, I would rank him as one of Slovenia's finest musicians, if not *the* finest Slovenian musician."

I stare at the door for the longest time, thinking.

"Do you have these?" Vlado asks. We're out by his garden. Something fat and oozy, the size of my thumb, is at our feet. A big copper-brown slimy lump of…

"That's a slug?"

"A red slug. Yes."

"But it's so big." It's splendid in an icky sort of way.

I lean over to see better. Mr. Slug's not moving. Maybe it'll move if I touch it, but the slug is so shiny, slick and gross, I don't know if I can do it. I stick my finger out to stroke it, but the "ick" part wins out.

Slug watching with Vlado. From *Rulet* to squatting down in the grass watching slimy things on an August afternoon. I grin up at him. He grins back.

The mosquitoes have found Vlado. Such a pity, because they aim right for his head.

"The bug spray—can you bring it? It's by the door."

I check by the front door but can't find it. He tells me to look in the car. Can't find it there, either. I know it's right in front of me but there's no bug spray. I return with the bad news.

Vlado waves it off.

"Stupid mosquitoes." I smash another one. "I wanted to walk down by the riverbank but there were just too many."

Vlado nods. "We had great water this summer. From the Mura. When the water gets over the banks, it stays in the off springs, and if it is autumn or whenever they grow, mosquitoes turn out in masses. Last year there were no mosquitoes."

I stare at the sky. "You'd think this place would be full of birds."

"Always full of birds."

"Not now."

"Oh, sure there are."

"Listen."

He stands in the middle of the porch, looking up and listens to… absolutely nothing.

Then he whispers, "Where are the birds?"

Vlado steps barefoot between the rows in his garden, watering each plant one by one with a huge red watering can. So intent is he on what he's doing that Attila the Hun could charge down the road and I doubt Vlado would notice. He's got coreopsis, comfrey and oregano down one end, marigolds down the other, and vegetables in the middle—cabbages, squash, and lots of tomatoes. At least eight red and swollen tomatoes hang on their vines, plus twice as many again in various shades of green. Huge wooden beams, neatly squared up, are laid out around the garden. They hold the dirt and plants in but a few unruly squash vines escape. With the ivy-covered fence and the long shed behind it, the tableaux looks like a postcard perfect country garden.

"Look at these! Haha! Just look at them!" Vlado gathers all the ripe tomatoes into a basket to take back to Ljubljana.

Vlado's out scything again, cutting the grass on the steep slope up to his barbeque. I glance at the sideboard. Right there in front of God and everybody are two cans of bug repellent.

I hurry outside. "Vlado!" I hold the can out in front like it was a talisman. He sprays himself down well, especially his head, and passes the spray back to me. I spray everywhere too, including my hat. I smell like Eau de Bug Spray but I don't care.

Vlado goes back to scything.

"You really like this," I say.

"Oh, sure. I do some, and then stop. A little at a time, or I get bored."

"But on a hill—won't you slice your foot off?"

He shakes his head. "You just watch the angle when you swing. Here. You try."

I stare at my bare feet. It's been years since I've walked barefoot in the grass. Stickers and all that. But Vlado's barefoot, and he hasn't found any stickers. I step off the patio onto the grass and, just the way he showed me, I swing the scythe.

Afterwards, when we're standing on the patio, I ask, "Do you come here often?"

"No. Not really." He looks down. "The family… eh, they're busy during the week when I have time off. When they have time off, I have to work doing concerts."

I almost say *it won't always be this way*, but I stop myself. When Ajdina turns eighteen, Vlado will be sixty-nine. But maybe he'll be like his father, who is still singing in his eighties.

Vlado goes back into the house. "Have some coffee," he says from the far side of the living room.

Coffee sounds lovely, but in an hour or so there's a picnic. It may be inside, may be outside, maybe there will be restrooms, maybe not. A mad dash into the corn might be entertaining but who wants to be remembered that way?

Vlado pulls papers out of a stack he found at his parents' house—newspapers and letters and magazines and posters. It's all sorts of memorabilia from the days when he was a youth. "My dad found these in his cellar. He was going to throw them away. *Jijijiji!!* So I grabbed them up."

"Today?"

"Yes, yes, today. Look at this!" It was a poster for Sanje, back when he was in the university. "There's more at his house. I'm going to save it all."

Happy as can be, he carries an armload of papers to the dining table and lays them out. "Here—you can read this."

"This" was a 1974 edition of the *New Musical Express*, a legendary magazine from Britain. Next to it was its Yugoslav counterpart, called *Đuboks*, pronounced 'Jukebox' and then *START* magazine, both from the seventies, with articles about Brooke Shields and Sonny and Cher, and a *Rolling Stone* magazine from 1972.

I was amazed. "Where on earth did you get these?"

"The English papers? Either Ljubljana or Trieste if Ljubljana was sold out. I don't remember which. *Rolling Stone* I brought from London."

"You could buy them? Just go out and get them?"

"Oh, sure. Why not?"

"But it was communist here."

"The Yugo passport was the most valuable passport on the black market, because with a Yugo passport you could go anywhere, to the east and to the west. We went to Trieste all the time; it was no big deal. We usually bought jeans there because we didn't have original Rifle or Levi jeans. I went to London to the Reading Festival in 1972. Saw Edgar Broughton Band, Ten Years After, Faces, Focus… Coming back, I stopped in Munich and tried to find a job at the Olympics. I got there the day the athletes were killed. You remember. Here."

Vlado shows me his blue pass into the Olympic village. "Well, after that there was nothing for me to do at the Olympics, so I came back home. But I could travel wherever I wanted to."

I flip through the Yugoslav magazine. Brooke Shields, Sony and Cher. The Yugoslavs did their best to follow our culture. We knew nothing about theirs, and didn't care. We didn't care about their stars or songs, couldn't even tell where Yugoslavia was, and here they were devouring stories about a fourteen year old American beauty, and singing, "I Got You Babe."

Tears prickle my eyes. I turn another page and wipe my nose. I don't know why this affects me so, why I'm fighting tears— embarrassment maybe, or guilt. I want to run away. Get away from here, from Vlado, and be alone. Who am I to be so oblivious?

Vlado goes through his papers with a half-smile on his face, blissfully unaware of my emotions. If he gives me one of those half-pitying, half-questioning looks, I'll blame my allergies for making my eyes wet.

But he keeps staring at something in his hand, and my emotions pass. The confusion taints the afternoon, though, even when Vlado passes pieces of his life over to me as he tells me each one's story.

He holds out a faded photo. A fan sent him her picture—this picture—years ago. A hopeful young lady poses in a formal portrait, her brown hair swept up in a bubble hairdo. Vlado studies at the photo for a long time, his eyes soft.

"Do you know her?"

"Eh? Oh, no. No," he says, but as he reads her letter, his face stays gentle.

Then it's hurry, hurry, hurry to the picnic. Vlado says they're having fish soup. I've never had fish soup at a picnic. Maybe they'll have some other Prekmurje dishes, too. Even *Prekmurska gibanica*? I'm up for anything.

Vlado jumps into the car. That's one of us ready. I have to run back in the house, keys in hand, one last time. Then out again, lock the door, err… lock the door. What is it with this door? Argh! I will not call Vlado, I can do this, I will not… The bolt relents and lunges into place. I dash to the car, toss the keys to Vlado and off we go.

"Where we're going is right on the edge of Croatia," says Vlado. "Over this stream." Just like that, we're over the stream.

It's back roads all the way, or maybe front roads. I can't tell. As far as I can see the world is one giant field of corn, with skinny roads making a checkerboard maze that cuts through the crops. Vlado knows which of the side roads to take, and soon we're out of the field.

The driveway is stuffed with cars.

We have incompatible philosophies on parking. I'm a fan of backing in. Vlado? He steers the car nose first into a narrow space between two other vehicles. I try to keep my mouth shut, I really do, but after his fifth attempt, I suggest that maybe backing in would be easier. Vlado nods. He gets the car into position, cuts the wheels hard to the left and guns it. No luck. The fence post, the tree, and a car next to his space conspire against him. Now he's stuck in a different position.

I jump out of the car. Outside might be a better place to navigate from. So, with much shouting and arm waving, I navigate. Too bad my navigation skills suck as much as my spatial imagination. Vlado, bless him, still seems grateful, although I'm not sure if it's the exterior navigation he's grateful for, or Little Miss Suggestion leaving the car. Either way, thanks to me, the car's wedged tighter than a tick, half in and half out of the spot.

But help arrives in the form of a dark-haired woman named Simona, who comes down from the picnic. In less than a minute, with her coaching, Vlado slips his car in between the two other vehicles. How did she do that? I sigh and resolve to keep my mouth zipped from now on.

The picnic is under the trees at Vlado Žabot's house. Two grills, maybe more, are fired up at either end of a huge table set up in a "U". So many people mill about that it's like swimming through sardines. Everyone's talking and laughing, and drinking lots of wine and beer. It feels like everyone knows everyone else. Except me, but that's okay. I know Vlado.

Someone asks Vlado if he minds doing an interview. A TV crew focuses their camera on him.

Vlado turns to me and says, "Ruth, will you try to talk to someone?"

'Talk to someone' he says. As if I speak Slovene. How many people here speak English? The younger ones, okay. But those with some history behind them?

So instead of bugging people like I should, I follow some distance behind Vlado and watch the taping. It takes all of five minutes. The reporter asks Vlado a question. The cameraman shoots from behind the reporter's shoulder. Another man fiddles with some kind of equipment. Vlado shrugs, says something, and the crew dashes off on their merry way.

Weeks later, when I get my courage up, I ask, "What'd you say at the picnic?"

"You mean what the TV asked me? Something like 'What is this? Mura Romances?' And I joked that it is a new genre that will take Manhattan and then New York.

"It is that Feri and Žabot organized a project of romance songs about Mura. We authors from Prekmurje should write songs and some amateur singers would sing them. I wrote a poem called *Two*, about two unhappily in love who jump in the Mura."

Love, death, the Mura—a perfect Prekmurje song.

All the tables have benches. I sit on the end of the one closest to the house. Timing is everything, and I'm just in time for someone to pass me a giant platter laden with meat. So much food, and whatever I'm served I'm supposed to eat because they might be offended if I don't clean my plate. I read this in a business article—you must always take what is offered and you must eat everything you take, or Slovenes will be upset. I take some of everything, even foods I don't recognize, telling myself that half the fun of going to a new place is eating new food.

Please don't let there be squiggly things.

The pile of food on my plate grows and grows. How am I ever going to eat all this food?

I must look bewildered because a voice next to me says, "You don't have to eat it all. Just eat what you like."

This is from the blonde-haired woman on my right. She has a merry face and she's smiling at me. Smiling faces I'm not so sure about but I'm a sucker for a merry face. She looks so honest and down to earth I'm sure she spends her life's work comforting people. Her name is Nataša, and she's a surgeon, specializing in facial reconstruction, although I don't learn this until later. She also speaks very good English, but like most Slovenes I've met, she constantly apologizes for it.

We jabber like grackles in between passing plates and scarfing food. We talk about books, including the one I'm writing, what she does and what she thinks of Vlado's music. Her eyes dance as she talks about him, telling me about her favorite song of his and how she listened to it over and over when she carried her son.

Vlado takes his seat across from me and asks, "You okay?"

I grin back at him. "Of course I'm okay."

"Haha!" He waves and goes off somewhere else.

Nataša moves on. I crawl down to sit on the concrete stoop.

Simona sits by me and whispers that the band setting up under the eaves is also from around Beltinci, that the whole area is a nest of creativity. Of course Vlado is the best-known chick from the nest. It's easy to imagine him in a nest with his bald head poking up over the twigs and feathers. The wine helps.

It also helps with my language lesson.

"I teach linguistics," says Simona. "I will help you with Slovene."

This is wonderful because I have a hard time with Slovene. Sounding like John Wayne's sister doesn't help. Simona works to teach me how to say *Cesta*, which is far more complicated than my tongue thinks it should be. It's not "Ses-tah" but rather "Ses-thah" with a pressing of my tongue to the back of my upper teeth. The result is me spitting. A lot.

Vlado looks over at us and raises an eyebrow.

"Go away, Vlado," says Simona, laughing. "I'm teaching her how to speak Slovene."

Cesta finally conquered, I scramble back up to my place on the bench. Vlado talks with his friend Igor, another writer and an old friend from when they worked together at Radio Ljubljana.

I ask Vlado, "You worked at a station? Really?"

"Well, it was just an extra job. I was the musical program director. Another extra job was when I read the weather report in foreign languages. Oh, and I even did some radio shows on Shakespeare. But I was regularly employed in the personnel department of Radio-Television Ljubljana where I worked with young new employees and students. Nothing to do with programming." He spies someone down the table and heads off again.

Igor and I talk about writing books and how he and Vlado actually first met when Vlado was in Sanje back in the seventies.

The band that's setting up under the eaves entices Vlado to sing, although, Vlado being Vlado, that isn't hard to do. There's a quick lead in with Gershwin's *Summertime*, Vlado joining in on the second verse. That segues into one of Vlado's older songs.

"That's from when he was in Sanje," says Igor. "In college. I knew him even then."

After Vlado, comes the vocalist for the band. She's a little thing, all sticks and angles. Her voice is a lyric soprano that could shatter Coke bottles for miles around. She stands perfectly still as she sings. It's probably the way her vocal instructor taught her. Her song is in Slovene so I have no idea what she's singing, but the people seem to enjoy it.

Vlado sits across from me again, this time so he can talk with Slavko, an old friend of his and a classical music composer of some renown. They nod, make faces, move hands. Vlado laughs. I like to watch them; I don't mind this invisibility I have.

Vlado looks over at me, and winks.

"We need to go," says Vlado, standing up, "but first I want to you to talk with Žabot. He's a famous Prekmurski writer."

He's also one of the hosts for this picnic. So Vlado Kreslin makes the introductions, telling Žabot that I want to interview him, and off Vlado goes. Žabot and I smile at each other for a few minutes.

"I'm sorry. No English," he says with an even bigger smile.

But Nataša speaks English, and Nataša is free. I hurry after her, asking if she'd be kind enough to interpret. Actually, it's more like pleading and begging but in a quiet, understated way. With many demurrings and apologies, she agrees to interpret for us.

But what to ask? Polite and safe… I don't know. I sense undercurrents here, an indulgent look on Žabot's face as he glances over at Vlado. Ah, yes, I think I see my way through this.

So I ask, through Nataša: what does Žabot believe is Vlado's contribution to Prekmurje literature? It's a loaded question, but why not ask the hard ones? Here are these authors and poets, making a name for themselves with their contributions to their country's literature. Along comes Vlado who can sell on the strength of the name he made in music. That's not to say that's why people buy his books, but I wonder if there is some resentment there because Vlado didn't have to jump through the same hoops they did.

Žabot looks at Vlado again as the latter, on the other side of the picnic table, launches into a story with some friends. Žabot smiles. He seems bemused at the whole situation, bemused at Vlado telling his story and bemused at this American asking pointed questions about Vlado. He answers, through Nataša, that Vlado's contributions are his lyrics that are both intimate and socially engaged.

Ah. Okay, that's nice and safe but… I cock my head to one side and watch Žabot. I wait.

He smiles again. He says that it's in his poetry that Vlado's philosophy is found. Vlado's friend Štefan once said that with Vlado, his poetry and his lyrics are the mist that floats above the Mura. This mist is his soul, and in this floating of the soul is his point of view. With Vlado, in his writings, human and god walk together hand-in-hand, and both equally are gods.

Curious. I ask about Vlado's contribution to literature and get a metaphysical answer that could take years to unravel. I've got to be missing something here. I'm good at muddling things up. I'm sure the fault is mine and not his, but even so the moment is pregnant with all the things he didn't say.

We talk some more about Žabot's work and Prekmurje writers in general. I ask Žabot if any of his books have been translated into English, and he tells me his latest *The Succubus* is indeed in English. I thank both Žabot and Nataša for their time and scribble all this down as fast as I can. I hope I can read my notes later, which is no sure thing.

But Žabot's words did paint a picture.

Vlado in a white straw hat, his shirt sleeves rolled up to his elbows, kneeling down by the Mura at the ferry landing. A mist, low and thick, covers the river. The newborn day shimmers like heated brass. Already the air grows hot, too still for this early in the morning. Mist, river—they're old friends, yes, indeed—it's hard to see where one ends and the other begins. Vlado points up to a kingfisher sitting on a branch, thin as his finger. The bird darts into the water and swoops up a tiny fish in his beak and flies away. The mist thins, spreads out and rises up until we can't see it anymore, and the Mura flows on alone. The mist carries the song the river sings—Vlado's words—and then it fades away, going wherever mist goes, until it comes back to the Mura to be birthed again.

So did Žabot answer my question? I don't know. Maybe it's better this way. To be a mist that rises to the sky and spreads out over the land— this is a good thing. After all, who knows who may follow the mist back to its source and drink of the Mura? Probably some crazy people. One, anyway.

Vlado says his goodbyes, his friend Feri walking with us. Vlado gives me his camera to take a shot of the two of them together. Then he gives Feri a copy of his new book of poetry, *Instead of Whom Does the Flower Bloom*? out in October. Getting Vlado to stay still for a shot, talking to Feri and laughing? It's easier to dam the Mura. But after many eyes-shut, mouth-open failures, I get it.

We climb into the car. Igor runs back to say goodbye and good luck with the book, and then we're off, speeding towards Logarnica to get our things.

"Look!" Vlado points down the road into the sun. A Prekmurje stork, flushed out of its hiding place in the cornfield next to us, scrambles across our path. It stretches out its black tipped wings, flapping like a gawky child until finally it lifts up and drifts into another field.

"The romance picnic has already been on the news," he says, as we pull up to friend Milan's house to drop off a T-shirt and pick up some vegetables.

"That was fast."

"It always is."

It's time to turn left and take the road for Ljubljana. At least that's what I think we're about to do.

Vlado has another idea. He turns right, and after a few turns that get me completely lost, he goes down a gray and empty road. I don't even know if we're still in Bistrica. He pulls up at a white house with one of the greenest lawns I've ever seen. "These folks may know why there is no birdsong. Come."

A young couple opens the door. Vlado makes the introductions, regaling them with the story of not hearing any birds singing—first in English, and then in Slovene. They nod, Vlado nods, and then they shake their heads. Even I can tell what that means. Vlado thanks them, and we hurry to the car.

"He didn't know. But there's someone else who might."

We pass a group out strolling after dinner. Vlado slams on the brakes. This time he jumps out by himself. Better to wait for an invitation, methinks, than to assume I should tag along.

"*Texasa*!" Vlado says, laughing. He looks more like a long, tall Texan than I ever will. "Come!"

Texasa? Maybe I should do a bow-legged mosey over to where everyone is talking. *Texasa*, eh? I cock my hat to one side and sidle up next to Vlado.

Once again Vlado introduces me all around. They talk mostly in Slovene, but every now and then they break out in English so I can join in. There's a whole lot of nodding going on, but no one does any head shaking.

Vlado smiles down at me. “My friend here tells me the birds all stop singing on Assumption, and that is why we don’t hear any bird song.”

“And today is Assumption.” Which means the last bird I heard was the dove in Martin’s garden last night.

Vlado’s friend nods, a big smile lifting up the corners of his moustache. “Every year they stop. All at once.”

With the bird mystery cleared up, we shake hands all around and climb into the car.

“You never knew this about the birds?”

“No, never,” he says.

Back at his house in Ljubljana I’m getting ready to turn in for the night. The taxi will be here at dawn, which means I have to get everything done now—packing, showering, repacking, setting out my clothes, packing one last time…

“Ruth!”

Vlado’s on the upstairs landing with a book in his hand—*Instead of Whom Does the Flower Bloom*. He inscribes it and hands it to me.

I look at the inscription, but I can’t read it. He has a very creative handwriting.

“What does it say?” I feel awful asking this, and I will feel stupid when he tells me, but I really want to know.

He says something, but I catch only part of it. I have tinnitus, a gift from a health scare a few years back. It sometimes makes it hard for me to hear. I haven’t told him. The irony is a bit much—someone writes his story, and she can’t even hear clearly half the time.

“I’m sorry. Can you please tell me one more time?” I make sure this time that I watch his mouth move.

He looks at me as if I’ve taken leave of my senses, but he says, “’To Ruth—On that sunny long day in August…Vlado.”

Chapter Sixteen

Cleveland, November 2012

Texas swelters. Cleveland freezes. Thus it shall ever be, world without end, amen.

Back home I sweated, bundled up for my destination. Here in Cleveland, I shiver at the airport taxi stand. Taxi drivers here must have an incredible union, because it appears no hotel provides a shuttle from the airport to their sanctuary. I dare not ask. The woman printing my chit so I can prove I didn't jump the line is too important for any unscripted questions. She makes sure not to look at me. God help her if she ever smiled.

"Destination?"

"Hyatt at the Arcade."

She rips the chit off the printer and shoves it under the Plexiglas barricade. My "Thanks" is swallowed up in her "Next!" I take the chit and pass through the doors to get properly chilled to the bone.

But the taxi driver? He's all smiles. A big black man, he ambles towards me. "I gotta tell you, my credit card machine doesn't work."

Cash is king as far as I'm concerned. That makes him a happy man.

Ninety minutes later I'm in another taxi, headed for St Mary of the Assumption in Collinwood? Cleveland? Wherever its home, it's on Holmes, which is how I made sure I was going to the right St Mary's. The one on Holmes had something written in Slovene on its website.

The driver pulls into the alley between the church and the rectory. I crawl out of the car, lugging boxes of pralines, a plate of rum balls and a birthday card, sans present thanks to my disorganized packing. Now where can I find Vlado? The church is lit up. I'll try that. I tug on a door. Nothing. I try another door. Nothing. I try the hall. That's locked, too. Even worse, I hear no music, not from anywhere.

Another man, another church. Here I am again, left waiting, all by myself. Thanks, Vlado.

The driver wants to stay with me until my friend shows up, but that's not fair to him. He's got a job to do, so I wave him on. I'm amazed at how brave I'm being. This is good fodder for the book. "Famous Singer Leaves Writer in the Cold".

I text Vlado. *At church. It's cold. Where are you?*

It's so cold I'd freeze to the fence if I leaned up against it.

My phone rings. Now if I can figure out how to answer it in time. Oh, wait. I don't know that number. I ignore the call.

The phone rings again. Same number. Maybe it isn't a random call.

"Hello?"

"Hallo! Hallo, Ruth? This is Jure!" He sounds like a hearty fellow, this Jure. Just the kind of guy for Vlado to hang out with. Jure tells me he and Vlado are almost here. At least I think that's what he says. With the wind blowing in my ears and my teeth chattering, it's hard to tell.

Then Vlado gets the phone. I mention how I can't get in.

"You can't get in?"

"No, and it's freezing out here!"

"Ruth!" he says. "Don't bother with that—just say a little prayer for me? Haha! Be there soon!"

'*Don't bother with that.*' That's easy for him to say. Not only has he given me a song that keeps looping in my head, he's warm right now. I'm so cold my face is numb. Vlado's used to this weather. He lives where it's cold. Me, on the other hand? I'm a delicate flower that blooms in warmth and sunlight and gentle breezes. If he doesn't hurry he may find me with all my petals turned to ice, huddled against the iron fence with snow dusting my opened, unseeing eyes. A casualty on the mountain of his tardiness. Yes. The notion cheers me right up.

My fingers hurt. I need my gloves.

No huddling for me, though. If I head down to the street I might see Jure and Vlado driving up.

I hurry down the alleyway with wind shoving me in the back. It's getting darker by the minute and here I am, a small pale person standing out in a "transitional" neighborhood. Dead-looking houses study me like a butcher sizing up a piece of meat. *Would she scream? Who would care?* God only knows what's there, watching me from behind those staring windows.

Maybe I'll wait by the back door to the church. It's got some kind of canvas thing around it. In this wind, that's got to be warmer.

A twitchy feeling starts in the middle of my back. I turn around. A man watches me from the far end of the alley.

I saunter back to the canvas enclosure. Sauntering shows confidence, something I sorely need right now. I'd whistle a happy tune but my lips don't work.

Come on, Vlado. Please.

I say a little prayer for him, too. He didn't need to ask. I would have done it anyway.

My rescuer doesn't come in the form of Vlado. The priest, who's standing with his dog on the rectory porch, asks me if I need help. I answer I'm waiting for Vlado and company. He laughs. With a quip about Vlado and Jure operating on Slovenian time, he lets me into the parish hall.

Inside, it's marvelously toasty. It's also empty but for one man on stage singing Neil Young as a means of doing a sound check. I find a table in the back, slump into a chair and peel my frozen fingers from the boxes of pralines.

"Ruth! Haha, you're here!"

Vlado charges into the room and throws his arms around me. He pulls me up from my chair to his face. Suddenly, I don't mind having to wait for him in the cold and dark. I kiss his stubbled cheek while he's got me close. He still has the softest whiskers. We both talk, our words tumbling together. It's okay. It's not so much what we say but that we finally get to talk, all those things that get bottled up from the last goodbye until the next meeting again. We're like two bottles of champagne exploding together, all fizzy and bubbly, messy and sweet, what with kissed cheeks and talking over each other's sentences, hands and hair—well, my hair anyway—flying as we talk.

"Here," he says, passing a gift sack to me. "Eva picked this out for you."

Inside is a Slovene cookbook. Bless her heart, not only are the photos beautiful, the text is in English.

"And this," he reaches into his pocket, "is a gift from Ajdina. She made it for you."

It's a clothespin, painted red, with a ladybug on it. The spring doesn't clasp the wood quite right but it's easily fixed by someone who has a knack for tinkering with such things. That leaves me out and, watching Vlado fumbling with it, it leaves him out too. Still, it holds well enough for Vlado to attach it to my scarf. The ladybug rides there in all her glory.

"Did you bring your recorder?" Vlado is determined to cure me of my electronics aversion.

I dig it out of my purse and lay it on the table. "I tried it earlier. It works, too."

"Let me see."

I press "Record", say something inane and play it back. Sure enough, there's my voice, all southern-drawly.

He nods, pleased that I've passed Recorder 101.

He spins and heads for the stage where the man is still working on the sound check. "Go talk to Jure, and take your recorder."

Oh great. Getting it to work once is no guarantee it will ever work again. I grab up the recorder and head to the foyer where Jure is. Better to try and have it fail than to never try and displease Vlado.

"Vlado's a legend. Thank God he's still alive, but he's already a legend. And I am really honored that he is my good friend."

Jure is the consul general of Slovenia. He's here in Cleveland because the largest group of Slovenes outside of Slovenia is right here. And since they came, Jure has come. Which makes Jure no small potatoes in all things Slovene. In fact, there is nothing small about Jure—not his size, not his personality, and especially not his laugh. He likes to laugh a lot. He could be a one-man mission to prove diplomats aren't stuffy.

"I met Vlado when I was consul general in Austria," says Jure. "There is a park near Liechtenstein in Switzerland. These Slovenians, they go there, but only Slovenians from Prekmurje. Good people. Hardworking. Honest. I wanted to do a little something for them, a little cultural. So I asked them if they would like something, and they said, 'Yes, we want to have Vladek.'"

Jure sighs with the burden of trying to get such a famous celebrity all the way up to this little park for the people.

"'Okay, I will try.' The husband of my cousin—he's a professor of saxophone at the music school in Vienna—I call him and I say 'The people asked if Vlado could come. Do you know how to contact him?' 'Oh, yes, I have his cell phone number.' So I call him up, and I say 'Vlada Kreslina'—it was… hmmm… 2001— and I said, 'My name is Jure Zmauc, I am the Slovenian consul general in Austria, and all your fellows and all your friends from Prekmurje want to have you come play at a concert…' 'Okay.' Just 'Okay'. My first meeting with icon Vlado Kreslin, and now he's staying in my house! And we're friends!" Jure grins with the enormity of it all.

A guy tries to pass us on the way to the parish hall, but Jure will have none of that.

"Štefan! This is Ruth, Vlado's friend from Texas!"

"From Texas! Ah, then you're the one…" and off we go, jabbering about all things Vlado, with a little photo-taking thrown in.

"Štefan is wonderful," Jure says. "He volunteers all over the place but he's usually found behind the bar."

Bar? As in selling alcohol in a church? This sure isn't Texas.

"But why Cleveland?" I ask Jure. "Why did so many Slovenes move here?"

"Because for Slovenes, it is just like home." Jure beams at me. "There are four seasons here, and they are all beautiful."

Plus, Cleveland had industry, and Slovenia didn't, especially in rural areas like Prekmurje. So the fathers and sons who sailed to America often ended up here. Most of them didn't plan to stay, but what with this war and that war, and a job that fed them and housed them, and more and more Slovenes showing up from both the home country and from around the US, they put roots down and here they stayed.

When Vlado comes to town, he talks with as many people as he can, writing down messages to take back to their relatives who are still in Prekmurje.

We head for the bar where Vlado's standing talking with Štefan.

"Would you like something to drink?" asks Vlado, sipping something copper-colored from a small glass.

That sounds wonderful. The last thing I had to eat was a bagel with cream cheese eight hours before but surely a little won't hurt. "I'll have what you're having. Err… what is it?"

"Whiskey." He hands me my own glass.

I've never had whiskey neat before. It's possible I've never had whiskey, period. But there's first time for everything. Besides, trying out new things because of Vlado is a tradition now. I sip it, and the whiskey burns sweet all the way down to my toenails.

Oh boy, this is going to be fun.

We carry our whiskeys back to the table. Vlado lays out his poetry book and the song list he's working on for tonight.

"Last night," he says as he puts his glasses on, "I played for a Slovenian group. SNPJ. In Pittsburgh. Eh… almost no one spoke Slovene. But it was great." He shrugs. "So tonight? I've been here before. It will be great, too."

He writes a few titles down. Flips through his book. Shakes his head. "For tonight? I don't know."

I suggest one, but he makes a face. "It wouldn't mean anything to them."

He picks up everything. "Come on."

Backstage, like in most church auditoriums, ends up being both a sound room and a catchall for anything that might ever be used in the parish hall. That means cables on the floor, and chairs and tables stacked all over the place. Lucky for us, the stack of tables is the right height to lean over and make plans.

"How was Washington?"

Vlado's just come from playing the Kennedy Center a few nights ago. It's arguably the most prestigious venue in DC; only the Oval Office is better, but the performers are often sub-par. Everyone who is anyone wants to play the Kennedy Center. I had no worries that Vlado could pull it off, but I did worry that the crowd wouldn't be very large, being the night before Thanksgiving. People on vacation, people cooking for the holiday, and Vlado not being known in DC—that's a lot to overcome. The weather had been downright nasty. Silly me. I shouldn't have worried. Vlado played to almost a thousand people. For his first time there, that's really good. Even better, the more he sang, the more people stopped to listen.

“Oh, I saw Dylan!” Vlado leans over our chosen a stack of folding tables, grinning. “After my concert I went to see him. I played in the same town!”

So much for finding out how his concert went. Seeing Dylan would trump almost anything for him.

“Where did he play? I bet it wasn’t as good as where you were.”

“Verizon Center downtown. Very big venue.”

“Ha! But you played in the Kennedy Center. That’s like the ultimate. You won!”

Vlado grins. “This town ain’t beeg enough for the both of us. Haha!”

New York, on the other hand, was big enough for a hundred Vlados and Dylans, with a thousand venues Vlado can play. This time he was at Café Marlene in Sunnyside. He read from *Instead of Whom Does a Flower Bloom* and sang his songs. The audience was enthralled, waving their hands and their bottles to the music.

“There was an Irish singer-songwriter,” Vlado says, “who was to appear there later in the night—Michael Brunnock. He’s great. We sang a few songs together.

The venue here at St. Mary’s is quieter. If nothing else, it’s a church, a place not usually known for being rowdy. But then they sell wine and whisky here, so maybe I don’t know what I’m talking about. I’ll find out tonight.

But right now Vlado and I are working out our schedules.

“Tomorrow,” he says, as we compare schedules, “tomorrow we plan. I can be at your hotel by nine, and we’ll have three or so hours to talk. Okay?” He pauses. “Let me see your recorder.”

“I recorded Jure.”

“Let me hear.”

I punch the button, searching for the conversation. It takes me a few false starts but I find it. Even better, I haven’t recorded over it. He listens for a minute.

“Good, good.” He lopes up the steps to the stage. “I’m going to do sound check. You stay here and watch.”

So I settle down on the floor, legs stretched in front of me, and do that very thing.

Ah, the elusive Joe Valenčič. After several email attempts we finally meet, thanks to Vlado. Joe is an affable guy with sharp blue eyes and an easy smile that lets you know he is just gosh darn thrilled to meet you. He’s happy to talk, mostly about Vlado, but my email address comes in for dishonorable mention as well. It’s got quite a reputation for losing random messages.

I like schmoozing with Joe. Vlado said he not only knew everything about the Slovene music scene in Cleveland, especially when it comes to Cleveland-style polka, but Joe knows everything about Slovenes in the USA, too. He's good about telling tales on Vlado.

"Here. Sit here."

Here is Jure's table, front and center. I'm not so sure about sitting here. I do much better sitting at the back of the room, where I can hide with my back against the wall and no one can see me. Here, the whole room sees me. This is the table that everyone looks at when they're tired of watching the stage. Not that Vlado isn't interesting to watch, especially when he's singing with his black hat on and guitar in hand. But sometimes after being dazzled by brilliance, you have to rest your eyes. Stage light glare, you know. What better way to do it than taking in the mundane glow of the people sitting front and center?

"Are you sure?" I ask. "The seats may already be taken."

Vlado makes a noise and pulls the chair out for me. "Sit."

The concert tonight makes me wonder if Cleveland is a suburb of Ljubljana. Even the birthday song for Vlado, which the crowd starts singing at the top of their lungs, is in Slovene. Vlado is incredibly pleased and a little abashed. The audience loves it and the more pleased he seems, the louder they sing. I sing, too, a half beat behind everyone so I can fake it.

Halfway through the concert I glance down. Ajdina's ladybug pin is gone.

In the grand scheme of things, where we deal with wars and famines and epidemics and gross unhappiness on an unfathomable scale, losing Ajdina's pin is not a big deal. It may not even be a big deal to Ajdina. But it is a very big deal to me. It's a good thing no one is moving around. Maybe it will be found intact before I leave.

A group of older women-- infinitely much older than me by at least five years—comes up. They scan me like I was a baboon in a zoo. The last time I got approached like this a gang of pre-teen girls threatened to pummel me into the ground. I doubt these women could muster up the nerve to do that but I'm leery. I don't want to die being gummed to death.

"Are you his groupie?" asks one of the women.

"Oh, hush, now," says another, giggling.

"But I want to know." They all stand back, sweet as pie, blinking. Waiting.

'*But I want to know.*' Oh, honey, I bet you do.

My brain goes into overdrive, trying to think of something witty and polite. I can't do it. Now is not the time or place to be snarky. Geesh. Did she really just ask that? Really? Ah, but she's never seen the way Vlado looks at Eva, how his face lights up when he talks about his children. He wouldn't mess that up in a million years.

"Do I really look like a groupie?" I try not to sound exasperated. It isn't what I want to say, not at all, but I don't want to offend anyone, especially since it might get back to Vlado. So I smile and shake my head. "No, we're doing a book together."

"Oh," she said, pressing her lips into a thin line. "Well. I just wondered," and then she gives me a tight little smile back. They all smile in formation and move on.

Now I wasn't born yesterday. I grew up in a small town and know exactly what that "oh" means. Believe me, my grandmother could "oh" with the best of them. And people will think what they want. I can't prove a negative. But, really…

Groupie?

"Ruth!" Vlado waves me over. "Come get some wine!"

Yeah, the 'groupie' could use some wine about now. I take a deep breath and look around.

Smack dab in the middle of a table sits Ajdina's pin. It's in perfect condition. Someone found it, toyed with it, and got it back into its spring. Thank you, thank you, whoever you are. I snatch the pin up and stick in my purse before it has a chance to disappear again.

An older woman, even older than the groupie gals, walks over to me. "I read where he's called the Slovenian Bob Dylan and I wasn't sure about coming. I don't like Bob Dylan."

"Ah," I reply. "Dylan can be an acquired taste." Dylan probably was a little after her time, but I wasn't going to point that out. She seems in a confessional mood.

"But you know? I like this Kreslin much better. Oh yes," she says. "Much better than Dylan." She winks at me and walks away.

The next day, when we're at the café, I tell Vlado about the woman who said he was much better than Dylan.

"She said that? Really?" He grins a big slow grin, and then throws his head back and laughs. "*Ojoj*. Much better than Dylan? Hahaha!"

Back at St. Mary's, Vlado plays an impromptu song that everyone knows. It's a Prekmurje song, and Vlado plays like a wild man. He hops, he spins, his arm pistons up and down as he strums—and he sings. Oh, how he sings—just for the pure joy of it. The people sing with him. For the umpteenth time tonight, Cleveland disappears. We're in Prekmurje, dancing with the *pozvačin*.

It's time to go.

"Tomorrow," says Vlado, "at the hotel. Ten o'clock?" He kisses my cheek good-bye, and Joe and I walk out to the parking lot.

Joe Valenčič is a man with a passion. He may be the go-to guy for all things Slovene in the US, but his heart belongs to polka. A screenwriter, narrator and local Slovenian historian, Joe's the president of the National Cleveland-Style Polka Hall of Fame museum and curator for their museum. He's an all-around good guy. We talk about Cleveland and polka, Slovenes and polka, and the Polka Hall of Fame awards that were held the week before.

He shows me the Christmas lights, filling the square and turning downtown into a brightly spangled fantasy land. They're almost as beautiful as the golden lit churches against the snow-covered hills on the way to Ljubljana that first night years ago. Almost.

Steps echo on the marble walkway in the empty arcade. My steps. I have some time before I'm to meet Vlado, but hanging around my room, waiting for a phone call, is boring. I'd rather be leaning over the balcony, watching people come in.

Except he's already here in the lobby, talking to someone behind the desk. I hear him ask for me. Good thing I came down early. The name I'm checked in under is not the name he knows me by.

"Vlado!"

He turns around, sees me, and with a cheery wave thanks the desk clerk without her ever having to say a word.

"Did I tell you what Desa Muck said about the wedding?" Vlado looks at me over the table, his eyes twinkling. We're working on the book—here is the coffee, there is the computer, our cell phones and recorders lying scattered among the spoons and sugar packets—but we're having too much fun, telling stories like kids swapping secrets. Right now, he's checking his emails on my laptop.

"She said it was like acting a supporting role in a Žika Pavlović film. He was a Serbian film author, part of the Black Wave in Yugoslavian film. The regime didn't like them but they allowed them. I sent you one, *Flight of a Dead Bird*. You remember. A Slovene film with the story from Prekmurje."

Oh, I remember. Cows being shot on screen, their carcasses burning. I grew up on a farm. These things happen. But to kill an animal for a film? Maybe they were only sedated.

"He shot the film in Gornja, Dolnja, and Srednja Bistrica, so with my friends we organized the viewing of the film at the ferryboat. Some of the men were going—'Do you remember this?' because they'd done stunts in the film.

"Pavlović was a very important director, and to be in his film was the biggest thing. Desa said our wedding was like being in his film. That it was that crazy. When we drove in a long queue of cars from Sv Vid to Žižki, we had to stop at every other house and have a drink and even a snack. It took a long time to get to Žižki…"

Vlado's phone rings. He chortles, answering it. First he presses it to his ear, then he jumps up and holds it next to mine so we both can hear. Eva and the kids are singing 'Happy Birthday' to… Cheski?

"Yes! Haha! They sing to 'Vladičevski Javor'. That's how they call me. Ajdina named me that. *Javor* means a kind of tree… a maple."

"That's your nickname?"

"Eh, I don't know. It is just not clear which one is a first name."

Vlado is a supremely happy man.

He checks more emails on my laptop. He's got tons of birthday greetings, and a few messages from his family. "Eva tells me Ajdina broke a glass. 'Ah,' she said, 'maybe it will bring good luck and Vlado will come home early.'"

"When do you head home?"

"Monday, I think. Soon." He types furiously. "This is from my father. Beltinška Banda is up for an award on the Vikend Gong of Popularity program. I was supposed to go as well but I am here, so I reminded my father to make sure they have their sunglasses. Haha!"

Our waitress pours us another round of coffee. It's kind of her, but it ruins the delicate sugar-milk balance I've made. In go two more packets of sugar and another dollop of milk.

"Ajdina didn't want to go to Prekmurje with me. So I said, 'On our way we can stop at the gas station.' And she said, 'And we can buy Kiki bomboni.' These were candies from the sixties and seventies. Then she said, 'They will put yourself back into your youth, and in the meantime I will sweeten myself.' Haha!"

Maybe I should drop some Kiki bomboni in my coffee.

"Did Štefan ever get to see Čarna?"

"When Čarna was born we took her to see Štefan." Vlado makes a cradle with his hands. He leans across the table, pushing his hand cradle towards me, his voice low and soft. "Štefan was laying down so we put her on his chest. Like this." Here he carefully lays an invisible baby down. "Štefan held her and said, 'So finally you came. *Skukureknula*… she pecked inside her shell, breaking her way out.'" Vlado grins and taps his finger against the air. "Peck, peck, peck."

So this is where the connection comes in between Čarna and Štefan, who gave her poppy pods, who got to see her after all.

There's a joke universities like to play—what is clarity to the cognoscenti is incomprehensible to the stranger, at least as far as finding certain classrooms. "Feeling lost? Feeling dumb? Want to know where CSU MC 122 is? Come matriculate and you too, will learn the secrets of the universe!"

Rick flies in from Dallas, just in time for us to get lost. Luka, head of the Slovenian Studies at Cleveland State University, told me precisely which building this particular classroom is in and even where we should park. We asked several student-like people where this building is, but were most helpfully snubbed.

A bored parking attendant, with a few mumbles and some pointing of fingers, indicates the building behind him. Happy as the clueless, we dash into said building. The doors we need open are locked.

Up the stairs we go. Locked. Down the stairs. Locked. What good is it to have a program for the public if the doors are always locked?

"Confusing, isn't it?" A cherubic face hails us from the landing above us. "You have to go down those stairs, take a left through the doors there and then go up one flight of stairs and then take a right through another set of doors. The room should be on the right down a little ways. I don't know why it's so hard to get there, but it is."

I know why. It's fun. It's the "Oh, look, there's another set of strangers; let's see how long it takes them to find the classroom" syndrome.

So, thanking the cherubic face profusely for saving our evening, we do exactly that.

What do you know—here it is: "Vlado Kreslin – CSU MC 122" right on the door. Lucky us, we're the first people here.

Vlado is nowhere in sight.

But soon, the room is packed with folks, all talking and laughing and grabbing a place to sit. Vlado's in the middle of it all. Luka keeps bringing in chairs, and the chairs keep right on filling up—and folks still are standing around. If this keeps up people are going to spill out into the main room.

As Vlado starts the concert, a gray-haired gentleman, with his overcoat precisely folded over his arm, comes in and takes a seat towards the front.

"Vodomec," says Vlado to the crowd. "Kingfisher. I had a friend, Štefan, who loved the river Mura, which is located where I am from in Prekmurje. He and I would often go to the river and look for kingfishers. We never saw one, at least never when we were together, no matter how hard we looked. When Štefan died, after the funeral I went with his wife and his daughter, and my wife Eva out on the river. And there we saw one, *vodomec*—kingfisher—with his beautiful colors, flying underneath the overhanging branches low over the water. So this next song was written for my friend."

Vlado sings *Ptič*, and his voice carries me to the Mura. Vlado is sitting there on the river with Valentina, Eva and Štefan's wife. The four of them together, alone in their grief. A blue flash whizzes by. For the few moments as he watches the kingfisher, Vlado's heart aches a little less.

The gray-haired gentleman shakes Vlado's hand after the concert. Apparently, he's one of the deans at the university. He, too, knows Vlado's music.

Everyone crowds around the back tables. Several have brought *potica*, a rolled sliced cake with walnut filling, and folks are eating it as fast as they can. I stay away from the table, talking with someone else who's avoiding the table. Tim is a friendly guy who's president of the Society for Slovene Studies. We talk mostly about Vlado and the concert tonight, but some about publishing and the pitfalls of translations.

Where to go? We're a small crowd—Jure, Janja and Nika, Luka and Erica, Vlado and us. Surely there's a place that will take us in and let us rest our weary bones for a glass or two of something. It's late, though, and there's not much within walking distance.

Luka takes off to see if maybe, just maybe… He comes back with the great news that yes, the bar in the student center is open.

A bar in the student center? We go where kids get can snockered and don't have to leave campus. What a radical idea.

"Wait." Vlado pulls out a chair at the nearest table while the others head for a larger one. "We can talk here for a little bit."

We put our heads together.

"I don't know how Eva's parents felt when we got married. We never talked about it but maybe they were not so happy about their daughter's husband being a rock musician quite some years older than she is. But then Eva some time after the wedding cited her mother:

"'You know Eva, I actually found out that Vlado lives quite a healthy life.'

"'What do you mean?' Eva hardly shared her opinion.

"'Well, I read that there is the highest level of ozone in the air early in the morning between 4 and 5 a.m. And that is when Vlado is coming home! Haha!'"

Vlado and I join everyone else at the other table. Talk is easy, lots of laughter, and enough beer and wine to make us relaxed. Vlado looks down the table at Rick. "So when will you come next to Ljubljana?"

In that strange synchronicity that highlights embarrassing moments, conversation stops. All eyes turn to Rick.

I'm touched that Vlado asked, since I have more than a little interest in his answer myself. But Rick says only that we'll have to see.

We'll have to see. The penultimate kiss of death to any request. Oh well, maybe next time.

Vlado smiles.

Then it's over. We all hug, say goodbye. I tell Rick that Vlado took good care of me but then he was *moj brat*, my brother. Vlado nods, and says, oh sure, sure. Then with a wave, we head for our cars, us to one parking garage and them to another.

At the elevator I turn one last time and see Vlado walking away, guitar in hand.

We fly at twelve o'something after arriving at nine a.m. for a ten-thirty flight. Vlado flies at ten-thirty, but he's flying internationally to Toronto. We're headed to Dallas, which only thinks it's in a different country. Still, a stroll around the concourses might be in order. Hopkins International Airport is no DFW. It's easy to walk from one end to the other. Stretch our legs. Find a friend, even. Not that I would plan to do such a thing.

So off we go, and at a fairly fast clip. The concourses are all connected so who knows? Maybe we'll run into…

"Look who's over there!" A tall lanky figure is desperately trying to corral his bags and guitar.

"Ruth! Rick!"

Vlado waves his arms and scoops us up, two little chicks who've made it back to Papa Stork. He hugs us as if he hasn't seen us in years, and then holds out his Godiva chocolate bar right at my nose. How can I resist? Rick is made of sterner stuff, so Vlado and I finish off the bar.

"Last night after you left, we drove somewhere in the middle of the night and they gave me a surprise birthday party! *Jijiji!* And the guys ran out of the bushes with their Dolenjska accordions and dressed as mariachis, woo-woo-woo…." Vlado waves his arms "…wearing these costumes. All sorts of people were there, and oh, the presents! There was a cake and we sang songs. I had the best time! And I thought 'Fuck! Ruth should be here!'" He wipes his cheeks as if wiping tears from his eyes. "Ah, it was great!"

Me there without a present? I'd be mortified, red-faced and begging the ground to swallow me down in one giant gulp. Still, it's nice to be missed.

So, the three of us heft our three bags, his three bags and a guitar case that's loaded with bricks—I know this because I tried to pick it up.

"Here, let me carry that," says Vlado. I not-so-reluctantly give it to him. So I don't feel left out, Rick passes a bag to me.

Carry-ons distributed, we step smartly down the concourse.

"Do you know what gate you're flying out of?" Rick asks.

Vlado looks at him. "Gate?" He checks his pockets and then his bag. "Ah. Here it is." He pulls out a paper. "Ten-thirty. Gate 26."

"Ah. Behind us."

We about-face and head the other way.

Vlado runs ahead, stops and pulls out his video camera. "Keep walking! Keep walking!" So we keep walking, laughing, passing by him and walking backwards now.

He changes cameras and crowds us all together for a headshot. "This camera always takes the best pictures."

Satisfied, we start off for the last time for his gate.

"Marija Ahačič Pollak is picking me up in Toronto. She was a very famous singer with Avsenik in Slovenia, and then right at the top of her career she left and moved to Canada. Tomorrow I am invited to jam with Walter Ostanek. He's won four Grammys, king of polka, a successor of the great Frankie Yankovics. I know him from before." Vlado grins like a little kid. "And then the same night there is an Indexi tribute concert in Toronto. Such a great band! I am invited there too, maybe sing *Žute dunje* as I did with the real Indexi band once in Sarajevo. So we'll see. It's gonna be quite busy, haha!"

"Mr. Kreslin!" The flight attendant glares at him.

"Uh oh." Vlado goes over and has a minor discussion with her. It seems his luggage is locked and they need the combination. He tells her what it is, which mollifies her, and he walks back to us, shrugging.

"Plus your concerts," I say, not wanting to lose the conversation.

"Oh, sure." He thinks for a moment and then, watching Rick, he says, "When do you think you'll be back to France?"

Ah ha, I know where this is going.

Rick, however, does not. He is such an innocent. "Probably March. Somewhere in there."

Vlado nods, looks thoughtful. Tries to be cool. "Perhaps it would be good if we got together again before the book is done. What do you say, Rick?"

Yes, Vlado is a most persistent man.

The flight has finished boarding. Vlado leans over and, pressing his face next to mine, kisses me on each cheek. Then he straightens up and shakes Rick's hand. "Take care. See you soon!"

Just as he's about to go down the jet way, he turns. "Duprés!!!!" he cries out and twirls his finger in the air, like he did that first night at the Hotel Slon. *Vsak se želi*, and the dance to heaven, a dance of adventure and joy, a dance of friendship.

I'm still dancing.

"Kreslin!!!!" I wave back, and then he's gone.

Epilogue

Vlado glances over at me. "Have you ever been to a recording session?"

Musicians must be crazy. They do some of their best work in padded rooms.

Gal's Studio HAD is a padded room. Egg-carton foam covers the walls, a thick white rug covers the floor, and everyone wears coats, 'cause, baby, it's cold outside. An electric piano and an upright grand with what seems to be a little steel drum sitting on top line one wall. Next to the upright grand is a Hammond organ. A contrabass and a row of guitars stand in a row, waiting, as do the trumpets, shiny and silent for now. There are mixing boards and computers, and a sofa for the weary or visitors who are clueless about where to stand. A treble clef hangs above the door. Water bottles, wine and cups, and even a candle for atmosphere. And there's music, music everywhere.

Vlado's baritone drifts through the air:

"Kakor da je zdaj, tisti mesec maj,
živel sem ga rad, neukrotljivo mlad,
mlajši kakor ti
in premlad, da prepoznal bi
rožo med umetnimi."

A huge microphone stands in the middle of the room. Seated in front of it is Milan Kreslin, looking dapper in his hat and tie. Gal, wearing his top hat, records him singing the harmony for "*Tisti bejli grm*." Vlado and Gal watch Milan; I watch his feet, swinging in the air as he sings:

"Če bi krila imel, takrat bi letel,
a če bi znal, ne bi se igral
starejši kakor ti
in prestar, da bi se znal
igrati z biseri."

And then Vlado and Milan sing together:

Zdaj tisti bejli grm pod oknom ne cveti,
jasmin ne ve, ne govori,

zdaj tisti bejli grm pod oknom ne diši,
jasmine ne ve
ne ve, kje si.

"You remember that song," Vlado says later. "At my parents' house last summer. You recorded the video."

"Outside with your dad, yes. I kept forgetting to take the cap off the camcorder."

"Yes!"

Vlado stops his dad and conducts the song, mouthing the words with great exaggeration. Milan sings again. More discussion ensues. Again Milan sings. This time they strike gold. The harmony blends, and the take is good.

"Zdaj je od tedaj že premnogi mlaj
in premnogo cest, nepozabnih mest
in še več sledi
z mojega na drugi breg
pokriva lanski sneg.

Zdaj tisti bejli grm pod oknom ne cveti,
jasmin ne ve, ne govori,
zdaj tisti bejli grm pod oknom ne diši,
jasmin ne ve
ne ve, kje si."

Later, over wine at his house, I ask, "Is recording always like this? So laid back?"

"Oh, sure. When I come into Gal's studio with a new song, I play it on a guitar or piano, usually just once, and he starts adding all those instruments that he can play. We talk about the world-- literature, history, politics, drink wine, and in the meanwhile we record a track, build a song. In the morning as the sun is coming up, I put the CD in the car's CD player as I drive home and my telephone rings—he calls me from his car listening to the same track in his car driving home as well—and he says, 'Not a bad minestra.'

"And I say, 'Yes, not a bad one.'

"What a great morning!"

I rush up the stairs and shed my shoes on the landing. What was it that bothered me about taking off my shoes? I don't think twice about it any more. Vlado pours the coffee, and along with cereal for him and bread for me, we sit at the table and become human again over breakfast.

Snowing still. This is where I came in three years ago, on the back of a blizzard, not knowing what this Vlado person was like. Throwing myself on the wind and hoping it would turn out okay. Music makes you do crazy things like that. I came to hear a stranger whose music moved me and found a friend. A brother. *Moj brat*, I called him. *Moja sestrica*, he replied.

And with the book, I had a reason to be here. *I have to go to Ljubljana, have to go to Beltinci, have to go to Cleveland. The book, you know.* It was a lovely frame, out of which friendship bloomed. Are you a groupie? No, just a friend.

But now the frame is gone. The little plant is on her own.

I shake my head. Sip my coffee.

Vlado watches me, his eyes bright as a bird's. "You okay?"

I shrug. "Oh yeah. It's just… we're done. It's over. The book, the interviews. Trying to get to Ljubljana." I give him a lopsided grin. "The creative synergy. I'll miss it."

"'Over'? Is that what you think? It's never over. There is the book launch, and then coming back for the concert series and…" He stops. Looks at me for a long time. And then he grins back at me and jumps up from the table. "Come on, come on."

"What?" I put my cup down so fast I slosh coffee over my fingers.

He laughs and grabs my sticky hand. "Let's go. I've got something to show you…"

Od višine se zvrti

Nikdar več, oh, saj ne more biti res!
Nikdar več, oh, saj ne more biti res,
krila so se mi stopila od strahu.
Nikoli več ne poletim na njih
in nikdar ne izvem,
da so samo papir –

zmaji,

ki že tol'ko let visijo nad menoj.

Saj že mama govorila je,

Da z višine se ne vidi vse,

Da nikdar de izveš,

Da so samo papir—

Smehjaji,

Ki že tol'ko let smejijo se s teboj.

Od višine se zvrti!

Skrij me v svojo dlan,

Svojo mehko dlan,

Svojo toplo dlan!

Vzemi me na sojo stran,

Skrij me v svojo dlan.

Lahki mi vrneš karto še nocoj,

Hočem le,

Da me vidijo s teboj.

-- fini --

Tista črna kitara

That Black Guitar

At every feast

In those early days of youth,

Our home resounded with song

Played by the mustachioed Gypsies.

My father, too, swept the strings of that black guitar,

The one he had bought

With his first wages.

Do you still have that, Sir?
Sir, do you still play that black guitar?
That, sir, was the greatest of all.

Years on,
When they would pass and reach out for a coin or two,
They'd ask him about the guitar.
Years on, as they stole away to the bar,
Far from their resting instruments,
Which enchanted the guests through the night.
Their women, too,
As they knocked on our door,
To plead for our garments, tattered and worn,
Would ask, eyes gleaming:

Do you still have that guitar, Sir?
Sir, do you still play that black guitar?
That, sir, was the greatest of all.
Once in a while, when back at my home,
I empty a few glasses,

Embraced by the shade of our chestnut tree,
I drink with my friends,
Whose lives are still bound to that land.
There, strings by the table,
The Gypsies would appear,
Play for us,
And ask once again,
With their childish eyes and voices deep and coarse:

Do you still have that guitar, Sir?
Sir, do you still play that black guitar?
That, sir, was the greatest of all,
Indeed, the greatest of all.

Tam daleč stran

There, Far Away, Over The Steppe

Translated by Vlado Kreslin

There, far away, over the steppe,
Over the wide flatlands,
The earth kisses the sky
Whispers in its ear.

There, far away, over the steppe ,
Over the wide flatlands,
Just one more time I would love to go there
There is my home.

Tisti Bejli Grm

That White Shrub

Translated by Vlado Kreslin

As if it was yesterday, that distant month of May
I lived it passionately, untamed and young,
Younger than you
And too young to tell the
Fair rose among the artificial ones.

If I only had wings then, I would have flown,
And if I knew, I would not play
Older than you
And too old to play with pearls.

Now that white bush under the window does not bloom,
Jasmine does not know,
She does not speak,
Now that white bush under the window does not smell,
Jasmine does not know,
She does not know, where did you go.

Many months of May, many roads and
Untamed cities since then have passed,
And many traces
From my own to the far riverbank
Are covered by last year's snow.

Violina

The Violin

Translated by Vlado Kreslin

I have never seen Janček
Leave his violin lying around.
At all times it was in his arms
Swinging softly like a newborn child.
Entire long bus ride to Lyon
In a plane to Olympics in France,
Or on his bicycle.
All the times, except that afternoon,
When we drove from Miška's place,
Where we played with Beltinška banda.

Janček was very generous
Last years of his life.
»C'mon, Vlado, let' s stop at Vili's
And have a drink of new wine!«
-You could not pass the inn
If you personally knew the owner.

It was the end of October
And in the days of boiling wine was not yet wine,
You seemed to be ok
But however you felt dizzy.

As I left him at his house and closed the gate
The violin fell off his hands in the garden.
They say never before was he so desperate
»Where is my violin?«
-She spent the night with cabbage-
And never so happy,

When they brought her back to him.

Cesta

Road

Long winds the road from village to city,
Long flows the river from first cry to the last sigh.
Scarred and pot-holed with yearning,
Snow-melt pools, desire and sobs,
Long as a wakeful night,
Long is this road from somewhere to once.

Namesto koga roža cveti

Instead of Whom Does the Flower Bloom

On a night when I share the vast skies with the storks,
Beneath the floating screen of haze,
Alone and silent I mingle with them,
Feet upon the rain-scented grass.

As the first sunbeam eats through the dark,
We are drawn from the pool of our dreams,
And new desires, once tied to the sheltering moor,
Now vanish, as they sail into the heavenly blue.

Instead of whom does the flower bloom,
Instead of whom does my heart pound.
What skin smells sweetest of all,
And what song needs my voice to strike the stars.

Should the grasses bloom above me,
Some eyes will melt in tears,
While others will see only a flower.

Instead of whom does the flower bloom,
Instead of whom does my heart pound,
What skin smells sweetest of all,
And what song calls for my voice.

Tam v meglicah nad mursko vodo

There In the Mist By The Mura River

The elders still remember
When the village was woven into one,
Even a stranger was welcome
To raise a glass with a word or two.

At times, when the sun sank deep
Up from the vineyard hills into our moor.
The echo of dulcimer allied with air,
The hamlet and meadows caressed by its flair.

Four men you were often to meet,
Mustachioed faces, clung to violins,
Their hearts imbued with soul-stirring music.
And if you gave away a daughter or two
The fiddle and double bass sharpened your heels.

At times, when dusk covers the earth,
And southern breeze ruffles the hair,
Then you might hear them play, vivid with lore,
In misty air above the moor.

Od Višine Se Zvrti

Vertiginous from the Height

No more, this cannot be real.
No more, this cannot be real.
My wings have melted with fear,
Never again shall I rise up upon them.
And never am I to learn
They are only paper dragons
That have, for decades, hung over me.

As my mother taught,
You cannot see it all from on high,
And never are you to learn,
They are only paper smiles,
That have laughed, for decades, with you.

Vertiginous from the height.
Let the palm of your hand shelter me.
Your palm, soft and warm.
Let me come over to your side,
Let me hide in the palm of your hand.
You can give me back that ticket tonight,
For all I want is to be seen with you.

All poems by Vlado Kreslin. Used by permission of the author and translator.

"Tisti bejli grm (That White Bush) ", "Tam daleč stran" and "Violina (Violin)" translated by Vlado Kreslin.

All other translations by Urška Charney and appear originally in *Instead of Whom Does the Flower Bloom—the Poems of Vlado Kreslin*, published by Guernica Editions Inc., 2012.

Acknowledgements

A book such as this is not written in a vacuum. So many people helped with this project, in ways big and small. I could not have done it without them.

I would like to thank my family – Rick, Aubrey, and Gabby—who supported me, cheered me on, and laughed in all the right places.

Thanks go to Mario Schneller who first introduced me to Vlado's music, and to Boris Jež, Ahmed Buric, Jože Hradil, Kester Eddy, Isabelle Kralj and Feri Lainšček who contributed stories about Vlado.

Thanks also to Allan Taylor for letting me use the lyrics to "Let the Music Flow".

To Carly Berg and Tina Davis Lollar, who read behind me and offered their editorial advice—thank you.

To Bob Schneller, Walter Briski, Jr., and Kurt Maloo for early encouragement—thanks.

And thanks to Johnny Srsen and Christian Zakelj, for letting me quote from their articles in Glas Naroda.

Thanks also to Sue Laybourn for being an outstanding editor and sounding board, and thanks to Anthony Kocmut for the authorial photo.

Thank you to Urška Charney for the use of her translations, and a special thank you to Dr. Noah Charney.

And to Vlado and Eva Kreslin, who opened their heart and home to me, and without whom in so many ways this book would not exist -- my words are too small to contain my humble and grateful thanks, but thank you anyway.

For further information about Vlado:

Website : www.kreslin.com

Facebook: https://www.facebook.com/vkreslin/

Youtube: https://www.youtube.com/user/vladokreslin

And if you'd like to contact me, here's the information:

Email: rpdupre@gmail.com

Facebook: https://www.facebook.com/ruth.dupre.5

Printed by Books on Demand GmbH, Norderstedt / Germany